"At Saatchi & Saatchi we believe that good ideas come from anywhere...and more and more they come from people without experience, without years of knowledge, and without fear. People who are ready to fail fast, learn fast, and fix fast. People driven by the 'I' words—Intuition, Imagination, Inspiration, and Ideas. People like Ben Barry. We live in the Age of the Idea...and this book will inspire entrepreneurs throughout the world to have faith in their ideas, and give them great insight on how to bring them to life and make them come true."

—KEVIN ROBERTS, CEO Worldwide Saatchi & Saatchi, Ideas Company,
and author of *Lovemarks: The Future Beyond Brands*

"Ben's socially oriented, profit-driven approach to changing the fashion industry illustrates how young, passionate entrepreneurs are changing the world. This is a compelling story and he is certainly a most deserving recipient of the CIBC Student Entrepreneur of the Year Award."

—IAN AITKEN, founder and chairman of Advancing Canadian Entrepreneurship Inc.
and Managing Partner of Pembroke Management Ltd.

"Part adventure, part activism, part business, part instruction manual. Above all, an inspiring story of Ben Barry's attempts to transform girls' and women's experience of their bodies so that anguish can be replaced by pleasure and self acceptance. Where will he go next!?"

—SUSIE ORBACH, psychoanalyst, consultant to DOVE and
author of *Fat Is a Feminist Issue*

"Like *Moneyball* did for baseball, *Fashioning Reality* takes on the time-honoured 'truths' of an industry—fashion modelling, in this case—and exposes them as nothing but stultifying myths.... Ben Barry combines a keen mind, an irreverent personality, and his own successful experience to show that for a committed and entrepreneurial change agent there is always a better way, despite the nattering naysayers! Readers old and young will gain the inspiration to forge a 'Balanced Contract' to change for the better a current reality they find unacceptable."

—ROGER MARTIN, dean of the University of Toronto's
Rotman School of Management

"Ben Barry's inherent chutzpah and intimate knowledge of the kind of drive, passion, and focus required to make it in the fashion industry is evident in his motivational writing. He's an energetic self-starter who's wise beyond his years.... His sheer tenacity alone is an inspiration."

—JEANNE BEKER, host of *Fashion Television*, and editor-in-chief of FQ magazine

FASHIONING REALITY

A NEW GENERATION OF ENTREPRENEURSHIP

BEN BARRY

KEY PORTER BOOKS

Library and Archives Canada Cataloguing in Publication

Barry, Ben
  Fashioning reality : a new generation of entrepreneurship / Ben Barry.

ISBN-13: 978-1-55263-820-0, ISBN-10: 1-55263-820-0

1. Barry, Ben. 2. Ben Barry Agency. 3. Modeling agencies—Canada. 4. Entrepreneurs—Canada—Biography. I. Title.

HD9999.M642B37 2006   659.1'52   C2006-901791-3

The publisher gratefully acknowledges the support of the Canada Council for the Arts and the Ontario Arts Council for its publishing program. We acknowledge the support of the Government of Ontario through the Ontario Media Development Corporation's Ontario Book Initiative.

We acknowledge the financial support of the Government of Canada through the Book Publishing Industry Development Program (BPIDP) for our publishing activities.

Key Porter Books Limited
Six Adelaide Street East, Tenth Floor
Toronto, Ontario
Canada M5C 1H6

www.keyporter.com

Text design: Marijke Friesen
Electronic formatting: Jean Lightfoot Peters

Printed and bound in Canada

07 08 09 10 11 5 4 3 2 1

For my mom and dad, who taught their son the art of turning cardboard boxes into cities. I love you.

Be the change you want to see in the world.
—MAHATMA GANDHI

ACKNOWLEDGEMENTS

MY ADVENTURE INTO THE FASHION world began with my family. They said "okay" when I asked them at fourteen if I could open a modelling agency in the basement of the family home. They sat front and centre at every fashion show without telling me how things are done. They taught me the value of never believing in never. They always let me be myself, and offered unconditional love along the way. For all this and more, I am thankful: Granny, Opi, Brian, Nicole, Ron, Iva, Peter, Deb, Gail, and Adam.

The lessons taught by Granny will influence me forever. Through your stories, you taught me about the pain of oppression. And through your actions, you instilled in me a desire to undo it.

I am deeply appreciative of those who have lent their support and faith to this book. Thank you to my literary agent Faye Bender, who always pushed for my ideas throughout the process. Thank you to the team at Key Porter Books—particularly Jordan Fenn and Linda Pruessen—for believing in the book before having read a completed manuscript, trusting the talents of a young and inexperienced writer, and respecting my desire to speak my message in my own voice. Kendra Michael and Marijke Friesen, thank you for your endless enthusiasm and creativity.

Thank you to my editor Louisa McCormick. You taught me how to show not tell, and shared your wonderful wit and way with words. I also thankful to Paul Crookall and Harvey Schachter, who have guided me from the time when all I had to show for this book was the title. You have both been inspirations for this young entrepreneur, and dear and trusted friends.

The success of my business, and advancement of our mission would not have been possible without the tremendous talents of my agency team. I thank each of one you for your creativity, dedication, and passion. I am particularly grateful to Matthew Choy and Erica North. Matt, whether you are creating business cards or business strategy, I trust that you will give your genius, and your heart to every project. Erica, your leadership and perspective have challenged standard business practice, and empowered me to always stay positive despite our many setbacks.

I am fortunate to have had teachers who challenged my worldview. To my teachers at Ashbury College, you taught me to believe in myself early on, and offered opportunities that developed my talents. To my professors at the

University of Toronto, and especially those in the women's studies program, each of you inspirited me to always question what is missing, and who is excluded. To my professors at Cambridge University, and particularly my supervisor Simon Bell, your commitment to research that makes a difference in the world inspires me. And to Erica Claus, Jeremiah Greene, and Mr. Wilson, you have helped me build on the lessons taught to me by my dad and mom.

I have been humbled to meet many young entrepreneurs who challenge the business status quo. Your struggles and successes have inspired this book, and motivate me on a daily basis. A special thank you to ACE and CIBC for their continued support of my endeavors, and those of many young entrepreneurs. I am also grateful to those exceptional individuals within fashion and business who graciously offered their support and guidance. Thank you, Elmer Olsen and all others who take time from their busy lives to share their experiences with youth.

My friends listened to my countless ideas and concerns about this book with never-ending interest and compassion. In your own way, you have each made an important contribution to this book as you do in my life. A special thank you to Omid, Lindsay, and Ginni for reviewing my work at various stages along the way.

Some names and event details in my book have been changed to respect the privacy of those involved.

When I was a young boy, my mom, dad, and I made routine visits to the grocery on Saturday mornings. We parked at the shipping entrance, and waited patiently for the clerks to pile up the empty cardboard boxes after unpacking the groceries inside them. When they had finished, we loaded the boxes into the trunk of the car. Back home, we unfolded all the boxes and spread them out on the basement floor. With scissors, glue, tape, and markers, we transformed the boxes into buildings, and the buildings formed our ideal cities.

There were two rules as to how the buildings were constructed. The first, "anything goes." And the second, "anyone goes"—anyone was accepted and protected in our cities. Turning cardboard boxes into cities taught me to always deconstruct the box in front of me, to re-imagine it, and to then use the same materials to reconstruct it according my own design. No box would remain intact once I laid my hands on it and put my mind to it, and I thank my mom and dad for sharing their gift with me.

CONTENTS

FASHIONING REALITY

THE RUNWAY STARTS HERE

THE WAITING ROOM AT ELITE MODELS is a head trip. Ten sleek black leather and chrome chairs line one wall. Ten black-framed photographs of beautiful young women decorate the other. The first time I was there I analyzed those photos like a mad scientist, trying to figure out exactly what made these particular female human beings the bomb. One hundred per cent wrinkle free? Check. Swan necks? Check. Teeny waists? Check. Mini hips? Check. Skinny arms and legs? Check, you-better-believe-it check. Smiles to make orthodontists weep with pride? Oh yes. And not only were all the teeth bright white, nine out of the ten models were white. I was either on Planet Clone or inside a top modelling agency, soaking up all the nerve, attitude, and action I could: the shuffled photos, the wailing phones, the horrified whispers, the cries of "Oh my God, *fabulous!*" It was action I wanted to get a firm grip on.

A herd of gazelles interrupted my inspections. No, wait a minute. Those were real live models, rushing by on their stilt legs with their portfolios tucked under their twig arms. I was seeing the same cheekbones, the same blonde manes and the same limbs for yards as the photos up on the wall. Except the real live versions seemed somehow less alive. They were tired, faded, not what you'd call vibrant . . . makeup bag let down, you might say.

Next a slim, elegant gentleman appeared on the scene. He was as willowy and bone structured as the ladies. He wore a pink and silver tie and a crisp, white, button-down shirt neatly tucked into sleek black pinstriped pants. Small silver curls were nestled tight to his head thanks to an obviously superior hair product. Everyone around here seemed to be worth a close look. The man stopped right in front of me.

"Mr. Ben, Mr. Ben, Mr. Ben. Welcome to Elite. Come to the boardroom immediately."

I jumped up and hurried. More framed pictures of more women so perfect it was hard to tell them apart: there was a glamazon factory somewhere (evidently Norway) and someone had placed a very big order. A long, oak table stretched the length of the boardroom.

"Take a chair, Mr. Ben."

The seat felt hot; I was having trouble keeping my cool. This was, after all, the big time. This was a room where deals were made with top magazine editors, advertising agents, photographers, and fashion designers. A single conversation in here could launch a top model—or sink a career. A top modelling agent has the power to control images that millions of people see on billboards, magazine covers, and televisions. Lately I had been dreaming of being a part of this world. And now, crazy miracle, I was.

I was sitting across a table from Elmer Olsen, vice-president of Elite Models, a.k.a. Industry Powerhouse. And I wasn't going to blush. No I wasn't. Yes I was.

"Well, Mr. Ben, how can I help you?" he asked.

It wasn't easy but I stared him down. "Sir, I want to steal your job."

Elmer smiled. Fourteen-year-olds aren't particularly diplomatic.

AN EIGHTH-GRADE FASHION INSIDER

I got that first meeting with Elmer during spring break of my eighth grade. I'd started my modelling agency four months before, pretty well by accident. It began as a simple attempt to do a favour for a friend, then swiftly evolved into a mission. By the time I found myself in Elite's boardroom I had five models under contract and I was determined to do my best for them. My mom had been planning a big trip to Toronto for months with museums and art galleries in mind, but I'd done some serious itinerary revamping. Now all I wanted to do was visit modelling agencies, so I'd looked them up in the phone book and requested meetings. Mom agreed to tough it out on her own with the Rembrandts and Ming vases. My father passed away when I was five, so it's mostly been just her and me. We've gotten pretty good at letting each other do our own thing.

When I'd communicated that I was the owner of a modelling agency visiting from out of town, big-city agents were delighted to make time for me. I dressed for what I thought was the part—my Sunday-best blazer, my shiny new black pants, and a classic turtleneck that I figured had continental flare. It was just too bad portfolios didn't come in smaller sizes. People could see either my belt buckle or my face; I arrived everywhere in the middle of a wrestling match.

I thought I looked pretty good but the receptionists weren't having any of it. When I showed up for my appointments, they did a fast double take and bounced Junior ASAP. No one was nice. No one cared about my lovely models. The best I got was, "Come back when you've finished high school, and maybe we can give you an internship." That wasn't going to do it for Nadia, Jane, Keisha, Sareena, and Sun-Yee, and it definitely wasn't good enough for me. My very last meeting was the one at Elite: the top agency in town with the largest roster of models internationally. It was do-or-die time. I was too young to die.

Elmer didn't seem fazed by age and attitude. He pored over the photos in my portfolio and asked questions about one model in particular: Nadia. "How tall is she? How tall are her parents? How big are her feet?" I was stumped. I knew Nadia's dress size and that was about it. Her feet? What was with the feet? I could only answer that she was thirteen and had tall parents. Elmer, however, had a genius grasp of genetics: "Thirteen, looks like a size 7 shoe, tall parents, so she'll grow. She should be okay."

He took me back to examine the pictures of the thin, white models in the thin, black frames, explaining how each met his criteria. He made comments like, "I scouted her in Turtle Lake. She's five foot ten and look at that teeny little body!" There was another model who made Elmer himself glow. "Isn't she gorgeous?" he asked. All I saw was a girl whom I might confuse with a couple of sticks and a smiley face. But Elmer saw the gold standard and if I was going to make it as an agent, I had to see the same: a thin, white, young, tall woman. "When you find a beautiful girl just like this, send her to me. I will treat her well. I'll treat you well, too," he promised.

I left on a high. Elmer Olsen, the guiding force at Elite, had spent a whole hour with me and had taken my small agency seriously. I'd been taught some basic rules of the game and was on my way to becoming a player. I'd been thinking that to make it as a model, charisma, personality, and basic hygiene would do. Now I knew the criteria for real success. Look out world: I had become a fashion insider.

THE COST OF BEAUTY

That was March 15, 1996—the day I boarded a roller coaster that hasn't slowed down once since, despite some highly unexpected twists.

By day, I was a high school student on the cross-country track team and the debating team, deciding whether it ought to be resolved that cartoons are harmful to children or if city councils should be given more political power. I openly loved French and drama class, secretly loved algebra, and was extremely proud of my vintage Pumas.

By night, I was in my office running a modelling agency—interviewing hopefuls, fine tuning contracts, and nailing down bookings. At 6 a.m. I had to wake up and call Europe to manage my models there. During lunch and spares, I was on the phone drumming up local business. I used school holidays to fly to New York, Los Angeles, Paris, and Milan. My agency expanded from representing five models to representing two hundred. Our client list grew to include MTV, Dove, Max Factor, Nike, L'Oréal, and Sears. Our models appear on the pages of *Vogue*, *Elle*, and *Seventeen*, and work catwalks all across Europe, Asia, and North America.

I started to get a lot of attention of my own. *Teen People* magazine recognized me as "one of twenty teens who will change the world." I was named "one of twenty-five leaders of tomorrow" by *Maclean's* magazine. I was interviewed on *Oprah*, FOX, CNN, *Fashion Television*, and in print for *Fashion*, *People*, and *Profit*, among others. Professionally, I appreciated the increased credibility and momentum. On a personal level, I loved the chance to travel the globe and to meet so many masters of their crafts. Trust me, if you approach it at the right time, in the right frame of mind, with the right aptitude, business is a thrill ride.

In the midst of all these glorious achievements, however, a crisis of conscience started boiling within me and threatened to overflow. The usual, typical, accepted standards for models started to seem outdated and harmful and grossly oppressive. Intuitively, I had once understood that beauty does not—and must not—depend on any one standard. I wanted my ideals back. I needed to challenge my mentor, Elmer.

The paradox would be ridiculous if it wasn't so tragic. The fashion industry takes pride in its creativity and innovation—season after season, year after year, designers find new ways of expressing their artistry—yet the kind of face and body that gives life to this art form remains the same. Modelling should be a positive reflection of our lives and our world. But it's not, not yet. It remains negative. It tells us, no, you don't fit the mould, you're not up to par, you're not thin enough or white enough or young enough. The average female model is five foot eleven, 117 pounds and white. The average woman is five foot four and 140 pounds and comes in assorted colours. Seems like a bit of a discrepancy, don't you think?

Well, fashion does that on purpose. Marketers purposefully create and maintain a gap between models and consumers. They believe that the disconnect helps to sell products. They destroy our self-image then persuade us to build it back up again by buying their cologne, shampoo, and jeans. As Dr. Phil McGraw points out, "It's always been that way, but it's getting more intense lately. Defining yourself through these images is the problem. Judging people on how closely they compare to the idealized model is the problem. It's the marketing machine—'if you have this, you will be glamorous too.'"

Business may be booming, but at what cost? The fact is, consumers will *never* look like models. (Most of the time, even the models don't look like models—they have zits, freckles, bellies, and, trust me I've seen it up close, cellulite.) Yet customers continue to buy advertised products as if they'll somehow turn into Kate Moss.

This is a lot bigger than that all-too-common and corrosive little question: "Do these pants make my butt look too big?" Currently, 80 per cent of women and 45 per cent of men in the United States dislike the size and shape of their bodies. Among them, nearly ten million women and one million men have medically diagnosed eating disorders. According to the National Eating Disorders Association, eating disorders affect people of every race, gender, and age. In a congressional briefing sponsored by the American Psychological Association, Dr. Lisa Berzins stated that, "The fear of being fat is so overwhelming that teenage girls have indicated in surveys that they are more afraid of becoming fat than they are of cancer, nuclear war, or losing their parents."

Celebrities are a long way from immune. Mary-Kate Olsen, Lindsay Lohan, and Victoria Beckham are just a few of the starlets who've discussed their struggles with body image. Being thin has become a top prerequisite for commercial success. Losing a few pounds to gain a lot of credibility seems like a leap in the right direction for some celebrities—and for those trying to emulate them.

The sad facts truly hit home for me when it came to my gorgeous, healthy young friends. One day, I would be sitting beside a runway in Paris, watching size 0 models strut their stuff in haute couture. The next, I would be hanging out in the school cafeteria listening to my pals complain about calculus and being tubby. Then Mia, my best friend—the one I spent every possible lunch, spare, and Starbucks run with—beautiful, healthy, strong Mia developed anorexia. The disconnect between my two worlds was heartbreaking.

ALTERING THE FASHION INDUSTRY (AND THE WORLD)

I'm not the first to notice the problem, of course. Hundreds of books criticize the fashion industry's obsession with skinny, young, white models. But those books stop one step short. They don't offer concrete, workable solutions. Fashion is and always will be a *business*.

I owed it to myself, and my world, to figure out a way to make fashion real while still establishing a business that thrived. I had to contemplate the industry with every ounce of insight I had going for me and work at affecting change from within. I had to wonder if fashion's leaders were simply out of touch—

isolated in their fancy Parisian studios and Manhattan lofts—or if there was something more sinister at work. How had this faulty paradigm been created? Why was it so resistant to change and how could I change it nonetheless?

Call me crazy but I was determined to run a modelling agency based on the principle that we are all beautiful in our own ways. I wanted more people to identify with models instead of getting forced into a narrow, uninspired, stereotyped understanding of beauty that's false the moment you think twice about it.

The business strategy I developed is surprisingly simple: people are excited when they see magazines and billboards with models they can relate to. Diverse models represent the people who will be buying and wearing the clothes. Advertising that reflects the consumer allows the buyer to identify with the brand. It builds loyalty and market share. It makes money.

In the beginning, I didn't know anyone would listen to someone new to the business, let alone a teenager. But I owed it to Mia and myself to try.

It was a big risk. But it paid off.

DOING WELL BY DOING GOOD

I wrote this book because I wanted consumers to get an insider's look at the changes I was able to make to the fashion industry. Also, I wanted to give other people working in fashion and beauty ammunition to blast through changes in their own firms. And I wanted to inspire potential entrepreneurs to enter fashion on brave new terms. Fashion *is* changing slowly, but it needs new energy and ideas to push it along.

But the story I have to tell is bigger than one young person and one industry. As the head of a company that makes a profit while also working for social change, I'm part of a growing movement. Many other entrepreneurs—especially young ones—have developed business approaches along similar lines and come up with innovative solutions to other social problems. So my second reason for writing this book was to prove that business can be a vehicle for social change and, furthermore, that business is sometimes even more effective than traditional activism.

Entrepreneurship is more accessible than you might think. If you're interested enough, it doesn't matter if you're young, or have the fancy degree from the snobby school. Anyone can make a serious contribution to the business world and thereby society. In fact, young people are natural entrepreneurs. We see the need for change around us and have the energy and imagination to take action.

With all that we know, at this very moment, we can transform our world. The stories I share in this book are going to prove that. When you're done, ask yourself: what are you waiting for?

Fashion your reality.

PART ONE

CHANGING THE FACE OF FASHION

MY PURSUIT OF REAL BEAUTY IN AN UNREAL INDUSTRY

CHAPTER ONE

MY CALL TO THE FASHION WORLD

THE BEGINNING OF THE BEN BARRY AGENCY

MY FIRST MODEL WAS LAUREN.

My family was over at her house for a New Year's party. It was an annual tradition, full of good times and, of course, good food—a sweet salad of apples, nuts, and cinnamon followed by roast lamb, grilled asparagus, and baked carrots with brown sugar. Dessert was carrot cake and French vanilla ice cream, my favourite. Lauren didn't mind it either. After two helpings of cake à la mode each, she and I excused ourselves. We waddled groaning to the TV room and collapsed on the sofa, hoping if we could only digest a little bit then we could have thirds.

Lauren and I had grown up together—sharing vacations, birthday parties, and milestones. Our families would get together five or six times a year. Being the only "young 'uns," we two would always be seated together, carrying on our own conversation amid the adult chitchat. In the past year, though, we hadn't seen much of each other. Lauren was sixteen, two years older than me, and already in high school. In some ways, flopping together on the sofa was as familiar as ever, but I couldn't help noticing a few intriguing differences.

Lauren had sort of grown up. Instead of jeans she had on a dress and *high heels*. Ponytails RIP, her hair was cut short and had been carefully styled for the occasion. Her makeup was something else again: her eyelids were shades of violet and mauve, her lashes were long and sooty, and her lips shone glossy pink. Lauren sparkled. Suddenly I was comparing her to Gwen Stefani, or maybe Gwyneth Paltrow, or both.

"Laur, you look like you should be in a magazine," I said.

Lauren laughed. "Dude, I wish! Actually, I took a modelling class. They taught us how to do hair and makeup, how to walk for fashion shows, how to pose for photo shoots, and stuff like that."

"That must've been cool."

"It was, but nothing's happened since. The course cost $3,000! Now I have a portfolio and the agency said they would find me jobs but it's been five months of zip."

I asked to see the pictures. The first one was a direct face shot. She was looking down and to the left. But she wasn't smiling for the camera; the photographer had caught her in the middle of a very Lauren laugh, the kind with an after-smile that lasted for hours. The next one showed her sitting on a park bench. In others, she was standing in front of a white wall or lying on the grass. I'd never spied anything so glamorous in my life.

"Wow, these are amazing," I said. "Modelling is totally meant for you."

"Maybe." Lauren looked uncharacteristically wistful. "I love to model, I love it all—taking on different personalities, listening to the photographer, getting my hair and makeup done. And I totally love the clothes and shoes. But the agency says I need to lose weight."

I couldn't believe it. It was one of the stupidest things I'd ever heard in my life. "No way! You're perfect! You shouldn't need to change a thing."

"The agency says I can only work if I'm a size 4 at the biggest and right now I'm an 8. I have no idea how I'm going to lose weight. My mom told me not to diet but I'm thinking about it. Maybe eating two meals instead of three?"

"Those modelling people are crazy! And that can't be good for you." I was remembering the joy with which we'd both just pigged out. "You should be able to get work the way you are."

Lauren was more resigned than I was. "Magazines and designers don't want girls my size. I'm not skinny enough."

"This doesn't make any sense to me." I said. "If I can imagine you in magazines, then I bet other people could as well. C'mon, give me your pictures and let me try."

"Ya, right. Thanks Ben, but you don't really know what you're doing."

"The *experts* haven't found you a job in five months, so let me try. The worst is that I won't get you a job, which is no worse than what's happening now."

I had her, I could see it in her big camera-ready hazel eyes. "Okay. I guess it couldn't hurt. But I still think you're nuts."

When we returned home that night, I headed straight to my mother's magazine collection. I scanned the pages and studied the models like I was boning up for a biology quiz. I focused on one local magazine. Its latest cover model was attractive, but no special energy radiated out from the page—unlike Lauren's stellar photographs. It was clear to me that this magazine needed her. I put pen to paper:

Dear Fashion Editor,

I am writing to inform you of an amazing model for your magazine. Lauren has the personality, energy, and look that would make her perfect for your fashion pages. I hope you will consider her for *Ottawa Magazine*. Please call me if you would like to hire her.

Thank you,
Ben Barry

I slipped in a couple of Lauren's photos and mailed the package the next day. Three weeks later, I was doing homework at the kitchen table one afternoon when the phone rang.

"Ben Barry, please," an extremely grown-up voice requested.

"Umm, yes, this is Ben."

"We really like Lauren. We'd like to use her. Is she available next week?"

"Yes!" I was ecstatic for a moment. But some tougher questions followed.

"Good news. So you must be her agent?"

"Her agent?" That threw me. I wasn't sure what I was. But an immediate answer was necessary so I mustered up some confidence and went with, "Yes, I'm her agent, sir."

"Great. We'd like to draw up a contract. What's the name of your agency?"

Another quick decision. "The Ben Barry Agency." It was the first name that came to me. It was mine after all.

"Where do I fax the contract?"

Covering the phone's mouthpiece, I yelled, "Mom, what's the number of your fax at work?"

With that one phone call, Lauren was in. And so, unexpectedly, was I.

SETTING UP BUSINESS

Word about Lauren's fashion shoot travelled as fast as teenage gossip—somewhere between warp speed and the speed with which a zit shows up the night before a dance. Soon, several other girls who had taken the same modelling course as Lauren asked me to be their agent as well. I decided to set up shop.

At school, I provoked a lot more uncertainty than excitement. I gave my business card to my grade eight teachers in case they could help. They smiled in obvious mystification. Since I studied hard, got good grades, and made it to the regional cross-country finals, most people accepted it as a phase I was going through, albeit a strange one. A modelling agency run by a fourteen-year-old? In sober, frigid Ottawa, Ontario, instead of New York or Paris? They figured I was playing a game.

Meanwhile, I needed to upgrade my work space. The family room in our basement wasn't cutting it. My mother didn't like the idea of strangers walking through the house, and the ping-pong table, shelf of track trophies, and two cats who licked anyone in sight weren't very professional. A friend's father was a lawyer who worked downtown in an old, restored Victorian building. It was elegant and hip, with converted loft spaces and exposed brick walls. He agreed to loan his office to me one or two evenings a week for free. He wanted to support my entrepreneurial spirit and boost my confidence, just like someone had done for him when he was starting out.

I'd arrive just as he and his partner were leaving, shouldering a backpack and carrying two suitcases. I'd take down all the law degrees and certificates from the walls—stuffing them into the suitcases—and replace them with my own accoutrements. My recommendation letters took the place of family photos. I'd tape my nameplate over the one that read "Williams and McLean, Barristers" on the front door. In minutes, the lawyer's office became The Ben Barry Studio.

To recruit models, I stapled flyers on lampposts and bulletin boards with dangling strips of paper that could be torn off with my phone number, as if I was selling a bike. The ad read:

MODELS WANTED
New modelling agency looking for men and women to represent for fashion shoots and shows. No fees. No modelling classes required.

It wasn't snazzy but it fit my budget and it was getting the job done. Each week I would meet with about ten prospects at my studio. My "receptionist" (one of a group of friends who took turns acting the part) would greet the candidates. Each one would be handed an application form. It asked for all the usual information that agencies gather: eye colour, body measurements, shoe size, etcetera. But it also asked about interests. I wanted to know if they studied or worked, what their hobbies and passions were, whether they could sing or dance or lion tame. I was sure that a person's diverse skills and experiences would enhance their modelling. I wanted the whole resumé.

The receptionist would then show the prospective model into my office. I would get up from behind the desk and conduct an initial interview in the leather chairs around the coffee table. Many prospects were initially suspicious, asking if this was someone else's work space or if I worked with an older partner.

"I own the agency," I would reply. "We actually have two offices; this studio, where we meet with our models, and a booking office where I do the paperwork." (I neglected to mention it was also where I ate cookies, played with my cats Spice and Russia, and watched *Beverly Hills 90210*.) I'd stress that since this was solely my agency, without junior agents, they could count on the fact they wouldn't be shuffled off to anybody less experienced. The head of the agency would personally work hard for them, seeing to their every professional need.

One or two prospects per night would seem worth pursuing. I'd show these ones the contract I'd developed instead of a standard modelling agreement. It surprised a lot of people. It gave me a 15 per cent commission, five percentage points below the standard rate in the city. And I didn't hold models exclusively to our agency: they could work with any other modelling firm they wanted. I explained our desire to be fair and also show how confident we were about our abilities.

"Once you start working with the Ben Barry Agency, you won't want to work with anybody else," I'd say. "We'll be getting you so much work, I don't know how you could."

A final distinction was that no classes or fees were required. "An agency should only make money when it finds you work," I'd let them know. "You shouldn't need to spend money unless it's for a legitimate cost, like having photos done or copying them to be sent to publications and designers. We only charge models for justifiable costs."

By the end of the evening, usually a couple of new models would have signed on or be seriously considering it. Once the last prospect had left the premises we'd pack up, hang back up the law degrees and I'd leave a thank-you note for the lawyer. My mother would pick us up as if we'd been at softball practice or catching the latest teensploitation flick.

In those early days, I was learning to be creative; to make use of my limited time and resources; to find advantages in my competitors' disadvantages—and in my own situation. I adjusted to what I learned to be the essentials of the modelling business. Nonetheless, I made sure to develop my own unique style. I was learning to be an entrepreneur but I was still just a kid. Somehow it was working.

AN EARLY ENTREPRENEUR

Thinking back, I realize I had always wanted to run a business. Sure, I was on the school track team but I never dreamed of the Olympics. At home I'd play executive instead. I was designing model cities with cardboard boxes way before *SimCity*, having a blast with pretend mergers and play acquisitions, crunching numbers for fun.

In fact, I started one operation when I was still in grade school. At the age of eleven, I decided to open a bed and breakfast right in our house. I developed a business plan. I bought an old Salvation Army uniform that I converted to a maître d' outfit, name tag included. I prepared a brochure that I distributed around the neighbourhood, advertising my services with printed menus and price lists. I set up my room and the spare bedroom as guest rooms, complete with guest towels and a chocolate on the pillow (After Eights). I did everything necessary to set up a viable B&B, including getting my first customer. Every detail had been looked after except one—I hadn't cleared any of this with Mom.

She came home one day to find a strange car in our driveway and a sign for Dorset Drive Bed and Breakfast on the lawn. The first customers had just arrived. They asked her about checking in. She was at a loss, and apparently stammered the first thing that came into her mind—which was to temporarily disown me.

"I don't know, I'm just visiting," she replied, as she got back into her car and left.

Mom needed time to think this one over. Soon enough she put her foot down, no doubt thanking her lucky stars that I was an only child and no one was screening movies in the attic or washing dogs in the garage. My mother wasn't willing but my grandmother thought the B&B was adorable. So when she came to stay I waited tables, set up the room, gave her the bill, and very happily collected a tip. Two years after my hotelier episode, I found a part-time job booking school bands. Then, at fourteen, I started the modelling agency. Third time lucky.

Many entrepreneurs start early. Something stirring within them leads them to sell lemonade, or build websites, or start clubs, or sell cool T-shirts. The ones that succeed, I believe, are driven by something apart from a desire to make money. Often, they want to help others, as I did with Lauren. They take a small leap and find themselves rocketing skyward. Entrepreneurs have a useful blind spot: they don't easily see limits—their own or anyone else's.

CHAPTER TWO

DISCOVERING THE MODEL

SCOUTING THE NATION BUT LOOKING FOR THE SAME GIRL

MY FORMAL EDUCATION in the fashion world began with an international contest run by Elite Model Management—the largest modelling agency in the world. Elite Model Look is a highly publicized annual search contest. The winner gets a modelling contract with Elite worth $1 million, and that's just her start. Nationals are held in fifty countries, then each winner represents her country in a worldwide run-off. Doors have opened wide for aspiring models all over the world. Brazilian superstar Giselle Bündchen got launched this way, likewise Canadian icon for the ages, Linda Evangelista.

Three months after I first met Elmer, he phoned me out of the blue to ask if I wanted to join him as a judge for part of the Canadian leg of the search. He said the whole process would teach me a lot about what great models look like and how to pick them. This was obviously a chance of a lifetime. Thankfully, this particular chance of a lifetime was taking place for the most part after school was out. I've never been one for skipping class if I can help it. I've had to miss so many of them involuntarily that I know all too well how the work just piles up and makes for more in the end.

I told all my girlfriends about the search. I told the ones who I was sure would make great models that they'd be crazy not to enter. Approximately ten decided to take me up on it. As it turned out, one of the first Canadian events was in a downtown shopping mall in my hometown: Ottawa's Rideau Centre. I left after morning classes, switching from my school uniform into my professional modelling agent attire of the time: black pants, shiny shoes, a black T-shirt several sizes too big and over that, yes, a purple dress shirt tucked into a big belt. Suave was my thought. I stuffed my school clothes into my backpack with my textbooks and gym clothes, threw on my puffy red winter jacket (the morning had been unseasonably nippy and Mom had insisted and now I had no other way of carrying it), and headed for the bus stop.

The mall was pumping to the manic beats of Britney and Christina with some Madonna thrown in for the sake of tradition. Huge photos of top models attracted onlookers. Crowds peered into the atrium, their eyes fixed on a runway set up in the centre court. I spotted Elmer at the judges' table and made my way over to him through a maze of tall, tall women in high, high heels. The air smelled of perfume, hair spray, and nerves. I felt for them. I couldn't believe I was about to judge them. I wondered who was going to judge *me* judging them.

Elmer laughed at my sweaty brow. "Off to the Arctic, Mr. Ben?" he asked as he led me backstage to get rid of my stuff. I was happy to dump the coat but kept the backpack nearby; I needed to work on my French homework during breaks. At the judge's table, Elmer pulled up the chair right beside him. He was elegantly garbed as usual, in black pants, a white waist-length jacket with zippers instead of buttons, and a black dress shirt—quintessential Armani chic circa 1998.

There were two other equally stylish judges who eyed me strangely as Elmer performed introductions. One was the editor of a magazine about the modelling industry and the other was the area manager of the clothing chain sponsoring the search. Glaring at me from the sidelines were all the other Ottawa modelling agents. They knew about me from a recent newspaper interview I'd given to the *Ottawa Citizen*. I'd offered to scout models for some of them but had been rebuffed because of my age. Obviously, I wasn't too young to make it to the head table. (Ha!)

There were five hundred contestants there that day, divided into groups of ten. They had to walk down the runway, stop and smile, then turn around and walk back. Then they'd have to line up in front of the judges' table. Elmer would get out of his chair, step onto the runway, and scrutinize each candidate individually. He'd examine a girl's pores, double check the proportions of her nose, inspect any blemishes to see whether they would scar and assess her overall bone structure. He was like an art connoisseur before a painting, with definite ideas about what is and is *not* in good taste. Except Elmer was staring at young faces.

Point blank, Elmer wouldn't consider anyone under five foot seven. I might say, "She looks great!" But he'd just smile encouragingly at the woman as she turned and then put a big X beside her name on the score sheet. "Yes, she has a very pretty face," Elmer might say, "but her hips are too big and they'll never be smaller." Or, "That one has a great body but she just isn't tall enough, too bad." And so on. "Too wide." "Too short." "Bad eyes." "Bad nose." "Bad skin." If anyone was wearing pants that covered her ankles Elmer would hoist up a leg. This also ensured he wouldn't accidentally pick a model whose height derived from her shoes: a dreaded "height-cheater."

Most of the hopefuls were immediately disqualified without being offered a single word as to why. Every single one received a welcoming smile from Elmer but that was as far as it went. They simply didn't meet "industry standards." Elmer kept telling me to look at ankles. He said if a girl had tiny ankles—and I still don't get the biology behind this—it meant that she had the potential to have a small waist. "She has beautiful ankles," he would say at times. "Get a load of those lovely ankles!" Sometimes he would even take out a measuring tape and check measurements—bust, waist, hips—to determine, I suppose, whether a model's dimensions were as small as her ankles predicted. At least he never measured ankles.

All this went on for about five hours while shoppers in the packed atrium gobbled up the spectacle. I couldn't understand why we weren't questioning the models about anything besides their physical attributes. I asked Elmer, "How do you know if they're good to work with—if they're professionally minded and show up on time? How can we judge what they're really like when they aren't even opening their mouths?" Apparently, that didn't matter at this stage. Right now, we only needed to know who had "potential."

Elmer was obviously in control. The other two judges didn't peep a word until he indicated that a girl had passed his standards. Then they pretty well restated his comments by switching up the fashion jargon a bit: "marvellous" in place of "fabulous" and "delicious" instead of "gorgeous," etcetera. Ever been in a situation where you suddenly realize that there are unspoken rules that everyone knows but you? Brutal.

I want to stress that Elmer's motives were genuine. He was looking for a top model by Elite's standards. Everyone got a fair chance to fit his criteria, which were, I would learn, the entire industry's standard. But the criteria seemed as narrow to me as Shalom Harlow. I was disappointed for the young women who I felt had potential but were being given a short, sweet no. Needless to say, some of them were those friends I had begged to take part. I felt awful. I'd been under the impression they all had the looks, presence, and personality needed to make it to magazine covers or runways. But no, not on this day and not according to these people.

I pointed out one friend to Elmer especially. "She's an amazing soccer player. She has a personality that everyone wants a piece of."

"Yes, she's pretty," he replied.

"But what do you think about her as a model?"

"Not tall enough."

If they weren't five foot eight or thereabouts, they barely stood a chance. The five foot sevens and six footers had to have perfectly symmetrical faces and exceptionally radiant eyes. Not a single one of my beautiful friends made it further than the first round.

ALLISON

During one of the breaks, a girl in the crowd caught my eye. She was different from any of the competitors. She had spiked, punky, bleach blonde hair and piercings all over the place (left eyebrow, nose, and chin at a minimum). She appeared to have an industry-standard physique, although it was hard to tell what was going on beneath her baggy jeans and yellow hoodie. What attracted my attention was her animation. Chatting away to her buddies, she was a total contrast to all the contestants in their tight tops and pants, heels, and makeup. This girl was chilled out—smiling, laughing, and drinking a huge Slurpie.

When I pointed her out to Elmer, he was intrigued, so I went over and invited her to join the contest. Her name was Allison. At first, she turned me down. She had no desire whatsoever to be a model. But I persisted, telling her how amazing the prizes were and what opportunities might lie ahead. Her friends joined in, urging her on, until she finally toppled. Allison told us that she would do it as long as we would all stop bugging her and never speak of this madness again once it was all over. We shook on it.

At 5 p.m., Elmer announced the twenty finalists, including Allison. They all got to take part in a fashion show that evening. The winner would be announced at the end. I quickly shrugged back into my backpack and hurried to join the judges for dinner. It was a chance to compare notes and fuel up. I ordered a burger and fries. Everyone else ordered a salad with a fancy name.

We passed around the application forms from the twenty finalists and discussed them in detail. "Not sure about that nose. . . . Eyes too close together. . . . Lips too small. . . . Features not in proportion. . . . Those cheekbones, not high enough. . . . She won't be able to lose any more off those hips . . ." The judges were incredibly observant. I hadn't remembered anything about gaps between eyes, or hip widths, or torso lengths. But I had noticed if an applicant had charisma. I commented a lot on what energy the models had exuded. Unfortunately, that didn't seem relevant to anybody else. I was a teenager among professionals, bright purple alongside basic black, a burger amid salads.

During the fashion show that followed, the twenty potential models strutted down the runway, no doubt trying their best to imitate models they'd seen on TV. For many, I'm sure it was their first experience in fashion. Some looked like scared baby deer. Others looked like prowling lynxes. Elmer made frequent comments regarding each finalist but I sensed he'd known since our discussion over dinner who was going to win. He wasn't jotting down notes, he was just watching intently. At the end, the judges and crowd turned to Elmer. He stood up to announce the winner.

"ALLISON!"

I was thrilled. The skateboarder—the only contestant who had been her own person—had won. "She's so cool and different!" I said.

Elmer nodded, but he had bigger plans. He liked Allison's edgy look but he wanted her scheduled right away for an extensive makeover. No more piercings and calmer hair; that was all "before" stuff and Allison needed to become an "after." She needed "development."

I was more than a little upset. So much for my discovery. Elmer wasn't picking Allison for who she was but because she would make a good canvas for his artistry. "Can't she keep some of who she is—at least some of her style?" I asked.

"Not if she's going to work," said Elmer.

Allison and the audience were oblivious to all this. My thrill at her win was mixed with guilt as to what it would cost her. As I slumped on the number 52 bus home, I wondered whether either Allison or I knew quite what we were getting into. At the same time, I had complete confidence in Elmer. Elmer knew exactly what it took to succeed in the industry. And I had what it took to help Elmer find excellent models. I had proven it that night.

The rest of the model search continued much like that initial episode. The judges would travel from city to city, station themselves in a prominent mall, and watch three hundred to five hundred young women parade down the runway, eager for their chance at fame, fortune, glamour, and *Glamour*. The vast majority had zero chance right from the start. Maybe five or ten in each show had what it took to pose for magazines and walk the runway. I felt bad that the other 490 endure a seven-hour contest that they had lost before even putting on their lip gloss and buckling their sling-backs. But Elmer kept on smiling at everyone, the whole way through—girl after girl, contest after contest.

As the search progressed, the cities blurred into each other and so, from my point of view, did the contestants. The judges all seemed to be looking for the same thing: Barbie dolls without the cleavage. Only one non-white woman was chosen as the winner for her city (not what I'd call ethnically representative of the nation I love). The only one I remember clearly today is Allison.

The grand finale was held in Toronto, in a huge downtown warehouse on the waterfront that had recently been converted into one of the city's hottest nightclubs. A red carpet at the entrance was burning up with spotlights. The contestants had all been flown in two weeks before for extensive makeovers.

Top photographers had shot them and they'd already been on auditions for magazines, commercials, and fashion shows. Canada didn't get much more chic than this.

A big invite-only pre-party for the industry was happening. I took a date: my aunt Gail. When we arrived at the door, the security guard asked me for my ID. When I showed him my student card, he tried so hard not to laugh that all he did was smirk. Nice guy. He told me that the event was strictly for people nineteen years and older because it was licensed. I proceeded to tell him that the majority of the models in the competition were under nineteen. Aunt Gail smiled at Security Guy while she soothingly stroked my shoulder. I took an article that I had torn out of a newspaper that day from my jacket pocket. It had profiles of all the models in show—a box with each one's picture, name, hometown, and age. I waved this under Security Guy's nose.

I got an "Umm...let me speak to my supervisor."

As the door opened, I heard music blast and saw people with champagne in hand. I was getting in there or else. Within a minute, Security Guy returned.

"Mr. Olsen, who is in charge of this event, has already given us a list of those under nineteen and my supervisor can't find your name on the list."

People were starting to pile up behind us. Aunt Gail's grip on my shoulder was getting tighter. SG got back on the radio with his supervisor. Five minutes later, Elmer popped his head out from behind the door.

"Let in Mr. Ben. He's with me. Sorry everyone, I forgot that Ben here is such a spring chick."

Aunt Gail and I finally made our entrance. We felt like we'd stepped inside the pages of *Vogue*: Paris, London, or New York. Sexy and sophisticated minimalism was all the range for summer '97. Partiers brandishing martinis wore tight, tailored, body-hugging items in solid colours from black to white to orange to aqua. Everyone's Vidal Sassoon hair glowed in a room lit only by candles and low lighting. A DJ spun remixes fused with Bollywood grooves. Some people looked like they were eternally posing for pictures. Others were making sure their hair stayed in place. Others were bouncing off the walls. A runway was raised high above the centre of the room.

Aunt Gail soon went in search of a sofa but I kept prowling. Elmer came up behind me and patted me on the back.

"This is no time to be jumpy, Mr. Ben. The fashion world is here. Let me introduce you."

Elmer and I did the rounds. I met editors, photographers, stylists, makeup artists, hairdressers, advertising agents, casting directors, and many, many models. After the standard double-cheek kiss (the firm handshake of the fashion world) I proceeded to ask my usual million questions.

Most people were horrified and gave me simple one-liners at best: "Thin is beautiful, baby." "Models are human coat-hangers," "Models are for showing off clothes, not themselves," "Models are busy running to castings, go-sees, fittings, shoots—they can go to school after their careers are over," "Oh no, I could never model, I'm too big in the hips . . . my eyes are too close together . . . my lips are too small . . . my ass is too big . . . maybe ten years ago but now I have more wrinkles than a Shar-Pei, lovey."

As I redirected my barrage of questions to each new group we met, Elmer smiled and said, "Ben's getting ready to steal my job." Then Elmer had to leave to get ready for the big show.

When each model did her final twirl of the night, her portfolio flashed on a huge screen. Allison didn't look at all like the Allison I'd first walked up to in Ottawa. Her bleached blonde spiky hair was tamed to a tightly cropped, sandy blonde shag. Her eyes were covered in liner and shadow, and her lips were glossed and pouty. The small scar on her right check was covered up and all of her piercings had vanished. She got roars from the crowd. Round after round of applause exploded from every balcony for every model. The suspense was killing all of us. Except Elmer; he'd made good use of the past two weeks to minutely assess the contestants as they were being groomed and polished and prepped. In the end, he announced his pick. Allison didn't win. I don't remember who did but I'm guessing it was a tall, thin blonde.

Yes, I had mixed feelings about the results but the search was a phenomenal learning opportunity. I was side-by-side with Elmer, pestering him in my charming teenage way: "What will happen to this model when she wins? What is it like to work in Italy? France? What types of models get work in those markets? What's the best way to find models? What look do you suggest for this model? Where do you think this woman should work?" Elmer was incredibly busy—he didn't just have contestants to deal with, he was organizing the entire event—but he was unfailingly kind and helpful and I will never forget that for as long as I live.

By the time the search and the gala final were over, I felt like a real, big-time agent. I knew what it took to find the right models. I had a Rolodex full of contacts in the fashion industry. I had a feeling and passion for the job. I decided to devote the summer to building up my business. If I succeeded, I would be able take on new models and international clients. If not, well, there was always grade nine.

RECRUITING THE INDUSTRY STANDARD

Although I remained a bit fish-out-of-water in Toronto's high-fashion enclaves, I was getting used to my role as an agent back home in Ottawa. I scanned streets, perused malls, and checked out all the high schools. When I found new models and signed them, Elmer would co-manage them with me, helping to secure work for them in Toronto, New York, and elsewhere around the world.

I learned how reliable and consistent an insider's criteria could be. Beauty was not in the eye of the beholder; it was a standard that any agent or scout could learn, and look for, and be respected for adhering to accurately. As I've been warning since page one, the criteria for a professional fashion model are extremely narrow. Take a close look:

- AGE: young. Most models are recruited between the ages of four-teen and sixteen, active from seventeen to twenty-four, and out of the business by twenty-six.
- HEIGHT: tall. But not too tall; five foot nine to five foot eleven.
- WEIGHT: thin. Dress size 2 or 4 (i.e., ten to fifteen pounds under the medically recommended minimum body mass index weight for her height.)
- SHAPE: slim. No more than thirty-five inches at the hips, with waist ten inches smaller than hips. The ideal is 34–24–34 with long legs.
- SHOE: sizes 8, 9, or 10.

- COLOUR: white. People of African descent are represented, but not in proportion to their numbers in the population. For other ethnic groups the representation level is even lower.
- PERSONALITY/INTELLIGENCE: incidental. Unlike musicians and actors, a model is rarely interviewed. The decision to hire her is based solely on her measurements and how she photographs or walks.

Men are recruited a little older. Their careers tend to run from eighteen to thirty years of age. But their physical requirements are just as rigid: six feet to six foot two; waist thirty to thirty-two inches; chest forty or forty-two.

How many of us could meet these criteria, even if we tried really, really hard? Not many. May I repeat: the average female model is five eleven and 117 pounds and the average American woman is five foot four and 140 pounds. Models are practically extraterrestrial. We're not used to them but the camera knows them very well when it sees them.

The ideal photogenic face is oval. Eyes have got to be large and also oval, spaced evenly apart and never too close together. Noses are straight: no bumps. Lips need to be wide and full, with both bottom and top lip around the same length. High cheekbones, strong jaw, clear skin, and a hairline beginning at the point just where the head starts to curve. This is what makes an industry model's face. Please, put the measuring tape down—your nose, lips and chin are just fine. Your mom loves them, your grandma loves them, and I'm sure I'd love them if I ever met you.

I started building my business and soon realized something big—that everything in modelling stems from the way that clients think of their needs. This continued to perplex me because I found a model's personality, hobbies, and interests very hard to separate from her effectiveness. I loved the way my actors emoted, I loved the way my dancers moved. All my clients wanted to see were photographs. It was simply a question of the right look and the correct vital statistics. A model's eyes weren't the windows to anywhere particularly important or useful.

The Elite model search had forced me to seriously rework my own MO. Prospects that I had considered excellent were no longer contenders whatsoever. Melanie, for instance, had thick, black, curly hair and a rambunctious charm that makes you want to stick close to her at a party. I'd spotted her at my high school fashion show and thought that she'd be fantastic in front of the camera or on the runway. Well, she was five foot five and maybe a dress size 7. The last thing I wanted to do was to waste her time or hurt her pride.

Luckily, I was finding excellent models who did fit the criteria. I spotted Élodie at a bus stop, in a downpour, shivering inside a huge raincoat. She was a university student in Hull, on the Quebec side of Canada's national capital region. She didn't speak English, so I made my pitch in high school French. I told her that she would make a great model and handed her my business card. She smiled. I assumed that would be the end of it. But, to my surprise, she phoned right away and came straight over to my house where we retreated to my basement office. We had a nice chat and I took some Polaroids. Elmer loved them. By the end of that week, he'd booked her for the cover of *Fashion*, Canada's most widely read fashion magazine. Wicked.

SHOOTING FOR *SEVENTEEN*

By the time I'd spent one-and-a-half years in business, I represented a group of twenty to thirty industry-quality models. Elmer had introduced me to contacts in New York and Milan and I had been energetically promoting the Ben Barry Agency to them. One of my models, Veronica, was five foot nine with long, black hair and green eyes. We teased her that she looked like Veronica from the Archie comics. What she really looked like was a traditional model. When I spotted her in a shopping mall she had already taken some courses but her agency had done nothing for her, focusing instead on the most recent crop of girls to enrol in their classes. I promised Veronica I could use her existing photos to get her work and I did. Veronica was selected for a main fashion spread in *Seventeen* magazine.

Now we were both off to New York on a 6 a.m. flight. It meant missing a day of school, but Veronica was the first of my models to make the big time in the Big Apple and there was no way I was going to miss out on any moment of the action. When we landed, a car with a chauffeur was waiting, courtesy of *Seventeen*. It was Veronica's first time in a limo but I'd shared a couple already so I tried to act suave. Soon enough we were delivered to a photo studio in a huge open space atop a building in Soho. Veronica and the other model in the shoot were sent straight to hair and makeup.

I used my time to chat up the editors of *Seventeen*, both fashion editors and booking editors—whenever they were on a break between cellphone calls, that was. With eighteen months of experience under my (patent) belt, I was feeling more comfortable in my skin. This gang all thought it was really cool that I was an agent at such a young age. I knew by then that youth had its enviable rewards. I could walk into high schools and scout the best prospects without looking perverted. My age also made me stand out, so I got remembered. Those are two great business advantages: the ability to go where your competitors can't and something special that leaves you etched in people's memory. Plus, I had a great and willing mentor in Elmer.

But I still had a lot to learn. The *Seventeen* editors explained that they were looking for models with "beautiful bodies" and a "healthy glow." I checked out Veronica as she got her makeup done. She seemed to have enough makeup on to make a hundred-year-old granny *glow*. I conveyed this observation to the beauty editor as diplomatically as possible.

"Your girl's not spending any more time in the chair than any other, darling," the editor replied. "That beautiful black hair gives her a real *exotic* look, don't you think? We're darkening the skin tone with foundation. She's just too pale naturally. It's so much easier to make a white girl look darker than a dark girl look lighter. Otherwise it can be a disaster. If she's too dark, she just won't photograph properly. She'll look gorgeous. Just wait and see, darling."

The photographer shot for about two hours—not that long considering both models spent fully four hours in makeup beforehand. The stylists and photographers were highly trained, there was no doubt about that. Each model had three looks to do. Two looks would be individual frames and one would be the two of them together. On went some classic Whitney full blast. The models were told to move, smile, and laugh. When the photographer liked a movement he asked them to hold it: "Beautiful, stay in it," and "Keep that, so sexy, baby, sexy."

At first, I could see Veronica trying not to laugh. Me, too. I doubt anyone had ever called her "so sexy, baby" before, especially not a strange forty-year-old man. I could also see that it was hard for Veronica to freeze her dance moves, especially when Whitney totally held a note. It looked a bit like she was playing Red Light/Green Light. But no one else laughed. This was fashion church. In between the photographer's verbal explosions and choruses of "I wanna dance with somebody," makeup artists rushed on the set to re-apply, and re-re-apply Veronica's foundation. It was smudging against her collar and dripping off her face. She kept needing to get darkened again. Eventually, Veronica and I slipped into career-minded moods and made this thing happen.

On the flight home from New York, I was on a natural high. I'd come a long way from getting Lauren into *Ottawa Magazine*. This was real fashion, true fashion, high fashion. I had a sense of where I was headed. Bigger, better, higher, more.

Cut to a few months later, lunch as usual in the school cafeteria—whoever had ordered a salad was trying to steal someone else's fries and speculation had started as to who was bringing whom to the spring formal. Then Jenn pulled out a fresh copy of the new April *Seventeen*. It had just hit the newsstands. I'd been sent JPEGs of the shoot but I hadn't seen it in context. Jenn ceremoniously handed over the magazine to me so I could flip to the pages that mattered while my pals beat out on a drum roll on the table. My satisfaction was rebounding off the walls, my grin was a half a mile wide, my mind was scrambling to savour every detail of every second . . . I had booked this model. I had helped this magazine bring its main photo spread to life. Here was proof that I had made it into the fashion industry and now I got to share it with my beloved posse.

The magazine quickly did the rounds, everyone wanted a good look. At first, the feedback was entirely dream-come-true: "Wow, she's so pretty!" "I love her outfits!" "Ben, this is so cool!" "That skirt is super cute!" "She's got great hair." But gradually, the remarks started to change colour, let's say from sunshine yellow to thundercloud grey. "Her stomach is so flat. Oh my God, the chick has, like, no blubber." "I wish I could afford those clothes but there's no way." "Has she ever had a zit in her life?" One friend complained, "My legs would look so chunky if I ever tried to wear a skirt like that." Another moaned,

"My hair is way too frizzy to wear it down like hers, nobody behind me would be able to see the blackboard."

Great. My big *Seventeen* spread was making all my friends feel like crap.

I had expected a huge celebration that would boost my pride somewhere up between Venus and Pluto: "Oh, Ben, this is so wonderful—so beautiful. Congratulations, Ben. Awesome, way to go!" I had expected a nice big helping of joy with plenty to go around for everyone. I had expected happiness. And definitely everyone was happy for me—while they were feeling inferior about themselves.

Without even realizing what they were up to, my friends were turning Veronica into a role model and then immediately putting themselves down for not living up to her. They didn't know anything about Veronica other than that she had the latest clothes, the latest hair, and expertly highlighted cheekbones. It didn't matter to them that they got dressed every day without stylists and makeup artists and studio lighting. It didn't matter that Clara was an all-star in dance, that Kishwar had just got an A+ on her English test, or that Lindsay scored the winning goal of the city soccer championship. All that mattered at that moment was that they didn't look like models. They couldn't. They had different bodies, different complexions, different priorities. And thank God for that.

I won't claim an epiphany. No light bulb went on in my head, no Hallelujah chorus. But over the next week, as I showed the magazine around some more and got the same sequence of reactions, I slowly began to reflect on how things had backfired. I'd had a hand in creating something that I thought was going to be wonderful all around and instead it had injured people's confidence and self-esteem. I was having a profound impact on people—but not the impact I had intended. I didn't yet know how, but I knew things needed to change.

CHAPTER THREE

QUESTIONING THE MODEL

PURSUING PERFECTION

FROM THE START I THOUGHT Mia was amazing. She was athletic, involved in school track and volleyball, and a phenomenal dancer. She started ballet and modern dance when she was three years old and was now regularly taking part in serious competitions. I always heard all about them. Mia and I had united over a shared love of clothing—basically over the fact that we were total, utter, hopeless trendoids. Our bond was forged in French class when everyone had to give a speech about somebody notable from France. The keeners could do François Mitterand and the eggheads could do Jean-Paul Sartre, but Mia and I both picked Coco Chanel. The teacher told us to work together on the presentation. Soon, we prolonged our time together from Friday mornings at the library to Friday afternoons at the bookstore, more specifically the magazine racks, poring over whatever fashion publications from around the world we could get our voracious hands on. We really liked French *Vogue* and Italian *Elle*. We really loved Christy Turlington and Naomi Campbell.

Mia was fascinated by the models. She would gush over how one looked in a certain outfit, or how she posed, on how simply beautiful she seemed. My attentions were more businesslike. I kept a small notebook handy and wrote down the names of the fashion editors and assistant editors, sending off letters advising them that my models could provide just as good a look if not better. I thought I was building international contacts but I never heard a word back. It didn't occur to me at the time that an editor in Milan or Rio de Janeiro would have no reason to call some guy they had never heard of in Ottawa. Innocence can be very time consuming!

Mia was always super busy. She was a diligent student but dance dominated her life. She had classes twice a week and a lot of weekends were taken up by competitions. But we generally made time to have lunch together. At first she would match my sandwich, cookies, and milk (yes, my food choices aren't typically on trend) with her rice, fruit, and dessert. After a while, though, I noticed some subtle changes. Eventually she was having only a yogurt, or perhaps some carrot sticks, or just an apple. Her lunch bag was still jammed with more substantial fare, but she ate little of it. If I mentioned anything, she would shrug it off with, "I'm not that hungry," or "I'm going to save it for later."

Then she started getting too busy to do lunch. She would drop by for a few minutes and then head off for a "meeting" or to "spend time in the library." Something would always pull her away. But she was an active, busy person, so I didn't make much of it.

Mia had been slim her whole life, but in an athletic way, with muscle tone and vitality. Now she was becoming thin and then thinner. Jutting bones took the place of the muscles that had formerly outlined her strong arms and legs. Her shoulder blades began to protrude. Her rosy cheeks began to fade and they no longer swelled when she smiled. They sank along with her eyes, which lost pretty well all of their twinkle. And Mia became cranky, often cutting me off mid-sentence or jumping on whatever I said and disagreeing with me. Her bursts of energy during our nightly phone call transformed into doldrums of pessimism.

I'd tell Mia that she was looking worn out, or that she was working too hard. I'd suggest she take a break and chill. But she always had an excuse. Schools are thick with grapevines and gossip soon started to spread about how skinny Mia was getting—that she wasn't eating, that it was a problem. I heard the chatter but I wasn't sure what to do.

One day, after Mia hadn't shown up at school for a couple of days, she finally called me back. Her mother had caught her forcing herself to throw up and she was in the children's hospital. Mia's parents had sensed what was happening, but like everybody else had been in denial or were unsure how to act. My mother drove me over to the hospital after a stop for flowers, the biggest most cheerful bunch I could find. Something told me not to bring magazines.

"I haven't been eating," Mia admitted. I'd never seen her look so small. I'd never seen her eyes look so big. I'd never felt so helpless. "I know I have a problem and I want to get better."

Mia stayed in the hospital for three months, in the Eating Disorder Unit. I had to keep repeating those words to myself to get over them. (Later, as an outpatient, she took part in support groups, which she still does to this day.) I visited her as often as I could. Finally we were talking properly about what had gone on. Mia said her eating disorder boiled down to three sets of related factors.

First, she wanted to be beautiful, and her idea of beauty was based on the images that surrounded her. In dance class, definitely, but also in the fashion publications we'd been religiously seeking out together every Friday afternoon. All the models were slim or underweight. Mia had been told in no uncertain terms that to do well in dance she needed to have the same body.

Second, those images of beauty were primarily of white women. The dancers around Mia—and the top dancers whom she admired—were white. Mia was not. She was of Chinese descent.

Third, Mia's life was busy. The chaos of tests, term papers, dance rehearsals, volleyball practices and family expectations became too much for her to handle. Being in charge of her eating was one way Mia could assert some control over her life. It allowed her to create a sense of order when her world seemed to have none.

The pressures added up and became intolerable. Race, weight, discipline: they all became interrelated, psychologically, and pushed Mia to become slimmer and slimmer as if that was her only chance at success and happiness, her only chance of feeling valued by her society and herself.

Over time, by working closely with counsellors, Mia became aware of all the complex issues dominating her psyche regarding food and eating. I'm so glad she had the strength to do so. Daily, she also tried to relay her feelings and experiences to me. Before Mia's experience, all I'd known about anorexia and bulimia were the clinical descriptions you get in health class. I didn't think an eating disorder would ever come alive and strike one of my dearest friends, or the young men, for that matter, whom I saw when I visited Mia in the hospital.

ART VERSUS REALITY

Every afternoon, Mia seemed to have something new to teach me. I would hear all about how this one model in Italian *Vogue*, who I thought was so perfectly glamorous and who always seemed to be putting on such a bravura performance, was sending Mia into a tailspin. Then I'd head home, eat dinner, finish my homework, and turn to business. As usual I'd interview prospects and book models. But Mia's experience remained at the back of my mind. As I sat in on photo shoots or checked in with magazines, I found myself viewing them differently. I was blending my old thoughts about glamour with my new feelings about Mia's suffering. I would lie awake at night trying to reconcile the two. I kept arriving at the same unhappy result: my work wasn't inspiring people, it was depressing them.

To me, the models in magazines were just models. I loved how they displayed stunning clothes in a stimulating way. It was an art form—a glorious performance. Yes, I had seen how my friends reacted when they flipped through *Seventeen*: comparing themselves to the models and feeling unworthy for it. But I don't think I realized how deeply this problem ran through their consciousness. I did know that by addressing these concerns too seriously, I could screw up my business. I had invested so much time, effort, money, and hope. I was an ambitious businessman after all, and I was finally getting my foot in the door to the big, exciting, competitive world of fashion. I wanted rewards. I wanted power. So, I'd set my concerns about my friends aside, downplaying them.

Until Mia.

I now realized that for many of my friends—and especially for Mia—these crazy fashion spectacles were having an effect that was crossing the line from external to internal so far and so deeply that it had the potential to become health threatening. Fashion spreads weren't in any way abstract for my gang. Furthermore, my friends didn't know how immature and whiny models can be, and how few of the clothes they modelled ever ended up in their own wardrobes, and how odd a good model can look in person—they're very gangly and angular. But for my friends, as for most people, the gap between model and self could never be closed—not even on a diet of yogurt and carrot sticks with diet pop to wash it down.

BODY IMAGE 101

Body image and eating-disorder issues are not very well understood, despite their widespread nature. We hear that half of the North American population is overweight, we hear that some models and actresses are anorexic, and we get used to it. Meanwhile, poor body image is devastating our culture.

Soon after Mia left the hospital, she began going to groups and workshops at Sheena's Place, a non-profit organization that provides support for people with eating disorders. One afternoon, when Mia and I met for our regular Starbucks, she told me about one group where she learned about the structure of her body and how it moves, and another where she got a chance to discuss how her family and the media had influenced her feelings about her body. Now she wanted to attend a group called Empowering Ourselves, and asked if I would come along.

"You got it," I said.

On a Tuesday evening, Mia and I arrived in front of an old, brick, three-storey, downtown house with a large front veranda and big bay window. I shot a questioning look at her as we climbed the steps to the veranda, thinking we must be at the wrong place. This looked like my grandmother's house, not a clinic. But, sure enough, there was a small sign to the left of the front door that read, "Sheena's Place, Providing Hope and Support for People with Eating Disorders." Mia opened the door and walked inside, and I followed behind. I definitely wanted her to take the lead on this. I removed my new Adidas trainers and Mia took off her spiked black knee-high boots, then we walked straight ahead into a small entrance hall. A young woman sat at an oak table in the centre of the room. She smiled, asked us to sign in, write our first names on a "hello" tag, grab some tea or juice from the kitchen if we wanted, and then to go to the living room for the workshop. The kitchen was busy with women making tea and chatting. They all looked up when we entered and said hi. Mia quickly introduced me.

"I brought a friend. My best friend, actually. Meet Ben."

I shook everyone's hand and then followed them into the living room. It was furnished with comfy sofas and chairs and a big cozy fireplace. The room quickly filled up. Looking around, I noticed that I was the only guy. Having been raised by a single mom and having spent countless weekends alone with Mom, my aunt, and Granny, I was pretty used to being outnumbered by females. One woman leaned over to me, and said, "It'll be great to get a man's perspective today!" I smiled back.

A woman in jeans and a T-shirt reading, "Fat is a Feminist Issue" closed the door behind her and sat down in a chair to the left of the fireplace. She had long, black hair tied back in a ponytail.

"Welcome to the Empowering Ourselves workshop," she said in a calm voice. "I'm looking forward to us locating our unique and enduring personal qualities today. I hope that by doing so, we'll discover navigational points to empower ourselves. Everyone's ideas and experiences are valued here. We want a non-oppressive environment of respect, comfort, understanding, and confidentiality."

It was kind of heavy, but I was in.

After asking each of us to introduce ourselves, she then posed a series of questions. For example, "What are your favourite qualities about yourself?" "What are your favourite leisure activities?" and "What compliment have you ever been given that stays with you today?"

I was getting a little nervous. Everyone else in the group was referring to their own experiences with body image when they spoke. I listened without raising my hand. Toward the end of the workshop, the workshop leader asked people what they thought "empowerment" meant. After everyone else had spoken, she looked at me as said, "Ben, what do you think?"

"I think...umm...empowerment is about feeling strong and confident... with who you are, and being comfortable with that."

She thanked me for my contribution and the conversation continued. When the workshop was over, a woman with shoulder length blonde hair and a warm, friendly smile came up to me and said, "I haven't seen you here before. Welcome. My name is Ann Kerr and I look after programs here."

"Nice to meet you. I'm Ben. I'm very interested in learning about body image."

"Well, there are some booklets on the counter that you can take with you and here's my business card. Feel free to give me a call if you have any questions."

I thanked her and took a leaflet. Later that night, I opened it up and read that body image issues flow along a continuum, ranging from not eating to overeating. I learned that an eating disorder can change in nature and degree over time. The term "eating disorder" usually suggests an individual medical problem, but Sheena's Place understands eating disorders as social issues. Diseases like anorexia or bulimia are influenced by an individual's cultural context and not necessarily just biological in origin. The social perspective recognizes that we get many of our ideas about beauty from the media, and that we internalize these typically stern and unforgiving images of beauty, to which our bodies don't match up. Based on the media's version of beauty, we no longer fit into the world around us.

I began to participate in other activities at Sheena's Place, attending workshops and book readings. I even spoke at their annual public conference and coordinated and facilitated my own workshops on media and body image, and men's body image issues. Ann and I became closer. I found out that in addition to her role as program director of Sheena's Place, she also teaches in the psychiatry department at the University of Toronto. I told Ann about my modelling agency, and she was excited about my work. We frequently discussed issues of body image and the politics of beauty. I always listened hard and learned so much from Ann. Gradually, thanks to her knowledge and experience, I developed a solid understanding of body image issues and the role of the fashion industry in influencing our understanding of our bodies.

Ann once told me that "1 per cent of the population is anorexic, and 2 to 5 per cent bulimic, but that people often develop a combination of the two conditions (like Mia). Eating disorders have the highest mortality rate of any mental illness—15 per cent of those diagnosed pass on." In other words, about one in seven patients with a serious eating disorder dies. And Ann thinks that fashion is becoming progressively more intrusive. To some degree, fashion has always been unrealistic, but twenty years ago, when Christian Lacroix said, "Haute couture should be fun, foolish, and almost unwearable," the look of a

Chanel or Dior model was well understood to be artistic and not by any means mainstream. Fashion was an art form, an exaggerated reality, and models were an accepted part of that. But these days, with fashion playing an increasingly important role within the media, more and more people are coming under its influence and mistaking it for reality. They're also taking it more seriously.

"Some women are influenced by the beauty industry and mimic its vision of beauty," Ann says. "Others are more influenced by peer pressure. And for others still, the need to control something is paramount." With limited control over our lives and little influence in a chaotic world, some people focus uncontrollably on one thing they can control—their weight.

Weight issues can fester in any climate. In 1995, American television programming was introduced to Fiji (a group of Pacific Islands that previously had limited outside influence), with many shows featuring ultra-thin actresses. In 1998, only three years later, 12 per cent of the teenage girls on the islands had developed bulimia, a previously unknown behaviour in Fiji. Welcome to the West.

Body image issues don't all concern weight. At least 35,000 Iranian women have had their noses reshaped beneath their hijabs. Women in China have had their legs broken and prostheses inserted to add a few extra centimetres of height. In our global village, one thing that seems to be uniting women is a single notion of beauty based on a tall, thin, white ideal.

Men are also threatened with an ideal, and are subsequently experiencing body image problems of their own. In the same way women strive to look young and thin, men are feeling a need to be more tall, toned, and handsome than ever before. The National Eating Disorder Association suggests that almost a million men in the United States are classified as having bulimia or anorexia (which would suggest about 100,000 men in Canada with these problems).

For men, there's also an opposite issue to contend with: muscle dysmorphia or "bigarexia" (i.e., the perception that one is too small and not muscular enough). Men with muscle dysmorphia often risk physical self-destruction by persisting in compulsive exercising despite pain and injuries. They continue on low-fat, high-protein diets despite being desperately hungry, or they gorge on bulking-up diets when they're full. A lot take dangerous anabolic steroids and other drugs. As with any eating problem—school, career, and relationships can be affected.

All of this for what? These images that tell us we are too dark, too fat, too old, too short. Trust me, these images are fantasies. Models can often spend five hours in makeup; often it's as many as eight. The resulting photos are airbrushed; with the stroke of a computer key, a cursor can remove scars, acne, and wrinkles. And we're not just talking about faces; necks, arms, busts, legs, and waists be reshaped. On a computer screen, hair, eye, and even skin colour can be changed in a click. Each step along the way makes the model look less and less like the human being who walked into the studio at 6 a.m. that morning.

MY NEW JOB

The bottom line is that advertising is contributing to widespread body image problems. Widespread because ads are everywhere and so many ads look the same. Solely valuing and representing tall, thin, skinny white beauty is tyrannical. The more I learned about the wider system at work, the less sense it made to me. The relationships that advertisers forge with consumers aren't healthy: they're emotionally and psychologically troubled.

After Mia was admitted to the hospital, I couldn't look at magazines in the same innocent way. I felt uncomfortable for taking pleasure from French *Vogue* when it tormented my friend. And I felt apprehensive about my role in modelling. The magic was wearing off and the point of being fabulous was being lost on me. At this point I got hostile; so much for optimism and enchantment. I was frustrated, cynical, and verging on angry with my vocation of choice. I decided that was it—no more moving forward in the fashion industry with only one eye open to the real world. From now on I wanted to get a close look at absolutely everything I was doing.

I decided that the fashion industry could and should change and I would be the one to change it. It meant rejecting a lot of my mentor Elmer Olsen's advice. It meant relying to a frightening degree on my own gut feeling. It was a risk, and it could end up costing me. But I knew that not taking it would cost me even more.

CHAPTER FOUR

BOOKING MY IDEA OF BEAUTY

HITTING THE RUNWAY

AS I APPROACHED MY THIRD year in business (and the end of grade ten), I knew I had a problem. I loved my job and I loved my friends but my two great loves weren't necessarily jibing. The *Seventeen* photo shoot in New York had been nothing short of exhilarating. The *Seventeen* photo spread, however, had been a huge letdown—once I saw how quickly it ignited insecurities around the cafeteria table. Seeing Mia battle an eating disorder was simply devastating. On the one hand, I was concerned about Mia and anyone else who'd been badly affected by the misleading images of beauty that smile down from billboards, jump out from magazines, scowl along runways, and relentlessly beam from TV. On the other hand, I'd worked really hard to get into the fashion business and abandon it. The important thing was that I'd become an insider. I knew I could make a difference that way. The hard part was going to be re-evaluating and redesigning the way I did business myself.

As a first step, I decided to start finally looking for models who *I* thought were beautiful. People with unique personalities and attitudes. People whose charisma and flare would reach out to customers and get customers reaching back. I had to recruit a full cast of diverse models that would include "non-traditional" model folk. Scouting traditional models was easy—the criteria couldn't have been more specific; all I needed to do was match it. There are so few very tall *and* very young *and* very thin *and* very pretty women that they're fairly easy to spot in a crowd. But how was I going to find real models? Didn't *everyone* classify as a real model? Did I stop every person I walked past and ask them to model?

I needed to determine exactly what I was looking for—real-model criteria—so I would know whom to recruit. I decided I wouldn't impose any physical restrictions—no limits on age, height, body shape, colour, ability, and so on. Instead, I had to make sure I represented as many different identities as possible so my clients could select from the widest possible range of models. I'd make sure to approach a mix of ages, sizes, and colours. If I'd already approached enough middle-aged black women, I'd look for middle-aged white, East Asian, and South Asian women. And so on.

But it wasn't quite that simple. How would I know exactly whom I should stop? The first three middle-aged South Eastern ladies who stopped to talk? I needed better criteria. I decided to look for people who had character. They needed to be singing to themselves, or smiling, or doing something that showed an interesting expression or emotion.

This time, I didn't stick posters on lampposts. Instead, I approached people in shopping malls, office complexes, grocery stores, and buses, just like I did when I was looking for traditional models. I'd pick a location and hit it up after school or after Saturday afternoon track practice. I'd start by hanging out at the front door, stopping people who looked like they had potential. Store managers and security guards sometimes came up to me to say that there was No Soliciting and firmly ask me to move on. So I acted as if I was shopping. I'd walk up and down aisles, pretending to check out the price of gummy bears, or I'd ride an entire bus route with my math textbook on my lap. I'd survey people around me and go up to those who I thought might make good models.

One Friday afternoon, I decided to target a grocery store. I was browsing the magazines when I spotted a woman bagging groceries. She was in her forties, Latina, lots of curves, short black hair, and rosy checks. She gabbed with each customer while she packed their groceries. By the time she ended six chats with six very different shoppers, she'd gone through a full gamut of expressions and I was still on the "Normal or Not" page of *Us Weekly*. She laughed when one woman made a joke about buying only one bar of soap. When one guy's grocery bag ripped and everything splattered on the floor and a huge gob of tomato sauce landed on his white shirt, she remained calm and sincere as she helped clean up the squished grapes and smashed glass. I was convinced she'd make a great Ben Barry model.

When things settled down, I walked over to her and handed her a business card, saying, "Sorry to interrupt you but my name is Ben Barry and I run a modelling agency. I think you'd make a fantastic model."

She looked at me in total disbelief, her mouth and eyes wide open. Then she burst into laughter.

"Me?! Honey, I'm old, fat, and short! This is a joke, right?"

"No joke at all. I'm looking for models to represent everyday people. I think you're beautiful."

"Gee whiz, this is some joke. How old are you?"

It was always like this. Me: "It's really not a joke. I've been in business for several years now. I've established many contacts in the fashion world." Them: "Shouldn't you be in class or something?" Me: "No, class is done for the day. My company is called Ben Barry Agency. Our models work in Toronto and New York."

Now this woman stood there even more surprised. The cashier glared at her, motioning at her to keep bagging up the baked beans, paper towels, and frozen peas. "I better get back to work," she said, shoving my card deep into her pocket sight unseen. "Good luck with your business, honey." She smiled once more and went back to the groceries.

She never called. And neither did most of the models I scouted this way. Most people just stood there in shock. I have to admit, I must have come off like a bit of a prank. Not only was I looking for models who didn't look like models, but I was all of sixteen years old (and looked all of fifteen on a good day). *I* might not have taken me seriously either.

Okay, I needed to revise tactics again. Now I decided to approach people through my personal contacts. I asked my friends at school to be models, and their brothers and sisters, and their parents, and their aunts and uncles, and their grandparents—basically the whole family. I even asked my teachers.

Mom works as a full-time therapist but she was doubling as my chief scout. She told all her friends, colleagues, and the gang at her gym about my agency. Every second Tuesday afternoon, she carpooled two of my friends and me home from school. Her maroon Toyota station wagon would pull up and we'd all pile in with our overflowing knapsacks, science projects, and muddy track shoes. I'd hop into the front seat and ask right away if Mom had spied any prospects. One afternoon, I was too exhausted from a debate team semi-final to hope for anything. But Mom had news.

Rita was a psychologist who worked at the same facility as Mom. I knew her from her summer BBQs—she made the best bison burgers ever. Rita was sixty-five, with wild orange hair and a face covered in freckles. She loved ballroom dancing and had a passion for stand-up comedy. Mom had told Rita about my big switch to diverse models and she was fascinated.

"Benji," Mom said, "If you want Rita to model, I'll give you her number and just give her a call."

"But Mom, you know her. She won't remember me."

"Yes she will. Do what you want, but if you want her, you'll have to ask her yourself. This is your business, not mine."

Yikes.

During morning break the next day, I called Rita from a payphone outside the locker room.

"Hello," said an elegant voice on the end of the line.

"Hi. This is Ben Barry calling. May I please speak to Rita?"

"Ben, hello. How nice to hear from you. Your mother tells me about all of your adventures. I think your business decision to use real women is just fantastic."

I couldn't have asked for a better opener. I jumped right in.

"Yes, well, that's actually why I'm calling."

"Oh?"

"I'm currently looking for models and I think you'd be wonderful."

"You do?"

"Absolutely. I want to represent you."

"I'm flattered. Thank you, Ben. But I'm not sure what to say."

The school bell rang in the background. Time for third period. I had to rush.

That evening I called Rita and we planned the next steps en route to her becoming a model. Rita ended up becoming one of my top models—shooting for catalogues, walking the catwalk for mall fashion shows—and one of my favourite portfolio photographers to boot.

I signed lots of models this way. My connections would explain that I was legit and people went for it. I'm sure most of them doubted anything would ever come of it but they were willing to help a friend of their son or grandson or whomever. How could they say no to a nice kid trying to do something good?

Once signed, it was the same procedure for my real models as with any new recruit: the first step was getting a portfolio of photos together. Elmer had introduced me to several fashion photographers who shot what's called a "test shoot" or a "testing." After I met with each model and determined what jobs they were best suited for (catalogue, fashion shows, or magazines) I would contact a photographer who I felt specialized in that model's strongest area and arrange a shoot. We would discuss what types of jobs I wanted the model to do so that he could get an idea of what clothes were needed and what style he should use. The model would then show up at his studio and spend five or six hours there. She would wear three different outfits, with separate hair and makeup to match. The shots looked like any traditional model portfolio except that the model was non-traditional. It was like taking the latest issue of *Vogue*, and replacing the tall, skinny, white, young models with ones who were shorter, curvier, not always white and frequently older. But everything else remained the same: the way the photographer asked the model to pose, the expressions he asked the model to give.

At first, the photographers told me the people I was sending over had no hope of ever getting a job. They just didn't look like models: too old, too short, too fat, too whatever. I bit my lip. I didn't want to argue. I needed these photographers if my models were ever going to get noticed. My models were already different enough from the norm, and I was so freakishly young. I had to show clients at least *something* they recognized. The photographers always went ahead and did the job despite their pessimism. My models and my agency were paying them, after all. (If my models could afford to pay for their photo shoots, then they did. But if they couldn't, then I paid and the models paid me back incrementally once they began getting modelling jobs.)

Once a shoot was over, I sat down with the model and the photographer and we selected the best images. Those pictures would then get enlarged and put into a bright orange binder with "Ben Barry" embossed in blue on the cover. Models would take this to their castings. The very best two or three photographs were also printed onto a card about half the size of a sheet of paper, along with the model's name and measurements, and my contact info. I sent these "composite cards" out to magazines, photographers, advertising agencies, international modelling agencies, and international magazines.

Nothing happened...unless you count rejection letters. "These people look great, but they seem more like actors than models," was the usual comment. "They don't look like they belong in the industry."

My clients wanted to attract consumers, sell products, and make a profit—they weren't especially concerned about my newfound cause. Let me stress that these are not malicious people. Nobody in the fashion industry wakes up in the morning and thinks, "How can I reduce people's self-esteem? How can I increase eating disorders?" Most of them are kind people who support charities, carry out volunteer work, and have no intention to cause harm. But they didn't see the merit of my argument because they couldn't see how it would help business. They perceived this as a social problem, but not a business problem—and surely not *their* problem.

I needed to reframe my case. I'd been using the language of social responsibility. Instead, I needed to use the language of business. I needed to tell clients how I could help to achieve *their* goals, not mine. I needed to address their concerns in language they found reassuring. The bottom line was that they wanted to hire models who would improve sales.

So I tried a new pitch: "You know who your customers are. What if they saw themselves in your models? What if they saw how great a particular dress looked on someone with their own body shape and skin tone, and liked what they saw? Don't you think they might be more likely to buy your dress that way? How often, after all, have you listened to potential customers say, 'That would never look right on me'?"

I painstakingly developed a new marketing kit. I called it "The Ben Barry Advantage." It featured all my arguments in succinct bullet points with dynamic graphics to match. I sent it out to every one of my clients. I followed up with dozens of calls.

Many calls were returned.

Some were returned like this: "Thanks, it's a nice package. But my models have to look a certain way." Others calls were returned with more feedback than that.

One afternoon, I returned home after a busy day at school to our beige, aluminum panelled house with hunter green trim around the windows and door. I'd lived in the same neighbourhood all my life, a suburb about a fifteen-minute drive from downtown Ottawa with five styles of houses that repeated in a routine pattern along its tree-lined street. But two things distinguished the house I lived in with Mom and Spice and Russia. First, we had a huge blue spruce tree on the front lawn. Mom kept Christmas lights on it all year round. All the other houses only put up lights in December. Plus, we were Jewish. My Dad had been Irish Catholic so Mom said we did it for him. At least it made it easy for people to find our house; looking down the street, our house was the one with the big, glowing big tree. Couldn't miss it.

The second distinguishing feature was the NBA-approved basketball net in the driveway. Mom had got it for me as a surprise for my thirteenth birthday. It was definitely a surprise. I know nothing about basketball. I played with it on the day I got it just to be nice, but after that it was mostly other neighbourhood kids. They'd ring our doorbell and Mom would move the car out of the driveway, sometimes stopping for a pass and dunk of her own. I'd watch from the window of my office while I was on the phone to models. Business was my basketball.

That day I jumped out of the car and said goodbye to Mom. She was headed back to work; she did couples therapy three evenings a week. It had been a crazy day. I'd had two tests in the afternoon, followed by intense interval training for an upcoming track meet. My head hurt from having crammed it with every section of the Canadian Constitution and the casts and plots of three novels. My legs were stiff and sore from super sets. But I knew from having picked up my messages at lunch that I had two calls to return. One was from a photographer who was working on a print advertisement for a jean brand. The other was from a marketing manager for a department store. Both had received my package and wanted to talk to me about it. Promising stuff.

After I turned on the tree lights, I switched from my shorts and track tank into pyjama bottoms and a T-shirt. Mom always left dinner in the microwave when she worked nights so I headed to the kitchen to heat it up. I brought my plate of chicken, rice, and broccoli to my office and put it on my desk. I took a couple of bites of chicken, picked up the phone, and dialled the photographer.

"Marvin here."

"Hello, Marvin. This is Ben Barry from the Ben Barry Agency returning your call."

"Oh, yeah. You sent me a package of models' comp cards."

"Yes, I did."

"The photography is excellent, really strong images. Your models shoot with great people."

"Thank you. I'm glad you liked the images."

"But the people aren't models."

"Yes, they are. They know how to pose, how to act on a shoot, how to walk."

"Well, they don't look like models. Like that one woman, what's her name . . . Ellen. She has beautiful shots, similar to the new Armani ads, have you seen those? But she's too old to model. How old is she? Forty? Forty-five? I can see all the wrinkles on her forehead and around her month. That's not attractive."

Okay, that made millions of sisters, moms and grandmothers unattractive. I needed to explain the deal to Marvin here.

"That's my point. My models represent real people. Her wrinkles will help customers relate to her."

"Sorry, but there's no way our client will go for an older woman. But, like I said, I really like your photographers. Send me some stuff of the young girls on your roster."

I had to agree, then I had to hang up. Okay. One call down but I still had another to make. I knew that the department store manager hired models for fashion shows.

"Good evening. This is Ben Barry, returning your call about the package I sent you on my models."

"Yes, yes, hi Ben. One second."

I heard him shout, "Make sure you fax the agencies the fitting dates." Then he came back to the phone. "Sorry, crazy here. Getting ready for a show. A million last-minute things. Listen, I called because I like Farzana. Really beautiful girl."

"Sareena is great. And has a really strong walk."

"But the thing is that I already have a black girl in the show."

I didn't get it. Why could he only have one black girl? Surely, there was going to be more than one black woman watching the show. And, anyway, Sareena wasn't black.

"Sareena is Indian," I said.

"Whatever. I have an ethnic girl already. But I like her. I was thinking I could lighten her skin? I've done it before and it works. As is, she's a little too dark."

"Umm, but, she's not white, she's brown. She's dark."

"Sorry, but that's not going to work for me. I'll keep your package on file."

I hung up again. I pushed away my chicken. Two calls down and neither wanted to try anything different. Neither wanted to try real women. They only wanted cookie-cutter action. I just didn't want to cook that way.

BAYSHORE

I'd finished grade ten and was on summer holidays. Now I could work full-time. No more returning calls only at breaks and lunchtime; now I could keep regular business hours. And I wasn't doing that alone. I had hired a part-time staff member. Her name was Paula. She'd heard about my agency from someone I represented and wanted me to meet her eight-year-old daughter who was modelling with another agency. That meeting lasted two hours and was followed by hours and hours on the phone with Paula over the next few weeks. Her daughter was very talented and I signed her, but the calls weren't about Samantha.

Paula had learned tons about modelling from travelling with her daughter to New York and L.A., what with all the models and agents she met along the way. And, like me, Paula was naturally curious. She questioned everything and everyone she met. Best of all, she had quickly formed her own ideas about the unethical practices of modelling schools and the rigid popular standards of beauty. But what really drew me to Paula was her energy. We could gab forever.

She was in her early thirties, a stay-at-home mom with three kids, and like me, she loved the creativity of fashion. Her hair, for instance, changed every time she went to the hairdresser; one month she had an asymmetrical bob and the next it was the infamous "Rachel" cut, bright red one month and brown with blonde streaks the next.

I'd been looking for someone to help me run the agency. It was getting to be too much to handle alone. Paula was perfect and the set-up I offered would be ideal for her now that all of her kids were in school full-time. She could work from home, and transfer calls to her cell when she was out. Sharing ideas and tips, it was as if we were already working together. When I asked officially, she said yes, on one condition. She wouldn't make any pitches or deals for her daughter. Only I would do that, to avoid a conflict of interest. Fair enough.

One mid-July afternoon, I was spending a typical day at the office: making calls to bring in business, sending out pictures of models, meeting new models, hoping to negotiate a deal. I'd just finished off a meeting with a model and her father to review her photos from a recent shoot when my phone rang.

"Ben Barry," I answered, my standard business greeting.

"Hello, Ben. This is Selma Hay. I'm marketing manager for Bayshore Shopping Centre."

"Hi Selma." I remembered her name and title from having typed it out on an address label for an agency package a few weeks before.

"Ben, I'm doing a back-to-school fashion show for the mall and I love the idea of using models who look like real folks. I'm looking for about twelve models . . . teenagers who actually look like teenagers and adults who actually look like parents. Is this something you can do?"

"Absolutely! I can do that!" I did my best to ration my excitement.

"Great. I'll also need you to produce the show—get the clothing, choreograph the sets, write the script, and host it. I'm sure you've done it so many times before?"

She was right if she counted coordinating my high school fashion show. But I wasn't going to let an opportunity like this get away.

"Of course. My agency can put the entire show together. It's no problem at all."

"Excellent. I need a proposal and budget by tomorrow morning."

"No problem. I'll have it on your desk first thing."

Selma thanked me and told me that she was looking forward to us doing business together. I was elated. Someone finally wanted to use diverse models. No problem—I already had all the models I needed for the job on my roster. But producing the show was another story.

I phoned Paula to tell her the good news. She was thrilled. Then I told her we had to have a proposal and budget ready first thing in the morning. We had no idea what and how to charge. We needed info fast. We hatched a plan. Paula's mother would call some local modelling agencies and event production companies and say that she was interested in organizing a fashion show and ask how much it would cost. While Jackie did this, Paula and I put together the proposal—which models we recommended, different themes for each set, our services we would provide, our timeline, and our budget. We knocked our heads together for the entire afternoon, and when Paula's husband Rob arrived home from work he helped us put the proposal into a standard business format.

My friend Omid is a fantastic graphic designer. I called him and said I needed a major favour. Omid had helped me before, with the graphic design for my packages and business cards. But I'd always given him plenty of notice. Not this time. I could get him the raw proposal by midnight; I needed it back a few hours later looking fantastic. Omid said yes. He was excited by the stress of the deadline and the fact someone had taken my ideas seriously.

By 3 a.m., Omid emailed the finished product, looking its best. I faxed it to Selma that night. She called at 9:30 a.m.; the proposal looked great, the project was a go—except we were undercharging. Selma doubled our production costs.

My first task was one I was used to: I had to check with my models for their availability on the necessary dates, give them details about the job, and let them know the rate. I'd made calls like this many times before but the reaction I received this time was completely new. For most of the models, this was their very first booking. They couldn't believe that someone had actually hired them. I'd say, "Hey, the mall likes you. They think you're beautiful." They thanked me over and over. Then I told them the pay: $90 per hour. They either screamed or went silent, and then screamed. They were being paid the standard rate, just like any other model.

The next stage of the project was more challenging. I had to put the whole show together. I visited stores in the mall to pick clothing. At the first store, the manager freaked out when I told her what sizes I wanted. "We know what we're doing, we've done dozens of shows!" she said. "We use the samples that get sent to us by head office—all 2s and 4s." I said I had an agreement with mall management to operate otherwise but she was sticking to her guns: we would either show the model-sized clothes sent by head office or none at all.

It was the same at the next store, and the next. The stores would give me only sample sizes. None of my models were 2 or 4. Thirty stores later, it looked like my vision for Bayshore Back-to-School '98 was doomed. Then, a realization struck. Sure, sample sizes hung neatly packaged in back rooms. But the racks at the front of the stores were already full of back-to-school items. I went back to the first store but this time I went straight to the racks. I picked out pieces and looks I thought would work, brought them up to the cash, and asked to sign them out.

Well, life is rarely that simple. The manager said I couldn't just walk into the store and take what I needed. I had to use those samples sent by head office or else. It was company policy and that was that; she had no discretion over the whole thing. I was so very frustrated. It made no sense. All those clothes were right in front of us, the same clothes that customers bought every day. After hearing the same thing from every single store manager, I asked to meet with Selma.

I explained the problem and Selma agreed that the stores' response was absurd. I sat quietly in the stiff chair facing her desk while she called every manager who'd told me that I couldn't take clothing from the front of the store. Every call went quickly. Selma explained that if they wanted products in the fashion show, they needed to coordinate with me and offer items that fit my models and my theme. As Heidi Klum will tell you—in fashion, you're either in or you're out. Each manager wanted in. I went right back to the racks and grabbed all the stuff I wanted in the first place.

We presented three shows per day over the last weekend of August. I emceed from the side of the stage, telling the audience about each outfit and sharing tips on trends. (I'll never forget that season—it was all about country club chic: sweater vests, mini kilts, knee-highs, polo tops, and button-downs paired with khakis.) Paula and her mom hustled backstage, making sure each model was ready to hit the runway. Mom and Granny watched every show, front row centre, clapping until their palms hurt.

Every show was packed. Rather than the usual token applause, we got massive cheers and huge buzz. It also helped that we juiced up the traditional runway presentation by choreographing scenes with a bit of a story line. For example, two girls came out dribbling a basketball, did a few fakes and shot into a basket. A man and woman came out with rakes. A couple of kids skateboarded the whole length of the runway.

Selma and I mingled with the crowd afterward so we could pick up directly on the reaction. Guess what? People were relating to the clothes and—miracle of miracles—identifying with the models.

"Those jeans are hot. That model and I have the same booty; I know they'll work."

"Mom, that model totally looks like you. You should so get that suit. You'll look great."

"That model and I have the exact same hips, and her pants fit all sexy. I need to get a pair."

After the very first show, one store manager said she'd immediately sold out of all the outfits the models had been wearing. Customers simply came in after the show and said, "We want what the model had on." Our innovations had translated into sales way faster and more directly than any standard fashion show ever had. Selma and I were euphoric.

A traditional mall fashion show operates on "bait and switch" principles. The show tempts customers with the "bait" of a classic model wearing beautiful clothes designed for her tall, thin body. But the stores often don't have that particular piece, and the customer rarely has that particular body. Even if a woman is size 2, a dress will not hang on her the same way if she's five foot three as it does if she's five foot ten. The shopper is therefore manipulated into a "switch" to other clothes. Or the customer often ends up buying nothing.

We got the contract for the Bayshore holiday and spring shows. Paula and I had our work cut out for us. My models now had jobs lined up for six months. We were making progress.

PANDA PLUS

I was giving the Ben Barry business plan a lot of thought. I needed to get my real models more than runway work. They needed print jobs with clients who could book them regularly. As I continued to re-conceptualize, I had Panda Plus in mind. It's a discount department store chain that advertised through widespread flyers. I knew Panda Plus catered to a wide demographic, from kids right up to seniors—real people, loads of them. But they used only traditional models in all their advertising. I wanted Panda Plus to use *my* models. Panda Plus might not have known it yet, but it wanted to use my models, too.

To truly understand the Panda Plus target market I decided to visit the five Ottawa stores for five days in a row, exploring each one in turn. I zeroed in on the clothes—the size ranges and the people doing the purchasing. I chatted with customers, asking why they shopped there. I wanted to know if they liked the store. If they seemed like they were in a mood to talk I asked what they were buying and why.

I'm sure some people were probably thinking, "Why is this kid staring at me while I buy a dress?" Or "Why is this guy shopping for ladies' dresses?" But before they could decide I was a little creepy I'd strike up a conversation. "That's a nice T-shirt," for openers, or "That colour would look great on you." Most women thought my compliments were sweet and the conversation flowed from there. After each trek I made careful notes. Whom did I see? How old were they? What sizes did they wear?

It wasn't a scientific survey but it cost me nothing and gave me a great feel for Panda Plus and its clientele. Once I was done, I made a list. I'd seen parents shopping with kids, seniors on their own, teenagers in packs, all of them in various sizes from a wide variety of cultural backgrounds. I couldn't identify an average. I did, however, find one common factor: not a single person in any of the five stores had looked like any of the models in the flyers. That gave me the push I needed to make a pitch.

First, I prepared a marketing brief. I detailed five groups: moms, children, senior women, senior men, and single men. I checked which store stocked what, and which sizes were selling. Then I matched my proposed models to these exact demographics. For example: men, fifty-five to seventy-five years old, thirty-four- or thirty-six-inch waists, or moms in sizes 12 and 14.

I phoned the Panda Plus marketing manager to set up a meeting. He didn't want to see me. He said they were happy with their current agency. I countered, "I've got something really different to offer. Anyway, can I just come in to talk about it?" He said he'd get back to me but he never did.

My high school had a membership at a local tennis club and I was adamant about keeping up my game. One day as I was walking in, I saw the Panda Plus marketing manager coming out (I recognized him from a photo on the company's website—thank you Google). I seized my opportunity and introduced myself. He appreciated my initiative. He said I could call him again.

This time, my call led to a meeting two weeks later. Now that I'd made the connection, you can be sure I was (politely) stalking the guy whenever I happened to be at the tennis club, just to, you know, say hello. When I finally got into his office, I presented my pitch: "Your flyer is great but the models aren't representing your customers. I spent a day in each of your stores doing the research." Then I outlined what I'd found and told him my real models would do a better job of connecting with his customers.

The guy was taken by surprise; I don't think he'd ever thought of models this way before. He was also amazed that I knew the inside workings of Panda Plus. I showed him my numbers. He looked them over and admitted that his data matched mine. At that point he asked me to explain in more detail how my ideas would work. He needed to know exactly why he should bother making any big changes.

I started with Mia's story and my subsequent realization that models in ads have a huge impact on people. He replied that this wasn't necessarily his problem. I said actually it was.

"Your goal is to attract consumers to buy your product. You obviously want people to feel good about themselves, to feel empowered. Your flyers need to be inclusive of the people who shop in your store. Otherwise they'll feel *dis*connected instead of connected to your products."

I stressed that I could provide the right models to accurately reflect his company's customers. "The same diversity of body shapes, ages, and backgrounds," I emphasized. "It's going to inspire your customers. More will come into the store and they'll buy more when they get there."

My arguments scored one point after another. By the end of the meeting he agreed to give my theories a try. However, his colleague, the one who actually booked the models, wasn't completely sold. For the next flyer, she selected only one of my models and four from the former agency. My model was Rupa: thirty-eight, Indian, and size 10. When the flyer came out I was so excited that I taped Rupa up in my locker. I felt like we'd accomplished something significant. I was proud of us.

For its next flyer, Panda Plus used two of my models. Store managers and associates had received a lot of compliments, even letters of thanks. There had been measurably positive outcomes in terms of sales. By the end of the year I won the full contract.

THE *OTTAWA CITIZEN*

Panda Plus wasn't my only breakthrough back then. Every Thursday, Ottawa's leading newspaper ran a fashion section using local models; I was determined to crack the lineup. I contacted Catherine Lawson—the newly appointed fashion editor who had a lot to prove herself. She took my call and politely explained that the paper had a contract with the city's biggest modelling agency. But I was persistent. I kept calling her every couple of weeks to see if she needed our agency. Catherine was remarkably polite and patient. I think she had a son my age and wanted to encourage me, but not to the point of taking a risk.

Then suddenly, after about six months and a dozen phone calls, she said yes. I'll let Catherine explain why:

> When I took over as fashion editor of the *Ottawa Citizen* newspaper, I inherited a long-standing contract with the city's biggest modelling agency. Ben called me, explaining what his approach was. I was leery. Newspapers don't have time to airbrush or retouch shots, or to reshoot a layout. We have constant time pressure. So I didn't want to gamble.

He kept phoning me, once a week. I kept talking to him. He was so nice, professional, interesting. No B.S., no big sell. No "you should be doing a story on me." I didn't have the heart to be mean to him or not accept his calls. One day, I was particularly flustered and in need of some models on short notice. It happened that Ben called in the middle of my panic attack. It was easier just to say yes to him on the phone than to call the other agency, so I agreed to let him do one booking. It worked. So I started a process of alternating between him and the traditional agency.

Ben had a huge impact on the fashion scene in Ottawa. His approach of not charging up-front fees for models was refreshing—I recommended any young person coming to me for advice to go to Ben. My own son even became one of Ben's models. It would be a good thing for the industry to adopt some of Ben's practices. And to realize you don't need to be obnoxious to be noticed or successful.

Catherine told me that readers enjoyed my models, but from her point of view their inexperience sometimes showed through. Once, a local fashion designer was opening a boutique downtown and the *Citizen* needed a model for the story. I suggested Sarah-Monica. She had the right attitude to show off cutting-edge fashions, being both very vibrant and very Zen, a combo only Sarah-Monica ever seemed to manage. Photographers needed to watch her like hawks because she transformed with every shot. She never needed direction. She knew her body; she knew how it moved. Five foot eight, bright-ocean blue eyes, wavy brown hair...and a size 6, that was her. Whenever we met with clients they told her that she'd be a superstar if she lost weight. She'd just laugh and say, "No way, man. I love my hips and butt. We're never downsizing." Catherine agreed that Sarah-Monica would be just right.

The shoot was at the Canadian Museum of Civilization: a building made of large dazzling walls of glass. Sarah-Monica arrived right at 8 a.m. She went straight into hair and makeup. Then she put on the first dress. She'd already met with the designer the day before to get fitted. She went over to stand by a totem pole for the first shot. As the stylist adjusted the dress so it creased just right she noticed Sarah-Monica's shoes. Correction: Sarah's sneakers. She asked her to change into heels, but Sarah-Monica didn't have any. She didn't know she'd needed to bring a pair.

I should have asked Sarah-Monica to bring some heels with her to the shoot (as every model always should). Did I mention that Sarah-Monica was a seventeen-year-old butt saver? She told the stylist that I had in fact told her to do so but she'd forgotten. Regardless, the stylist and the photographer were zooming fast toward crisis mode. They thought maybe they wouldn't shoot Sarah-Monica's feet and the image could get cropped at the knee or waist. But then they'd lose the full impact of the dress's beauty. And how would they photograph the pants? While they debated, Sarah-Monica quietly walked over to a woman selling tickets and asked whether she could borrow her sling-backs. The woman was flattered. Her shoes would be in a fashion shoot! Not *Vogue*, but close enough. The shoes were a little big but Sarah Monica slipped them on and got back on set just as panic was really starting to set in. The stylist was about to call a shoe store and beg and the photographer was about to cancel on his afternoon client. The shoot ended perfectly on schedule.

Sarah-Monica called me right afterwards to let me know what had happened. (I always asked my models to call me after a job so I'd be prepared when I spoke to the client.) I thanked her for covering for me and thinking on her feet. I'll never forget what she said: "That's why I eat breakfast—totally keeps me on the ball." I called Catherine, and apologized that Sarah hadn't brought any heels. She said I should always remind my models to come prepared. The honest truth? I was still learning myself. I had no idea models needed to bring heels to a shoot. I thought the client would always have shoes on set. I thanked Catherine for her understanding, and told her that I would charge only half of Sarah-Monica's rate and assured her that it wouldn't happen again (of course, I paid Sarah the full rate). Catherine appreciated the gesture and immediately began to discuss the next shoot. It was sunglasses; heels were not required.

MODEL SEARCH

The following August, another mall—Billings Bridge—asked us to put together a fashion show and model search. By this point, I had fashion shows down pat; I was a seasoned pro at picking clothing and coordinating with store managers (while Paula kept busy working the phones, and negotiating and organizing other bookings). Billings Bridge wanted to attract people to the mall by promoting the idea that beauty is diverse. Its search would be open to anyone, no modelling classes required. The judges were a television host/former model, two clothing store managers, and me.

A lot of people dream of a career in fashion and it showed—around three hundred would-be models turned up for the contest. Some had traditional-model looks but most didn't. I was running this model search differently from Elmer's for Elite. Every contestant walked the fashion runway, but once they reached the end it was a completely different experience. They weren't physically scrutinized but were instead asked a series of questions: Why did they want to model? Were they in school or did they work? What were their hobbies and interests? What did they consider beautiful? Who did they think would going to win the upcoming federal election? (That last question was totally mine; I've always been a politics geek.)

The event stretched into a very long day. The other judges and the mall management wanted me to speed things up. I resisted. The questions were important. I needed to get to know these people, to get an idea of their personality and interests. It was important to their success as a model . . . at least with my firm. The marketing manager kept pointing to her watch and looking at me with terrorized eyes. I just smiled back and kept the questions going.

After five hours it finally came time to pick the winners. Each judge suggested his or her top picks. The other judges all had crossovers. None of my choices matched anyone else's. A fierce debate began.

"We need winners who have a chance of actually being successful in the modelling business," one judge said.

"But my choices *will* be successful," I countered. "These models will start with a one-year contract with the mall."

"They're not models," another judge jumped in. "They don't look like they could ever be in *Vogue* or on a catwalk."

"Not today, but maybe some day, if we take these kinds of opportunities to change who models can be. We have that power right now—let's have the guts to do something with it."

I was hoping my motivational speech techniques would stimulate a consensus if not an ovation. The third judge just shook her head sadly. "We'll be seen as a joke by the media and public. No one will believe our winners have any hope of working."

"Then let's help them change their ideas of what models look like. That's why we spent so long on our questions. We got to know each model. The three winners I suggested are fantastic. You *all* said how much you liked them."

"We liked their answers, sure. But, Ben, the media and public will think we have no clue about the modelling business if we pick these ones."

"Your agency will look amateur and unprofessional."

"They just don't look like models."

"For once, people will feel included in the fashion world. They will support us and thank us. In the end, I'm the one responsible for getting them work. I know what types of people my clients want to hire. And they're them."

The three other judges couldn't argue with this.

We agreed on the winners. My winners, that is.

The female winner was Kosa, a fifty-something journalist. She had recently immigrated to Canada as a refugee from Kosovo. She had silver hair down to her shoulders, and moved with complete elegance. What really made her jump out to me was her response to my question "What does beauty mean to you?" Kosa said, "To me, someone is beautiful when they are able to be to give and care for someone else . . . to be selfless in their actions for others." I liked how she didn't define beauty as a physical feature, as most of the other contestants had done.

The male winner was twenty-five-year-old Joey, who had competed as a wheelchair racer in the Paralympics. As soon as he got in front of us judges he gave us a smile. A smile to get drunk on. I think we all blushed before we smiled back at him. When we asked why he wanted to model, Joey said: "I

want to show people how beautiful it is that we all move in different ways."
Joey got it.

Each winner received a photo shoot, a contract with our agency, and a lay-out in the *Ottawa Citizen* fashion section. By the time the newspaper shoot happened, a new fashion editor had taken over from Catherine—a woman who wasn't familiar with my work. She was nervous about using my winners. Nervous about Kosa's age for one thing. Would her visible wrinkles photograph well? Would she offend readers by showing her bare arms and legs? The editor was worried that Joey was in a wheelchair. Would he be able to change in and out of his clothing alone? Would he be able to handle the speedy shooting schedule and take instructions from the photographer? I assured her that the models would perform as well as any models she'd used. In fact, they'd be even better because they were untainted by the modelling industry and so excited to be part of it. The editor was rattled but obligated so she went ahead.

After the photo spread was published, she called in amazement to tell me about the resounding response. She said the *Citizen* had never received so many complimentary letters to the editor—all of which said something to the effect of "the models you used were great," and "we can actually relate to them." Even the two local news stations did features on the fashion spreads on the evening news. The use of real people in fashion was so unusual it was newsworthy. The headlines said that Ottawa was becoming a modelling trend-setter. Further stories showed people's glowing reactions. There was also an interview with the fashion editor. She said that it was the first time she had ever used non-traditional models, but that they were as professional as any other models she had worked with. She'd received great support from readers. She had already hired the models for another layout (she had to call me to negotiate this booking!).

So—my new business model *was* working. I was using real people—people you might see waiting for a bus or buying a pack of gum—and getting my clients both great media response and increased sales. I'd created a buzz. And none of this was subliminal—people were openly talking about how much they liked seeing themselves reflected in models and how it helped them build a relationship with a product.

MY BUSINESS STATE OF MIND

At this stage—three years into the business—I wasn't especially profit driven. I was a teenager living at home, with a mom who bought him all the fruit, cookies, burgers, milk, ice cream, and chocolate sauce he needed. Whatever I made was mine to spend—no mortgage, no medical bills, no student loans. Young people naturally take risks, but it's great when you can afford to act on your ideals.

That was my situation, in any case. It was just as important to me to do good work as to make money. I'd realized that the fashion industry could have a negative impact on morale; I'd wanted to change that. I reversed traditional reasoning and promised that using diverse models could promote sales—and then proved myself right at the cash register. I hadn't read a single business text; I was just a kid who saw a problem, came up with what seemed like a logical solution and figured out how to apply it. Consumers themselves had taught me what the industry didn't know: the huge disconnect between the image and reality is often really painful for people. That pain can make advertising seriously unproductive.

Fashioning a new reality wasn't easy but there was no way I was giving up. Not having got this far and definitely not with such a long way still to go.

CHAPTER FIVE

TRAVELLING TO FASHION MECCA

LEARNING TO SELL FANTASY AS REALITY

I WAS IN GRADE ELEVEN, the Ben Barry Agency was in its fourth year, and my new approach to business was going strong. I felt bolstered by my victories at the local level. But it was time to see my models up on billboards and in big magazines. Everybody I spoke with told me large campaigns were handled by head offices. New York is the epicentre of fashion in North America: it's the shiny hub of advertising, cosmetics, and design. All the major U.S. runway collections are created and presented in New York. All the key decision-makers and creators are based in New York. The excitement and energy are in New York. I needed to go to New York.

I had hardly any contacts in Manhattan. But I'd successfully overcome that hurdle before by cold-calling anyone I could think to target. Time to log on to 411.com again. I'd start by phoning reception to get the name of the marketing director. Then I'd fax a letter explaining that I was going to be in New York and wanted to present models. I tried ten firms. One agreed to meet with me. I was what you'd call psyched.

Mom didn't share my excitement. Something about sending her teenaged son off alone to one of the biggest cities in the world didn't thrill her. I needed

Mom onside—otherwise, no New York deals, no future, no big time. I explained why I absolutely had to take the trip and gave her my prospective itinerary, complete with every phone number from the hotel to the taxi company to a contact at each scheduled meeting (I made her promise to pretend to be my assistant if she called). I also swore to call home three times a day to confirm I was safe and sound.

Mom was hesitant, but knew "no" was never a good colour on me. I would just keep chipping away at her, trying to hammer out a compromise (i.e., get what I want). It was spring break so I wouldn't be missing any school, so that helped. That was Mom's one unyielding condition: I could do whatever I wanted with the business as long as I kept up my grades. She finally agreed to the trip, dropping me off at the airport with my maple-leaf embroidered suitcase. Day One of spring break...Big Apple here I come.

BECAUSE YOU'RE NEVER QUITE WORTH IT

That very first meeting I had in New York was with L'Oréal, the fierce powerhouse of the beauty industry. Umpteen top-selling brands under one roof, or more accurately, under one Manhattan skyscraper: Biotherm, Garnier, Kiehl's, Lancôme, Giorgio Armani, Maybelline, Ralph Lauren, Redken, Vicky, and, of course L'Oréal, L'Oréal Paris, and L'Oréal Professional, among others. I was happy just to get in the door.

L'Oréal's reception area displayed the usual swanky black leather furniture assembled around a large stylish coffee table stacked with magazines. The foyer walls were plastered with photographs of L'Oréal models. A company that sells makeup and hair products deals mainly in head shots, so I was bombarded with images of large eyes, flowing hair, full lips, and flawless skin. I could take it.

One of the numerous L'Oréal marketing managers greeted me and led me up to her office on the twenty-eighth floor. Before we even sat down (why waste any time?) I asked her what types of models L'Oréal hired. She explained that she looked for two types. The first were "spokesmodels"—the top celebrity models, singers, and actresses like Milla Jovovich, Andie MacDowell,

Aishwarya Rai, Natalia Vodianova, and Beyoncé Knowles—whom I'd seen adorning the lobby. The second were publicly unknown but professional models who were featured in L'Oréal print campaigns, websites, and other promotional material.

Since I wasn't representing any famous faces, I knew that my models and I would have to squeeze through the door in the second category. The marketing manager thumbed through my portfolio, simultaneously asking all the familiar questions about my age and whether I was really, truly, actually running my own modelling agency. Every initial meeting with a new contact involved this mandatory five minutes. Yes, it was repetitious for me but it was memorable for them, and it also helped break the ice.

As the marketing manager flipped through my photos, she noted my selection of diverse, real-life-looking models. I explained how I had come up with the idea and why it worked. She conceded that it was a fine idea, but said that she would never use those models herself. Beauty advertising especially, she explained, calls for flawless skin, big lips, evenly spaced eyes and a nose in exact proportion to the face.

She explained that if consumers saw a perfect face in a L'Oréal ad, they would be motivated to buy L'Oréal products, believing they could thereby achieve the same perfect hair, perfect lips, and perfect eyes. The perfection was supposedly a result of what L'Oréal had to sell.

This struck me as amusing coming from someone who wasn't wearing a lot of makeup herself and whose eyes weren't perfectly symmetrical or lips grandiosely bee-stung. In other words, a real-life woman. The marketing manager resisted that logic. She told me that my models might work for something like a chain-store flyer, but not for the utter fantasy that L'Oréal was trying to sell. I asked whether she wanted her brand to relate to her customers or not. I told her more stories about my agency. "It sounds nice," she repeated, "but L'Oréal's advertising just doesn't work that way."

I didn't give in. "Women will never look like the models in your advertising. My friends will never look like that. The woman on the street will never look like that." The woman was getting seriously frustrated. Trust me, I was trying to be polite. But I wasn't going to leave without displaying some Ben Barry chutzpah.

The marketing manager said that women would always want to be part of the fantasy, to buy into the L'Oréal slogan, "Because You're Worth It." In other words, they would always aspire to be *worth* more but would never feel like they were (it was a fantasy they were chasing, after all). Consequently, they would keep buying more L'Oréal products.

I was fuming. How dare L'Oréal imply a woman's worth was defined simply by her physical appearance—measured against that of an impossibly beautiful L'Oréal model! So much for her intelligence, sense of humour, talent, and soul. Nothing mattered besides owning a lot of eye shadow.

Was a woman not a judge of her own worth? Did a woman need L'Oréal to embrace her? Shouldn't she embrace herself? But how could she, when L'Oréal's influence was so huge? L'Oréal taught the beauty standards. L'Oréal's advertising was on so many billboards, in so many magazines, on so many store shelves. L'Oréal dominated.

I kept all these irate questions running through my mind, not my mouth. I stayed quiet and kept a smile on my face. The marketing manager was clearly frustrated enough with me; I didn't want her kicking me out on my ass.

I thought it best to agree on something. I knuckled under and showed the traditional models in my portfolio. The marketing manager liked Kelda, a five foot ten, size 2, twenty-one-year-old with long brown hair, green eyes, and ivory skin, and requested more information on her. I'd already scored Kelda jobs with Miu Miu in Milan and Procter & Gamble in London, but I knew her dream was to work in New York. She'd been modelling for five years now, three of which had been with me, and she had always told me that she wanted to make it to fashion's fabulous HQ. She would be so excited that L'Oréal in New York was asking for her materials. For Kelda's sake, I had to chill.

The marketing manager asked me how much longer I'd be in New York. When I said four more days, she asked if I wanted to hang out at a photo shoot for an upcoming ad. I was thrilled and told her so. "I'm learning," I said. "I'd love to see how the industry works in New York."

Right on! I *was* a L'Oréal insider—a member of the beauty industry elite.

A MANHATTAN MIRAGE

I'd attended Veronica's shoot for *Seventeen* but this was different. This was a beauty ad. And I was older and a little less dazzled. And I wasn't accompanying a model so I'd be able to pay attention to details that I'd missed the first time around.

I arrived at 1 p.m. to be asked if I minded getting coffee for everyone. I didn't mind. They had been there since 4 a.m. and were on their sixth coffee run of the day. Everybody was busy, in a rush. It was an odd rush, however—a slow, painstaking rush. The models had been in makeup since 5 a.m. Eight hours later, they were still getting that makeup perfected. Every line was smoothed. Every strand of hair was untangled and straightened. I was more absorbed than most people would be watching their *own* hair get styled.

Finally, at 3 p.m., the models were ready for the camera. But now the lighting had to be adjusted (and readjusted, and re-readjusted) to capture the wonders of the makeup. Another hour and a half passed before the first photo could be taken. The photographer positioned the model's head, checked his digital camera, and checked the lighting one last time so that her features looked as symmetrical and proportional as inhumanly possible. The shoot itself lasted about two hours, actually quite fast compared to the ten hours of extended preparation.

The results of the shoot that I saw up on the computer screen were gorgeous—phenomenally striking. But they still weren't perfect. Next, I watched the art director get to work, touching everything up. Every crease, every line, every bump was smoothed out. Basically, the model was digitally sandpapered.

It was mind blowing. All that preparation plus lengthy post-production to turn this woman (actually this sixteen-year-old girl) into a fantasy. By the time the work was complete, she no longer looked living and breathing; she looked like a marble statue, or maybe a top-of-the-line android. Again, I kept my inner monologue to myself. I watched, listened, and thanked everyone profusely for the experience.

Anthony Cortese, in his book *Provocateur: Women and Minorities in Advertising*, expresses his belief that all this work on a model—intended to make her look perfect—ends up detracting from her humanity. "The exemplary female prototype in advertising, regardless of product or service, displays no lines or wrinkles, no scars, blemishes, or even pores . . . [she] is not human; rather, she is a form and hollow shell representing a female figure."

I second the motion.

I was learning on two levels. One was the mechanics of a photo shoot at the highest level of the industry: the fastidiousness and brutal hours fuelled by nerves, technology, and a river of lattes. But I was also learning about the odd disconnect between the result of all that work and real life. The studio itself revealed it. All the makeup artists, lighting technicians, hair stylists, and computer specialists—this huge team of about twenty-five professionals all bent on the illusion of female perfection—nobody looked like the final picture. Not even the model. She was a bright, professional, extremely patient girl who in real life had a few zits on her chin and forehead, a crooked smile, and brown freckles on her nose.

Nobody else seemed to pick up on this discrepancy or care at all about it. They were so caught up in the creative process and so accepting of industry mythology that they could no longer understand how unnatural their end result was. Nobody felt it was at all strange to spend that much time on hair and makeup, let alone then fine-tune the photographs until they represented something that never has and never will exist. When somebody would say, "Hey, there's a bump, take it off," it got done immediately. This was the major league. These were New York pros at work. I was a long way from my basement in Ottawa.

Ultimately, this was how the industry thrived: fantasy construction. Obviously, many women in the real world were enraptured by that.

Truthfully, I was feeling a certain joy, too. In a few months I'd be seeing this very ad in all the top magazines. I was at the white hot centre of fashion advertising: music blasting, specialists working to the max—mixing, colouring, shadowing. The shoot was a kind of performance art—the star model working one-on-one with the star photographer while the supporting cast crowded around them, everyone delivering. It was a beautiful team effort. No one person (not even a few people) could have achieved it alone. So, yes, what they were doing was bewitching. But I thought it was also nuts.

I began to wonder if I was the crazy one, since everybody else seemed so polished, professional, and assured. I questioned the marketing manager from

L'Oréal again, but she simply reiterated her basic message—women don't want to hear about reality. They want to see a fantasy portrayed and offered to them through a L'Oréal product. They buy into it precisely because it is a fantasy. And new product lines *always* need to be launched through fantasy. They need to create a new problem. Why would a woman buy something new to erase the lines on her eyelids if she was happy just using her old shadow?

Eventually, I tumbled out into the fresh night air, shell-shocked but happy. Spring had arrived early. The air was warm with a light breeze. I decided to take advantage of the weather and walk back to my hotel. When I got to the lobby, I headed straight to the payphone. I told Mom all about the photo shoot, about how much work it took it make the L'Oréal model look like the L'Oréal model. She listened as I recounted each minute of the shoot, detail for detail. Mom didn't know anything about fashion or care much about it before I started my agency; she's more of a sports fanatic, tree-hugger type. But she listened intensely, picking up on my own excitement. Granted, she also asked the standard Mom questions: What did you eat today? Do you have enough money? Are people being nice? Are you sure you're eating? Buy some food!

The next day I headed to H&M's huge North American flagship store on Fifth Avenue (for some wardrobe boosting of my own). I couldn't help it; I listened in on two women trying on jeans. They were saying things like, "How come the model's butt looks so much better in these?" or "No wonder these look so good on the model, she has, like, no hips!" They definitely hadn't internalized the fact that to create the perfect butt in the perfect jeans it takes a long day, a team of twenty-five specialists, nuanced lighting, and advanced computer retouching. I heard them loud and clear: consumers internalize the fantasy, make it a reality of sorts, and then feel disenchanted when it doesn't work for out them.

Was I going bipolar? Half the time I felt like a real insider, part of an industry that creatively drew people to stores. Leaving the L'Oréal shoot I'd felt such an insider I thought Karl, Stella, or Marc might be calling any moment. But when I absorbed people's true feelings about the shopping experience, I felt like an outsider, like I was the only person within a thousand miles of Madison Avenue whose ideals made sense.

How was I going to change an industry that refused to admit any change was needed? How would I get fashion insiders to see that millions of women's self-esteem was suffering? How could I get them to understand that the harm being done *was* their problem? How could I get them to realize that they didn't need to tell women that they weren't thin enough, white enough, and young enough in order to stimulate sales, and to see that their tried and trusted messages were damaging their brands' relationships with their consumers? How could I convince the beauty industry that they could tell women that they were worthy in all their glorious diversity and still sell lipstick, eyeliner, and hair colour?

UNDERCOVER IN PARIS

I'd actually spent some time in another fashion capital a few years prior. Back in grade nine, I'd visited Paris on an exchange program with my school. When we arrived at Charles de Gaulle Airport, we were picked up and chauffeured to our billets, most of them with upper-class, white Parisian families. The kind of families you expect to host elaborate dinners in beautiful townhouses located in ritzy enclaves full of poodles and private parks. However, I was placed with a newly immigrated Algerian family. My host, Amine, was on a scholarship to the prestigious private school based on his outstanding academic achievements. Amine was also streetwise. His family couldn't afford a car so we rode the subway for an hour to get to their apartment building in the suburbs. They lived in two rooms—mom, dad, brothers, sisters, grandparents, and now me.

I was lucky. Instead of signing up for organized trips to museums and tourist traps with the rest of my class, I was getting my chance to sneak up close to the fashion hotbed. Paris is the city of lights, sure. But I wanted those lights to be camera flashes and runway spotlights. And in addition to the Paris I craved from Audrey Hepburn movies and French *Vogue*, I was treated to a taste of Amine's Paris. He took me to Algerian markets, twenty-four-hour cafés where people argued until dawn, and fragrant, bustling neighbourhoods left way off the tourist maps.

One day, we decided to stay up all night to walk along the Seine and watch the sun rise. We arrived at a little café filled with overstuffed bookshelves at around 2 a.m., ordered *les chocolats chauds*, and kept talking. Amine was the same age as me, fourteen, with long, shaggy black hair and big, dark brown eyes. I asked him if he ever felt different, being the only non-white person at his school. He told me that when he'd first started there, he got especially close to this one girl. She invited him to eat lunch with her and her friends every day. They sat beside each other in class and they helped each other out with homework. One day, he overheard some other kids chatting about what they were going to wear to her birthday party. Amine had known nothing about it. When he asked her what was up, she said that her parents would be furious if she ever invited an Algerian home. She'd thought it best not to say anything to Amine so as not to hurt him. That had made him feel different. He said that was the point at which he began putting all his effort into his grades, to show everyone he was just as good as them.

Amine asked me if *I* had ever felt different. I had. I was born at less than two pounds and spent the first six weeks of my life in an incubator. I explained how I was a late learner, always getting the lowest mark in my classes, always the last to understand a new concept, always the last to be picked for a team. I was frequently called dumb and picked on because of my size. I told Amine that a large part of my drive to be successful with my agency was to prove to myself that I was as good as anyone else. I also told him that I wanted to represent models that weren't standard because at my core I understood being excluded and feeling different, and I never wanted anyone else to have to feel like that. That drove me, and the fact that at the end of the day I'm a privileged person who's always had a roof over his head and food on his table. Since I had the tools and the ability to do something about some of the problems that surround us, I felt I had an obligation to do so. As I still do.

Before I'd left home, I'd sent off faxes and letters to see if I could worm my way into anything going on during Paris fashion week. No responses, *rien*. So I decided to visit some French modelling agencies just to see how they did business. Maybe an invite or two would come my way.

I called to set up appointments, speaking a mixture of French and English. I was in Paris to learn French, after all, so this was a great language exercise. I did my best with my dictionary handy. At one of the agencies, the person I was talking to was interrupted by a call about an upcoming show for Chanel. I made a mental note of where it was going to be and when (my French was clearly improving). I asked Amine if he wanted to tag along. Amine had nothing against model-gazing so we looked up the address on a map and there we went.

It was an old warehouse building, with a huge lineup outside. TV crews and photographers were on the lookout for celebrities. It was drizzling yet the women were all in high heels and big hats: *très chic*. People were milling around, coming and going, but security was tight. We didn't even look like we had a ticket, not in our wet sneakers, jeans, and soaked hoodies. Not with our bangs stuck to our foreheads.

Amine asked one of the security guards about getting in, but he just laughed, a laugh that was every bit as condescending in French. As we watched people streaming into the show, we realized that we would have to come up with a plan B. "Why don't we just go around back and see if there's another entrance?" Amine suggested. Trying to mask my nerves, I said it wasn't *that big a deal* to see the show. But Amine insisted it would be a cinch to find a back entrance and I agreed to take a look. Sure enough, around the back of the building we discovered a loading area with one of the garage doors open. Makeup artists and hair stylists were standing around smoking with racks of clothes behind them.

"Don't make eye contact, just follow," Amine instructed in a clipped tone. He headed for the door, said, "Excusez-moi madames," and walked in. I shadowed. Nobody batted a mascaraed eye.

Things were buzzing and humming backstage. Rolling racks of clothing were hustled down the corridors. People were yelling in broken English and French, "*Vite, vite* . . . let's go, *mes amis!*" "Does anyone have *un dessiccateur de coup* [blow dryer]?," "*J'ai besoin d'un* streamer," "*Noir* pumps, size *huit*, please." Models rushed barefoot down the halls in bras and underwear, with completely styled hair and no makeup, or with a full face of makeup and a tangled mane.

I was scared witless, convinced I was going to be caught and tossed in jail in a foreign country with nothing to eat and drink for years but Evian and dry baguette. But Amine knew to stay calm and act like we belonged. It was an excellent strategy. The only people paying a lot of attention to us was us.

We weren't quite sure where to go from here. We noticed an opening on the left of the corridor where we'd been loitering. Looking out, we could see white folding chairs in tight rows on either side of the runway. The audience members were squeezing their fitted tweed skirts into their seats, fanning themselves and chatting on cellphones. People with clipboards were rushing past. We avoided eye contact at all costs.

We waited for about five minutes until the room went dark. Depeche Mode blasted, spotlights shot on, and a phalanx of models stormed the catwalk. Amine grabbed my hand (his dry, mine soaked) and pulled me behind the rows of seated *invités* until we reached the middle of the hall. We pressed our backs against the wall. Everything was dark, except the glowing runway and flashbulbs.

It was all so gorgeous. Each model strutted down the gleaming white runway in true Naomi Campbell style. I felt myself learning more and more about the garments that adorned each body—how they moved, their texture, their cut interacting with the human form. At first, there was nothing else to possibly pay attention to. All the lights in the room, each pair of eyes, focused on the couture. The clothing stood out so beautifully. Yet the models started to seem hazy and identical. After about ten outfits, I wasn't paying any attention to any of them. From Chanel's perspective that must have made sense.

But it didn't make sense to me. As beautiful as the clothes were, I couldn't imagine them on any of my friends or family. The clothes were all fitted to a young model with no hips, a small bust, and a tiny waist. Shouldn't the department store executives, celebrities, and socialites be allowed to see how the clothes would look on other body types, too? Surely the goal was not just to show off the clothes, it was to sell the clothes?

Amine was getting bored. His eyes drifted away from the runway. He looked around the room, at the floor, at me watching the show. Eventually, my gaze began to shift, too. I knew from my snatched time backstage that this was pure stress on display. It all started to feel too high-strung. I thought the show might have been more interesting if live music was incorporated. Or if the models did something other than simply strut back and forth—maybe dance or do something acrobatic. That would be more fun to watch and the clothes would get real human life breathed into them, instead of being worn by walking hangers. Diverse models were needed in *la belle Paris*, obviously—not only to make fashion accessible but to jazz things up.

FRONT ROW IN PARIS

I was headed back to Paris Fashion Week the winter before my last year of high school. This time, there were Ben Barry models taking part in the shows, *les défilés*. I invited Amine to come to the Dior spectacle with me. No more sneaking in the back door; we walked right down the centre aisle this time, invitations in hand. No more hoodies and sneakers—we were dressed in our avant-garde best: me in distressed jeans, a seaweed green shirt with a graffiti design, and chocolate brown leather boots; Amine in fitted black pants, a dark red T-shirt, and aviator glasses. We brought umbrellas this time. Now we could make eye contact with whomever. Now we belonged.

Our section contained a bevy of fashion journalists who talked openly throughout the show as they took notes. "Oh, she's good." "Ooh, why did they pick her?" "She's looking a bit lardy." "That one's on a champagne and laxative diet." Standard fashion-journalist gossip. None of the female journalists looked like models. They thought of models as products to shop for. Their job was to size them up to determine if they were worth hiring.

The models might as well have been the same ones I'd seen a couple of years before. Astonishingly thin. Astonishingly young. Astonishingly other-worldly. Same with the presentation of the clothes. Models stalking the runway, again, and again, and yet again. Amine and I didn't really notice a difference between our first *défilé* and this one, except for our second-row seats and the fancy after-party we were invited to, where we guzzled Moet & Chandon and boogied the Paris night away. I'd describe the whole experience as exquisitely detached from anything that I continued to understand as reality.

In New York I felt like an alien. Back in Paris, I felt like an alien again. Clearly, I needed to open up some offices abroad. Time to storm fashion's capitals with my fresh eye.

CHAPTER SIX

THE BILLBOARD
BIG TIME

MY MESSAGE TO MILLIONS

IT WAS THE END OF MY SECOND-to-last year of high school. I had a downtown office with three full-time staff members, a hundred models on my roster, and almost five years of experience in the business. I'd met with numerous other entrepreneurs; I really liked learning first-hand about what they'd been through and what they'd learned—I got tons of good advice that way. And I'd read literally dozens of business books. But I had yet to take a formal business course. I thought maybe it was time.

I ran the idea by my accountant, Mr. Levine. He had an MBA and had been in business for more than fifty years. He came with a strong recommendation from my most-trusted source—my grandmother. Mr. Levine was a close family friend, having met my grandparents when they'd first arrived in Canada after escaping Nazi Germany. I always listened to him carefully. Once a month we met at his office to discuss my finances. Being under eighteen, I still wasn't allowed to sign corporate cheques or draw up legal contracts (which infuriated me). But I trusted Mr. Levine and Mom to sign for me when necessary.

Mr. Levine always said that in order to make money, first you need to spend it. "I've been doing this for over fifty years," he'd say, "and if I've learned anything it's that business is about constant change. Just about anything works. If you want to convince me that an investment will generate income, then all you have to do is explain every possible outcome scenario to me and have proof to reinforce your points." I always went into my meetings with Mr. Levine armed with proposed expenses—and detailed arguments to back me up.

BEN BARRY INTERNATIONAL

One Friday afternoon in May 2000, I headed right from school to Mr. Levine's office. It was in an old limestone building on a tree-lined street packed with boutiques and cafés. His secretary always gave me what I suspected was her biggest smile. She'd announce my arrival over the intercom and then ask me to go in. Mr. Levine would be reclining in his favourite chair behind his big oak desk. His office was lined with bookshelves loaded with hundreds of business manuals and filled with photos from the different companies he had worked with, or been in partnership with, over the last half century. Most visits, he would share a story from one of the photos, or lend me a book to help me better understand a difficult decision I needed to make.

My agenda for this meeting was crystal clear: I wanted to study business officially. I had my mind set on a six-week summer course on management and entrepreneurship at LSE: London School of Economics. Not only would I learn about business, but also I'd get an international perspective. That was going to bolster my case with the formidable Mr. Levine.

"I've developed a successful company without any formal training, Mr. Levine," I began. He nodded; that was always good. "Now I want to take it to the next level, beyond Ottawa and even Canada. I believe that studying business will enhance my practical experience and help me grow the agency."

Mr. Levine wanted to know more about the expenses; London and foreign tuition fees don't come cheap. Right off, he had two big questions: "Firstly, you're going to be in London for six weeks. Can you meet with British clients who might hire your models? I'd like to see you maximize this trip. Secondly, how will you manage the agency's activities while you're away?"

This time I was two steps ahead of him. London being a major fashion centre, I'd already drawn up a stellar list of contacts. I took it out of my courier bag and passed it across the grand desk. I told Mr. Levine that Paula would manage the operations while I was away, just like she'd done whenever I had an out-of-town debating tournament or a track-and-field meet. Plus, I'd be in contact by email and phone every day.

"Fine," said Mr. Levine. "Agreed."

And with that, I was off to England.

The course at LSE focused on "tactics and techniques for creating and developing a business plan." We'd learn about every section of a plan by working in groups to develop one of our own. For the final, we'd present the plan to three venture capitalists whom the professor had invited to watch the presentations. They were going to test us with the very same questions they'd ask anyone looking for real capital to start up a real business. Fifty students from around the world were taking part.

The very first day, we were invited to reveal our business goals to the class. Some of us had business ideas of our own while others didn't. You can guess who wanted to create a plan for an international modelling agency representing diverse models. Then we were asked to divide into teams.

Most people couldn't get over my age. I was so used to being in business with older people that I hadn't even noticed that I was by far the youngest person in the course—I still had a year of high school to do and everyone else had finished high school, many were already halfway through university, and some were already professionals in the workforce. (Normally I wouldn't have been allowed in, but my high school principal had written to attest that I was a good student who had run a successful business since grade school.)

I embarked on yet another detailed explanation of my business history, but this time I was cut short. Everyone quickly sussed out what I wanted to do. Four people jumped at the chance to grapple with my plan: Kristina from Sweden, Maria from Spain, Shauzab from India, Dave from the United States, and yours truly from Canada.

Afterward, our group went to the LSE campus pub, The Underground. We were all new to London and wanted to celebrate our first day of class. The lounge was in a basement. The walls were painted silver and midnight blue, and rainbow-coloured spotlights cast weird rays around the room. Sofas and chairs, the kind that you fall into really deep, were filled with people gabbing away with beers in hand.

"Ben," Maria asked, "What motivates you to go up against the rules of the fashion world? I mean, industries don't get much more judgemental, right?"

Dave jumped in, "Yeah, models are so ingrained in our culture . . . everyone knows what a model looks like. That kind of thing is so hard to change. What makes you think you can do it?"

I told Mia's story. Each head nodded in recognition. They'd all heard of, or had, similar experiences.

Shauzab said, "In India, beauty is about being as white as possible. The whiter your skin, the more attractive you are. All the models in magazines are super fair and girls want to copy them. There's so much pressure on my sisters to use skin lighteners and bleaches. The chemicals in those products are so harsh that they cause blisters and rashes. Sometimes even burns. It's so sad."

"My mom just wants to be young," Dave said. "In California, women think they need to look twenty-two forever to be beautiful . . . no wrinkles, no grey hair, no fat anywhere. My mom goes for surgery to get rid of any lines and sags. It's become kind of an obsession for her. Man, it seems like every few months there's something to get done."

Maria was worried about her brother: "He goes to the gym every day for an hour and a half and still thinks he's a wimp. He's always showing me pictures of guys in health magazines and saying he want those quads, those pecs."

"In Sweden, beauty is all about thinness," Kristina said. "Mothers put so much pressure on their daughters. My mom kept showing me fashion magazines, saying how great the models looked and why didn't I try to look like them? Sorry, but I'll never be a stick. I have an athletic body. I struggled with anorexia for about four years. Nowadays, I'm fighting hard to feel confident with my size but it's hard. Especially when I never see anyone remotely like me in any damn magazine."

After three hours of sharing stories we were drained, but buzzed at the thought of our task. No matter where you lived, the media idealized an unrealistic standard of beauty. No matter where you were from, people faced intense pressure to conform to this standard of beauty. No matter where you found yourself, people's health and self-esteem were being harmed by this standard of beauty.

I went back to my dorm that night and sank right into my bunk but I stayed awake for what felt like hours. I was fired up with more motivation than ever. The people in my class had all been immediately convinced of my idea, and my group had seen similar experiences to that of Mia. The fashion industry needed to change globally. Obviously, the Ben Barry Agency had to go worldwide.

We worked together every day over the next six weeks—for at least six hours and sometimes twelve—brainstorming, researching, and writing the business plan. Breakfasts each morning, lunchtime conversations, tea and sandwiches, evenings, and midnight oil—all spent in the computer lab. Each of us worked on a different section of the business plan based on our expertise. I oversaw the entire project, rotating every day to work with each person in turn. We weren't just writing a business plan: we were creating a manifesto with which to conquer the fashion industry and make it equitable and inclusive. Our own stories from that first evening fuelled us to keep pushing, no matter how sleep deprived (or exhausted from dancing away the stress for hours at our favourite new Soho clubs).

Hundreds of hours later, our project was finally complete. We had a comprehensive hundred-page outline for the launch of Ben Barry Agency International with thirty offices worldwide, complete with five- and ten-year projections. What a score.

The group wanted me to present the plan since I knew the most about the business, and they thought my enthusiasm and passion would sell it. I thought they were just way too tired to give a presentation and asked me because they knew I could talk about the industry in my sleep. In any case, I said yes. We stayed up all night to finish the PowerPoint slides. David and Kristina went on caffeine and juice runs. By 5 a.m., we had printed out the finished project. Maria and I thought sleeping at all that night would just make us more tired so we headed to Kinko's to bind the project, then went out for a three-hour breakfast. I practised the presentation and we tested each other on possible questions.

The presentation went really well. I was calmer than my usual bouncy self but still delivered the plan with conviction. The judges seemed persuaded.

One said, "The current environment is right. The body image crisis, the increasingly aging population, and the multiculturalism of the world make your offering a good match for the marketplace."

"True," our professor said. "There is a very real opportunity now and your business is designed to effectively capitalize upon it." I'll never forget that.

Then they probed us on how we would adjust our financial projections according to different rates of acceptance of diverse models by clients. We had expected this question and had devised different financial scenarios based on how many clients had hired us. The projections were based on theoretical models of clients more open to using diverse models. We'd gleaned this from my own practice in Ottawa.

"We've placed companies prone to hiring models along a scale. The left side represents those companies open to using diverse models, from most open to less. Examples on the left side of the scale include commercial clothing firms and TV commercial production houses. The right side represents those who are resistant to using diverse models—fashion designers and fashion magazines."

One judge asked, "How do you plan on penetrating the clients on the right side, the resistant ones?"

"We'll promote traditional models to them in order to build a trusting and professional relationship. Over time, we'll begin to promote diverse models as a way to better attract their consumer."

The judges liked the fact that we'd thought through different scenarios and devised a strategy to develop and grow no matter what. They nodded their heads in agreement and in the end we got an A and received business cards from the judges and I even got a couple of offers to invest in Ben Barry. We celebrated—in our rooms, in our beds (sound asleep). I had some pretty sweet dreams.

As promised to Mr. Levine, I didn't just go international academically. I had daily meetings with British fashion designers, advertising agencies, and modelling agencies. And I took daily Tube rides.

Each day, when class ended at 3 p.m., I opened my London Tube map and took a train to a different part of the city. This was the first time I'd lived in a major city with a subway at my disposal and I loved it. Seeing so many people of different ages, body sizes, colours, and abilities crammed together was an inspiration. Everyone defined and redefined beauty with their individual style. I looked at one Indian woman who had deep wrinkles spread throughout her golden skin and thought she was beautiful. Then I looked at a white teenage girl with wavy brown hair to her shoulders and thought she was beautiful, too.

This watching continued. I would sometimes miss my stop, or get strange looks from people who caught me staring at them. But I was so stimulated. Beauty was fluid and it flowed all around me. The fashion world, and all the audiences reading magazines and watching runway shows—they were missing out terribly. I wanted everyone to see the beauty of the Tube on the catwalks. And every once in a while, maybe someone else did, too.

I had a meeting scheduled with a marketing director at the house of Alexander McQueen. I was thrilled. McQueen is renowned for expertly bending the rigid rules of fashion, earning him titles like *"enfant terrible"* and "the hooligan of English fashion" (and also frequently "genius"). He was one of the youngest designers ever to achieve the title British Designer of the Year, in 1996, and he's gone on to win it three more times since.

We met at McQueen's flagship store on chic Old Bond Street, where all the top designers have London shops. The store's interior mirrored the beautifully tailored designs. The entire store was white and the walls curved gracefully; no sharp edges. I wore black dress pants with a grey AC/DC T-shirt. When I entered the store, the sales associates eyed me, letting me know that I was being watched. I'm sure they were thinking, this kid *so* can't afford a thing in here. But I walked up to one of them, smiled, and announced I had a meeting with one of their marketing directors.

The marketing director and I settled on a rounded bench at the back of the store. I gave him the story of my agency, told him I was taking a business class at LSE for the summer, and showed him the photos of my models. He flipped through the portfolio, whipping past every diverse model *and* every traditional model I represented. But then he stopped short at Joey. "Tell me about *him*," he asked.

"Joey won our model search last summer. He's done shows and editorials since then and also completes in the Paralympics."

"Alexander has used models with disabilities before. He used Aimee Mullins in several of his shows."

Mullins broke world records in the 100-metre and 200-metre dashes, and long jump at the 1996 Paralympics. She was also one of *People*'s Fifty Most Beautiful People. The marketing director grabbed some photos of Mullins from a McQueen fashion show.

"She has such a strong presence," I said.

"Alexander carved wooden legs for her to look like long boots. No one guessed. We didn't tell the press about her disability until the following day. Then their fur started flying! Article after article. It was madness."

"Why didn't you say anything at the show?" I asked.

"Alexander and Aimee wanted her to be seen as 'Aimee Mullins, the athlete and model' instead of 'Aimee Mullins, the disabled athlete and model.' They wanted to challenge the audience's prejudices, not have them get hung up on her disability."

"I get it. But I think you should have exposed her disability," I pronounced.

He gave a puzzled stare. I went on.

"Showing her disability could have shaken up people's expectations. I mean, she looks like a regular model in every sense. She's tall, young, thin, white, gorgeous. Yet she has a disability. You'd be putting two opposite expectations together."

"You're so post-modern . . . go on."

"I mean, when we think of images of disabled people, we typically think of charity campaigns."

"And medical books and circuses."

"Exactly. Not fashion. But by putting the body of a traditional fashion model and a disability together, the image challenges expectations about who and what is beautiful. You open up discussions on beauty." I was still thinking about the Tube.

"Alexander's done that. He edited an issue of *Dazed and Confused* a few years back with Aimee on the cover." He quickly rustled up the magazine and showed me the cover. The knee joints of Aimee's artificial legs were showing.

"This is what I mean! This kind of thing helps people with disabilities to imagine themselves as a part of the ordinary world. I'm sure it also helps reduce discrimination. What was the reaction like? Sales?"

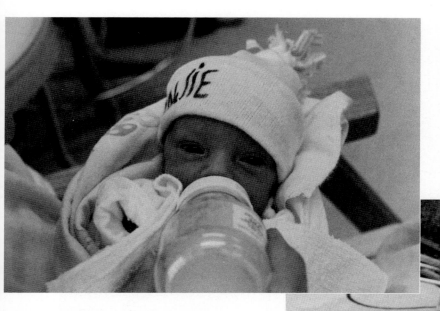

From Feeding Bottles to Feeding Models
Me, at one month, drinking from a bottle. (I was less than two pounds when I was born.) And, yes, the little toque on my head says Benjie.

Snuggling with Granny
Four-year-old Ben laughing, being held by my granny at the beach.

I've Always Had a Short Attention Span
Reading with Dad at age three.

Always Curious
Seven-year-old Ben, eyes wide open.

Ben & Breakfast
My so-official B&B sign on the wall of my house (I cut the computer-made sign into a circle, stuck it onto blue paper, and hung it on the wall of my house).

Oh Captain, My Captain
Standing in my school uniform behind a plaque listing the names of all school captains (my name is not up yet).

Les Rues de Paris
Fifteen-year-old Ben standing on a Paris street.

Who Wears Short Shorts?
My track team and me after a race. Why is everyone else wearing their pants but me?

What Did You Eat Today, Ben?
Mom

Six-Hour Meetings Make Everybody Smile
The Toronto Youth Cabinet Executive posing
after a Friday night meeting at Toronto City
Hall: Me, Clara, Rahel, Mandy, Tanika, Vinni,
and Estée.

Welcome to My Studio
On the phone in the lawyer's office that I transformed into my model agency studio.

Monopolizing the Phone
In my basement office at fifteen.

Mr. Ben, Mr. Ben, Mr. Ben
Elmer Olsen giving a pep talk at the Elite
Model Look, 1998.

How Big Are Her Ankles?
Showing Elmer my newest models at Elite's
Toronto office.

Asleep on the Job
A group of my models, the photographer,
and I taking a break from a photo shoot …
and I have a big yawn.

Misses and Kisses
I have a big red lipstick kiss on my cheek and am standing with my models and Paula from my Ottawa office.

Feeling Appreciated
Joanne, left, and Erica, right, kiss my cheeks—I am seventeen here—at a diversity fashion show coordinated on Parliament Hill.

Spreading the Word
Doing the television media circuit
(I was pretty beat by the last one).

BEN BARRY
18 Year Old Entrepreneur

Top 20 Under 20
Posing ever so fiercely
for *Teen People*.

"Sales have been consistent every season we use Aimee and we get ridiculous amounts of attention and reaction. Mostly supportive, thanking us for making disability visible in the world of fashion. But some negative. Most of that is from activists, critiquing us for exploiting disability to sell our products, or saying we should have used a disabled person who didn't look like a typical model. But all press is good press!"

The conversation seemed to be going just my way. This guy was interested in diversity. Time to move in with my killer sales pitch.

"So, do you think Alexander might want to use a disabled male model? Like Joey?"

"Normally we only use models who have representation in the U.K."

"Joey can travel here."

"Well, sure, send more images of his work and maybe a video."

"I'll call my office today and get them to courier it right over."

"Oh, there's no rush. We've done disability. It's basically over."

Now I was confused. Disability was old? Over? How could disability be passé? There were millions of people with disabilities living in the world. We'd just had an entire conversation about exactly how to portray them in fashion and why it was so important. I'd thought the guy was onside.

"Okay, well, I'll deal with it when I get back to the office if you want. But I think it's still a great idea, even if you've done it before. Maybe you could make a tradition of always having some models with disabilities in your shows?"

"That would get dull and then no one would care. We'd just be copying ourselves."

"You keep using typical models and that hasn't stopped you from continuing to be original."

"It's not the same. They're not in the show to provoke reaction."

I was dazed and confused myself. Just when I thought the international fashion world was open to using diversity, I realized diversity was seen as a trend. For this marketing director, it was something to create shock value, to grab attention, and to cause a stir. It wasn't meant to attract disabled consumers or promote positive images of people with disabilities.

I thanked the marketing director for the conversation. He'd spent over an hour with me, which was generous. As soon as I got home I sent him a package on Joey. When he received it he emailed to thank me. He said Joey looked great but that for now disability was definitely *done*.

The rest of my meetings in London went the same way. Most clients weren't interested in diverse models, except for two modelling agencies. Two top London firms thought it might be interesting to represent a few of my more mature models for the British markets. They agreed that with the aging boomer population, a need might just develop for older models. They would split the commission with me, just as Elmer had done.

I headed back to Ottawa with fifty new email addresses from all over the world, a few contracts in hand, and utter determination to take my company global. But I had one big thing to finish before I implemented my expansion plan: high school. I had been voted School Capital, which was my school's name for head of the student body. Plus I had a ton of studying to do. In any case, Kristina, Maria, Shauzab, and Dave all needed to finish their education as well. Our international plans had to wait . . . for now.

TEEN PEOPLE

By August I was back in Canada, feeling confident about life in general and my business life in particular. My main focus was getting ready for the school year: meeting with other prefects to plan the Buddy Day, the early social stuff, and the welcome-back picnic. From a business point of view, I was most concerned with raising my profile. I was curious and hopeful about who might come looking for Ben Barry once they knew we existed. Boosting your brand is an important part of any business; I'd known that since my first *Ottawa Citizen* profile back when I was wondering if I'd ever grow any facial hair or stop talking like a choirboy. Fortuitously, during February of senior year, I was given the opportunity to get my message out wide and clear.

I got a mind-blowing phone call from *Teen People*. They had picked me as one of "Twenty Teens Who Will Change the World." I was the sole businessperson and the only Canadian. Other teens on the list included a queer-rights activist, a female Paralympian, and actors Kirsten Dunst and Mandy Moore. As gangs go, I thought it would do nicely.

Everyone kept asking me how *Teen People* in New York had found out about a modelling agency in Ottawa. I had no idea myself until I got an email from one of my models, Sara, congratulating me on being selected and divulging her role in the adventure. Sara had spent the summer as an intern at *Teen People* (I knew she was interning at a magazine because she'd told me she couldn't model that summer, but I didn't know which one). She had written a sample article about me and shown it to one of the editors for feedback. The editor told her that she wanted to consider me for the "Twenty Teens" list but asked her not to say anything to me while the magazine was still deciding. Sara said in her email it had been insanely hard to keep her mouth shut while she listened to all the editors at the magazine discuss Ben Barry. I wrote Sara back a thank you in forty-eight-point type.

All twenty teens got invited on a two-day trip to New York to attend the awards ceremony. There were going to be several events leading up to a gala lunch: a welcome dinner, a tour of *Teen People*'s offices and the AOL Time Warner building, and a press conference. Mom was also invited to come along and hang out with all the other proud parents. I was really looking forward to meeting other rebels with valid causes.

But I was stressed about missing three days of school. Test season was fast approaching and missing classes meant missing new material. My grades were now more important than ever. Mid-year marks were being sent to universities in a month and these grades would be the final factor in deciding where I was accepted. I wasn't sure whether or not I wanted to go straight to university but I wanted to keep the door open at least. When I told my teachers about my fears, they offered to meet me over lunch or after school to review what I was going to miss. So before my trip, I spent some extra hours with Ms Allen in math class, Mrs. Jowett in the English department office, and Madame McNairan in the language lab. Then I crammed my calculus text and the latest print edition of *Julius Caesar* into my bag along with a bunch of model portfolios.

I'd planned to arrive in New York in the morning, take some time to walk about the city with Mom, have lunch with a potential client while Mom checked out a museum, and then get ready for the big welcome dinner. But a good old Canuck snowstorm delayed our flight. We landed at the airport just minutes before the dinner started. Thanks to Taxi Guy's complete disregard for public and private safety, we got there only ten minutes late, not including any time to change. I had to go into dinner wearing a massive pair of snow boots and a bulbous down jacket. Mom was equally decked out in Canadian winter attire. Nobody commented; I guess they thought this was all the rage in the Great White North.

At the dinner I sat beside a marketing director from L'Oréal. The company was a sponsor of the awards, offering each winner a scholarship for their studies. I couldn't have asked for a better dinner neighbour. Mom was beside another mom and I could hear her contentedly chatting away about Bloomingdales and Broadway. I had the perfect icebreaker to start the conversation: that I had met one of the marketing director's colleagues a year ago and been invited to watch one of the L'Oréal photo shoots. I raved about the experience, about how much I had learned, and how friendly everyone was. He was happy to hear it. He leaned back on his chair and took a big chomp out of his pizza slice with a pleased look on his face. Now for the attack.

"I've looked at many of your ads and wondered why they all feature women with traditional model looks, like Milla Jovovich, your main spokesmodel. Why is that?"

He sat up, a bit startled. "Well, everyone can relate to Milla Jovovich," he said. "She's so beautiful it's almost beyond human."

"Hmm, beyond human," I repeated. "How do most people relate to someone who is *beyond human*?"

"Women all want to be like Milla...have her ivory skin, high cheekbones, long lashes, bright eyes, lush lips. She's perfect. They want to be perfect, too."

Here it was all over again. L'Oréal wanted to tempt the average woman with the idea that beauty had one definition: young, thin, and flawless. It wasn't the greatest dinner convo, but I countered that nobody is perfect and that L'Oréal customers were far more likely to end up feeling dissatisfied with their bodies if Milla Jovovich was who they were being asked to compare themselves to.

"Nonsense. Women want to aspire to be more beautiful. We fuel their dreams and give them hope. You know our slogan, 'Because you're worth it.'

Our customers want to be worth it and we're helping them be worth it because we believe that they are."

Nonsense? Nonsense?! I'd show him nonsense. All my feelings after my first meeting at L'Oréal were coming back to me now. My blood was going from simmer to boil. My heart felt like a bumper car. I heard red-alert sirens screaming in my brain. This time, I wasn't going to shut up.

"How can women feel *worth it* if you persist in showing them an image that they'll never achieve? If a forty-five-year-old woman looks at a billboard of Milla, she'll never feel she's *worth it*. She'll just compare herself to Milla and feel old and unattractive."

"But she'll want to look like Milla. She'll dream and fantasize about it. And she'll buy our products in hopes of it."

"But it's *false* hope. It's *not* achievable. She'll never, *ever* do it." I was holding back the foam that threatened to spill out of my mouth. I was almost hurling my slice of Hawaiian pizza across the table. The other people at the table looked over nervously. Mom and the other lady weren't chitchatting about *Phantom of the Opera* any more. I offered up a twisted smile then mouthed "sorry" to Mom's new friend.

"I sometimes get a little heated in debates," I said to my tablemate. "Excuse me, please."

"Hey, it's okay. You were starting to remind me of my brother at a Yankees game."

"Thanks...I guess. Anyway, this woman I'm describing to you, she probably has some wrinkles, she probably has a few grey hairs, right?"

"She probably does," he said.

"Okay. So you're telling her that she can be worth it, and then never allowing her to be worth it. And you're doing this knowingly."

"I hear what you're saying, Ben, I do. But I'm working for a business here. Not the UN or the World Wildlife Fund. In business, we exploit opportunity. And frankly, if women's low esteem gives way to an opportunity, well, then, so be it. Not that it's our goal to make people feel bad about themselves. But I'm in business here, not the charity sector."

"I'm also a businessperson. At my agency we make people feel beautiful. We make a profit doing it and our clients do, too."

I explained how my agency supplied clients with models who reflected their consumers and how their consumers felt good about their own bodies as a result, and related well to the brand and kept buying into it.

"That just won't keep our consumers product-hungry, I'm afraid. If they're happy with themselves, they won't buy. Our ads keeps dreams and hopes alive."

"But what if your dream and hope is to be the best possible you instead of trying to be someone else? What if people were to buy the products because they feel like they're a legitimate part of beauty and want to enjoy that? What if their hopes and dreams about being beautiful were actually fulfilled?"

Before the L'Oréal marketing man could reply, the chairperson of AOL Time Warner addressed the crowd to deliver a welcome speech. He told us about the history of the awards and how excited he was to be honouring us. L'Oréal Man leaned over to me and whispered, "Sit beside me at the awards luncheon tomorrow and we'll finish our conversation." I smiled back, trying to chill, and nodded in agreement.

After dinner, Mom and I walked back to the hotel. I began to describe my dinner conversation. She said there was no need, she'd heard every word. In typical Mom style, she reminded me always to be polite, even when I didn't agree. "I know, Mom," I said, "I was polite. And I *soooooo* didn't agree."

The next morning, I awoke to a TV crew in my room. The Canadian media got right on my story when they found out I was the only Canadian on the *Teen People* list. A reporter from the *Ottawa Citizen* came to New York, the local news station set me up for live feeds, and *Fashion Television* was going to follow me around all day for a story. My day started while I was getting dressed in my room. The first question the FT reporter asked: What was I going to wear to the luncheon? I'd noticed that most New Yorkers wore black, so I put on black pants, a black shirt, and a black jacket. When we arrived at the gala luncheon, I found half of the guests wearing black clothes—all the New Yorkers and me. Right on.

I also grabbed a chance to talk with the publisher of *Teen People*. The magazine had made the decision to use only real teens as models when it launched in 1998 and had stayed true to this commitment. Right away I congratulated the publisher on her vision and commended her on *Teen People*'s innovative fashion and beauty editorials. They always had a box beside each teen model listing his or her age, school, and fashion tips. As soon as the cameras started rolling, I asked her if she would ever consider requiring the advertisers to use real teens as models. She said she didn't have control over the ad design; the advertisers simply supplied them to the magazine. I suggested that maybe she should persuade her advertisers to use real teens by showing them the positive feedback *Teen People* got from doing so.

I also suggested she could create guidelines regarding what type of ad was allowed in the magazine. She responded that *Teen People* did have such guidelines. They didn't allow cigarette companies or alcohol companies to advertise because they didn't want to promote teen smoking or drinking.

"That's great," I replied. "So, similarly, you could insist that models be a certain dress size and be ethnically representative if you don't want to promote negative body image and exclusion."

She looked at me. She looked at the camera. She gave us both a big smile and said, "Ben, maybe we can speak about this more later. I need to speak with some more people before the lunch."

"Definitely!" I said.

Business hint: never stop working your angles.

I was presented with my award by Todd Oldham, a big name in design. When he introduced me, he said that my vision for the fashion industry was "a needed change, indeed." I took the podium, too stoked from the past two days of confrontations to be nervous. I talked about the harmful impact of the fashion industry and how I wanted to transform that into a positive force. The audience agreed, extremely passionately it seemed to me, although I admit I didn't have an applause-o-meter handy.

After the awards presentation, I went looking for the marketing director from L'Oréal. I hadn't sat down once all day. None of the winners had. Instead, we'd gone from table to table greeting guests and then we'd waited by the stage to receive our awards. I found him speaking with the *Teen People* publisher. Great, now I had the opportunity to follow up with both of them. I loitered nearby. The marketing director saw me first and motioned for me to come over.

"Ben, I've been thinking a lot about our discussion last night. I think certain L'Oréal consumer brands could benefit from your approach. Possibly Redken and Maybelline."

"Fantastic!"

He said he wanted to discuss my idea with the various L'Oréal brand marketing departments. The *Teen People* publisher mentioned that she wanted to discuss my idea about model guidelines for advertisers with her editors and advertising department. She agreed that banning ultra-thin models would be in the best interest of the readers and the *Teen People* brand.

"Great! And it'll increase your readership and allow more teens to connect with your advertisers' products. These are smart business policies for both of you." I thought about the support I'd just received from the audience and decided to press my advantage. "Actually, I think all the L'Oréal brands would profit from my approach. And I think *Teen People* would benefit by setting advertising guidelines for using models from diverse cultural backgrounds." Another business hint: if you're going to press, press as hard as you can without bruising.

No bookings resulted directly from the *Teen People* event. No *Teen People* advertisements. No L'Oréal billboards. But the award offered me a lot of legitimacy and opened doors in the States. I no longer had to bang on those doors, introducing myself as an unknown. People were beginning to recognize my name and accept my company's diverse roster of models as serving a real need. An article about the awards soon appeared in *Teen People*, which led to yet more U.S.-based model and client contacts. This wasn't typical for a Canadian firm in the hard-to-break-into American market. Also, many *Teen People* readers were inspired by my story and connected personally by writing to me asking for advice.

My enthusiasm had always burned pretty bright but at this point it was flaming high. It helped to realize I wasn't alone, that my message resonated with people as an important issue. But some people still didn't get me. They couldn't figure out why I was aiming to create positive change in society while running a business. At the *Teen People* gala—and in correspondence afterward—people echoed the L'Oréal marketing director's questions: Was I in business with the chief aim of turning a profit or was I running a charity organization with a primary goal of solving social ills? Over and over, I was asked to decide on a priority for myself: profit or social change? I knew there wasn't necessarily a choice to be made; I was convinced I could do both. So what if my business model seemed like a paradox? I understood it perfectly.

One of the ceremony attendees, however, seemed unfazed by my approach. She was a producer with the *Oprah Winfrey Show*.

OPRAH CALLS

It was a May evening, a Monday night, one month before my high school graduation. I was in my basement office studying for finals, decked out in my ultimate study gear—flannel pyjama bottoms and my track team sweatshirt. Textbooks were spread open on my desk. Calculus practice exams were scattered on the floor. I was working on sample questions on scrap paper, hammering away on my calculator, and wiping eraser scruff off my desk. Shoved deep into my knapsack, under my history and geography notes, my cell started to ring. I put down my pencil and dug into my bag.

"Hello, Ben?" a voice said. "I'm a producer from the *Oprah Winfrey Show*. I was at the *Teen People* awards and I caught your acceptance speech. Oprah's doing a show on people with cool jobs and she thinks you'd be a great guest."

The *Oprah Winfrey Show*? Oprah thought I could be a guest? A *great* guest?

"Cool," I stammered, my brain quickly switching over from solving for X to scheduling an interview with a talk-show empress.

"We'd like to shoot some background with you tomorrow and then fly you down to Chicago for a live show the next morning. Can you do it?"

This woman wasted no time. I liked her. I thought fast. Obviously, an immediate decision was required. Most CEOs are constrained by their shareholders—I had Mom and a bunch of teachers to appease.

"That should be just fine but can I call you back in ten? I just need to change some previous plans."

"Sure, but ten minutes at the most."

I hung up, opened up the phone book and found my principal's home number. He answered, thank God. I asked if I could reschedule my exam and if Oprah's crew could film at my school. He said yes. I called my debating coach and asked if I could arrive late for the weekend tournament. She said yes. I ran upstairs to the kitchen to talk to Mom. At that point she could hardly say no. In eight minutes I called the producer back: "I can do it!"

Not only was it a massive personal thrill to be a guest on *Oprah*, it was also one of the best, most gigantic PR opportunities going. Not that I fully realized this until after the show had aired. Everything happened at the speed of strobe lights.

In order to introduce me, the producer wanted to pre-film a three-minute montage of my life as a student-slash-modelling agent. It's not like I didn't have a lot of time to prepare; I'd known about this since, oh, 6 p.m. the night before. My cross-country running team graciously permitted the film crew to capture our sweaty early-morning practice, grunts included. Hanging out with my friends Jon and Omid during lunch was crucial; that was where I was most myself. We sat in our usual spot outside the gym, munching on subs and laughing away, almost forgetting that we were on camera. And definitely I had to get my calculus class filmed: being on *Oprah* was the excuse I was using to get my exam postponed.

After school, they filmed a magazine shoot that two of my models were involved in. It was supposed to be a few days later, but since Oprah wanted to catch a shoot I called the fashion editor and asked if we could do it sooner, say in twenty-four hours. She kindly agreed and coordinated the photographer and stylist. How did anyone say no to Oprah? The shoot took place in Ottawa's historic Byward Market, in front of sidewalk cafés with the Parliament Buildings in the background. Two of the first models I'd ever signed were in the shoot: Elizabeth, a forty-five-year-old full-figured model with fiery red hair, and Sarah-Monica. Both models laughed, strutted, and gave seductive poses for the camera. I did what I normally do during photo shoots: watched quietly from the sidelines, thanked everyone working on-set, and complimented my models.

Then we dropped by the agency office. Normally, it would have been dark and locked up by that time of day but I'd invited a bunch of models to "meetings." It was my acting ability at its very best. I faked interviews with new models, reviewed pictures from photo shoots, did runway practices, and conducted a staff meeting. I told my guys there was pizza in it for them, premium toppings, as well as the chance to be on *Oprah*. When Mom finished up with her patients for the day, she came by the office with three extra larges. After filming several of my meetings and conducting a few one-on-one interviews with my models and staff (and one longer one with me) the camera crew plus the agency staff, models, and Mom all tucked in. Just the end of one of the more intense "typical" days of my life.

The next morning I flew to Chicago. A limo driver greeted me at the airport and drove me directly to the Omni Hotel where the show had booked me a spectacular room. The taping (that was to be broadcast as if it was live) wasn't until the next morning so I had a whole afternoon to myself. I decided to follow up on some of the Chicago-based contacts that I'd made during the *Teen People* awards. On short notice (dropping Oprah's name like anyone in their right mind would) I was able to meet with a marketing manager and three potential models. So what if it meant having a jam-packed afternoon? Keeping busy would keep me from getting eaten up by raging Oprah nerves. Business hint: face-to-face meetings make a huge difference in building relationships,

I arrived back at my hotel in the early evening. The producer had insisted I order whatever I wanted from room service. After some enjoyable pondering, I opted for a steak dinner with chocolate cheesecake for dessert. T-bones and cheesecake generally taste pretty good but never has a T-bone and cheesecake tasted better. I was up on the thirty-fifth floor; the imposing Chicago skyline twinkled in the dusk. Never had a city seemed so compelling, so welcoming, and such an important place to be.

Once I was sufficiently fortified, I had to think about what to wear. Millions of people would be judging me for that. (Whoa, big mistake: I didn't want to be making too much use of the word "million.") I laid out several wardrobe options on the hotel bed. I wanted to look professional, yet my age, yet fashion-industry appropriate. A suit was out—too business. All black was too New York, and would look blah on TV. I went with a French-cuffed black dress shirt, shiny red pants, and even shinier black shoes. Red pants were a risk, I knew that, but I wanted some serious snap. It was actually a good thing that my day had been so busy because I went right to bed and right to sleep, once the red pants had been safely transported to the armchair.

Five a.m. I got my wake-up call. I quickly showered, ate breakfast (a bold move, but I figured a vital one) and made it to the lobby. Another limo ride, this time to Harpo Studios. I was given a security badge and shown to the green room. The producer met me there to discuss the format of my interview with Ms Winfrey. Luckily, I was good for only fifteen minutes in makeup. High-end television makeup is air-brushed on nowadays. It's slightly freaky, but a real time saver.

Sitting across from Oprah felt surreal. Yes, that was Oprah, but was this really me? Two days before I was in calculus class; now I was in the crosshairs of five camera people. Was I looking at Oprah a bit like a puppy checking out its new owner? This was a woman who had worked tirelessly to promote self-empowerment, just as I wanted to do in my business. At least she made it seem tireless. Was I going to tire out the tireless Oprah? Could we do a Take 2 in a crunch? I knew I might mess up on some answers given my slight need to barf.

During the interview, I told Oprah that as far as I was concerned, when a model poses in front of the camera or stalks a runway, it's not about her shoes, makeup, or dress. It's all about her personality and charisma, about effervescence from within. I acknowledged that most of the population associates the glamour and allure of fashion with drugs, infighting, anorexia, and bulimia. I mentioned that inferior agencies add to the negativity by charging wannabe models thousands of dollars in training fees and then failing to procure them work. I said I'd seen first hand the harm inflicted on young women's health and sense of self by such practices and that for those who do get to be models, there's prestige to be had but also the feeling of being more of a commodity than a human being.

I told Oprah's audience this needed to stop, that the fashion industry needed to revamp its representation of the human body so that more people could identify with models instead of being forced into a narrow, false stereotyped understanding of beauty. The dominant images put out by the industry were (and still are) a power to be reckoned with, but I said I was challenging that power. I was running an unconventional modelling agency based on the principle there is no single standard of beauty, that we are all beautiful in our own way.

But Oprah dug deeper. She was Oprah after all. She asked what fuelled me, what kept me going. I explained that for me, it was important to wake up every morning and to know that I was doing something that was helping people. I was driven by a desire to leave the world better than I'd found it. (As I suspect a lot of people are, whether they remember that over their morning coffee or not.)

Oprah finished things off by saying, "Well, aren't you something!" I took that as a good sign.

On the way home from the airport I could hardly wait to check my email to see if there was any feedback from Oprah's viewers. My server had crashed... that's what happens when you get 500,000 messages at once. Five of my friends, including Mia, helped me to reply to every one. We divided the messages into three groups.

The first group were emails from people who'd wanted to share their personal experiences with body image and the media. I felt really honoured that so many souls had shared such intimate stories. One story particularly stands out. It was from a woman who had recently immigrated to San Diego from Nigeria. She said that her full figure was seen as beautiful in Nigeria but that her American friends told her she needed to lose weight, that she was too big. She'd tried to look like the models in fashion magazines but said no matter how much she exercised and dieted, her body wouldn't get smaller. She also wrote that her boss suggested that she relax her hair if she wanted to get promoted. From her African point of view, the American beauty ideal was something she didn't fit into at all. She would never be "beautiful" in America.

As to the second group of emails: hundreds of potential models living in the U.S. sent photos requesting representation by Ben Barry. Potential U.S. clients also began contacting me to inquire about my services. I knew I couldn't let all this opportunity go to waste. I reviewed all model applications, conducted phone interviews, and then travelled to Boston, Los Angeles, even to Wichita, Kansas, to conduct in-person interviews. That way I could offer American clients diverse Ben Barry models in every major American centre, in addition to our Canadian-based roster. All models and clients would continue to be managed by my Ottawa office.

The final group of messages were from people who wanted to express their appreciation for what I'd done so far. Just to say thank you. This always makes you want to do more and keep pushing for change. Oh, right, we also got lots of requests from people who wanted tips on becoming model scouts. After all, it is a cool job.

The exposure I got from *Teen People* and then the *Oprah Winfrey Show* made me seem a lot less fanatical. People now wanted to pay attention, figuring that

I must have something important to say if Oprah cared to listen. But when it came to the major New York fashion and global beauty brands, Oprah only got my foot in the door. Some of them did hire diverse models for fashion shows and one-off ads in local regions: L'Oréal hired my models for some new product launches and Hugo Boss did so for a charity fashion show. Not, however, for Fashion Week or major billboard and magazine advertising. Most marketing directors still held the conviction that a traditional, thin, white girl was the only valid model for major projects.

In five years, I'd developed the experience, contacts, and credibility needed to make change. Something, however, was holding me back from signing major deals. Was it not having enough business education to handle international projects? Was it living in Canada's capital instead of a fashion capital? Was it not having a marketing strategy and business model that was sufficiently compelling and thorough to gain clients' trust? I had to figure out the problem and I had to fix it fast.

CHAPTER SEVEN

DEVELOPING MY STYLE

HAVING IT BOTH WAYS

I WASN'T LANDING ULTRA-HIGH fashion gigs in Paris or New York but other clients were hiring from the Ben Barry Agency. Banks, car companies, hotel chains, and the Canadian government all booked my models for their major campaigns. Even MTV hired one of my guys, Quddus, to host their flagship program *Total Request Live*. Things were definitely starting to take off.

A few days before graduation, I was all alone in my Ottawa office. I'd shifted operations to the downtown core by then, to the fifteenth floor of a building otherwise full of government offices and NGOs. I sat back in my black bungee-cord chair at my frosted glass desk (I was very proud of both) and stared at two pieces of paper. My two worlds were literally facing off against each other. In one hand, I had my models' booking schedule for the upcoming summer. In the other hand I held my acceptance letter from the University of Toronto, including the offer of a four-year scholarship. High school was over and I had a huge decision to make. Did I take time off school—with the possibility of never going back? Or did I put my business on hold and go on to university?

I decided to call a mentor, Kelly Streit, to discuss the honking big fork in my road. When Kelly was nineteen he'd decided against post-secondary school and started up a modelling agency in Red Deer, Alberta. Twenty years later he has two offices in Canada and one in the States and can take credit for discovering models as top as Tricia Helfer and Heather Marks.

Kelly listened closely and put it this way: "I've been successful in business and learned a lot of things that I could never have picked up in school. But I still regret not going to university. There's something life changing about being at university when you're young," Kelly elaborated. "I know I could always go now but it wouldn't be the same. When you're an adult, your mind isn't as open to being shaped by new ideas. You're more decided about what you believe and who you are."

I didn't want to regret anything. Neither did I want to be confined to a choice that was either/or. I thought that I could study *and* keep my business running at full force. I'd done it all through high school.

So I said goodbye to Mom, Spice, and Russia, and accepted my scholarship to the University of Toronto. Yes, I'd be in a different city, but I didn't think anyone at the agency would be troubled by the difference. Things would run the same way as they always had. I would still negotiate the bookings and manage the models via my cell and email. My staff could still call me any time with questions, and I would still check in each morning and at the end of each business day. New model photos could be emailed to me daily as usual. Now, I would just be on the other end of a line in Toronto instead of Ottawa. And I'd be back in person once a month for meetings (and Mom's famous cinnamon chicken).

The only big difference about not being in Ottawa was that I couldn't sign cheques and contracts on a day-to-day basis, a power that I hated to give up now that I was finally eighteen. I decided to hire Mom part-time as a manager with the authority to co-sign for me while I was away. I trusted her more than anyone else: she was Mom after all. And she was the most qualified candidate, having signed my cheques for five years already.

I was excited by the move to a new city and a big city. I'd lived my entire life in Ottawa. I'd gone to the same school since grade five. I'd only ever lived with Mom, since dad died when I was five.

Mom met my dad and married him in a whirlwind six weeks. He was a professor of psychology at the University of Ottawa and Mom was a newly admitted grad student who was helping out in the department. One week, my dad was preparing to give a talk in Florida, but his research assistant was away on holidays. Mom was assigned to help him prepare his lecture, and then he went away for a week to deliver it. When he returned, she picked him up at the airport and he proposed. A month later they were married. Nine years later they had me. Mom was devastated when Dad got sick. After he was gone, I remember feeling like it was my job to look after her and protect her. It forced me to mature fast. It also brought us closer together.

But Mom was thriving now. All parents and kids have to part ways eventually. Time to say goodbye and do my own laundry. (Well, most of my own laundry.)

I admit that I was looking forward to the chance to discover more about myself. I hadn't really explored the world outside of work, family, and a few best friends. It had been years since I'd been able to hang out without being recognized as the kid model agent and then having to talk business. Toronto had over four million people; U of T alone had sixty thousand students. No one would know who the hell I was.

During my frosh year, I lived in the Trinity College residence. The University of Toronto is divided into colleges and Trinity is the smallest, located in a Baroque-looking building beside Queen's Park. My room was on the first floor. There were nine single rooms on my hall with a common bathroom at the end. Like any dorm, each room contained a bed and a desk with two inches of discretionary space between them. But the rooms had tons of character. Mine had a huge window with fancy carved stone moulding around it, overlooking a soccer field.

My room tripled as my study space, my sleeping space, and Ben Barry Agency Toronto. While the other guys on my floor put up posters of their favourite hockey teams, rock bands, or swimsuited *Sports Illustrated* girlfriends, I decorated my walls with pictures of my models. By the time I was done, there was no wall space left blank. And while the other guys had no problem making do with one phone line, I needed two; I had a fax machine to hook up. Before the phone company would install it, I had to get permission from the college. I met with just about every residence don and administrator, explaining how a fax would "allow me to focus on my studies since I won't be spending time running to Kinko's." Not the most convincing argument, but I got a yes in the end. Model contracts arrived and departed while I studied poli-sci. And offered up my room as the bar whenever we had a floor party.

That first year, I didn't set up an actual office on purpose. I wanted to be a student full-time—to live in a dorm, go to class, and hang out with new friends. And that's what I managed to do, at least for good chunks of time. Admittedly, it was a total test of my willpower to stay focused on term papers and the campus pub when things were transpiring with the agency. Every once in a while I absolutely had to slip away to finesse a contract or sign up a new model.

I'd constructed a course load heavy in business studies. After all, I ran a business and had really gotten into my entrepreneurship course at LSE. But after a couple of weeks it seemed like all my classes were focused on matters strictly practical and routine. Yes, it's important to get a handle on finance, accounting, decision making, and marketing. But none of my professors were addressing the larger political, economic, and social issues that I knew were critical when developing business ideas and making business decisions. So I decided to shake up my class schedule a little. I didn't want to miss out on any key skills, but I sure didn't want to be bored.

THINKING FEMINIST

It was three weeks into term. I wanted to replace accounting 101 with another course but most of them were completely full. I kept checking online but couldn't find anything that grabbed me. Until one evening at 11:50 p.m., ten minutes before the system shut down for the night and I could toss aside my books and head to the pub. One place had opened up for one last student in a course that dealt with gender, class, and race in the media. Not a bad fit at all, so what if it was women's studies? I registered immediately and blew a good-bye kiss to Principles of Accounting.

The next day was what I call busy. After breakfast, I headed to my three-hour marketing class at the business school. It was in a brand new building named after a multi-million-dollar donor. The outside was all glass and chrome and the inside had leather chairs and sofas and televisions in the lounges, all tuned to the latest stock market quotes. Students were busy on laptops and Palms, or reading the latest issue of the *Financial Times* while downing lattes from the Starbucks in the lobby. The lecture was in a theatre-style room, with three large screens for PowerPoint presentations. The class was about 50/50 male and female, mostly in their early twenties. The lecturer entered wearing a tailored black pant suit, glasses with modish red frames, and her hair combed back in a sleek, low ponytail. She plugged in her laptop and "The Fundamentals of Marketing: Target Markets and Brand Positioning, September 23, 2001" flashed up on three screens. She tapped her mic.

"Good morning. I'll be lecturing on market segmentation and brand positioning."

Thus followed a two-hour lecture on how companies divide up the marketplace according to age, ethnic origin, income, interests, and opinions, then design advertising and promotions to resonate with said targets. They select slices of the market based on demographic, psychographic, and behavioural criteria. Demographics include age, gender, family life cycle, education, income, and ethnic origin. Psychographics included a person's activities, interests, and opinions.

I realized this was how I'd been convincing clients to use diverse models. I'd explained to clients that standard models didn't match their demographic criteria. The psychographic criteria demonstrated that consumers wanted to see real models.

The screen changed again. We learned about "positioning": a company's attempts to distinguish itself favourably from its competitors in the minds and hearts of consumers. I got that, too. Using diverse models helped my clients effectively position themselves.

After the lecture came my tutorial, led by the prof. We were doing a case study on Parasuco Jeans. Five-hundred-and-forty million pairs of jeans are produced annually in North America: getting denim to the checkout counter is no easy task. It's done by developing a personality for a brand through advertising. The prof handed around a sheet with info about Parasuco. It was started in Montreal in 1975 and now sells two million pairs of jeans annually in Canada, the United States, Italy, and Japan. About 75 per cent of its U.S. sales are to black and Hispanic consumers.

"Here's your challenge as marketers," the prof said. "Parasuco is adding a new apparel line for young career women. Who should the target markets be and how should the new line be positioned?"

One woman raised her hand. "The demographic should be women between twenty and thirty-five who work in professional roles and live in urban centres."

"They care about fashion and beauty, and want to look good," another person suggested.

"So we need to attract them by creating a sexy and beautiful image," a guy said.

It was time for me to jump in. "Yes, but we should also look at body size and ethnic origin. We can attract them by creating sexy ads, but with models who represent the demographics. Models who reflect the customers' ages, ethnic backgrounds, and sizes."

"But we have to convey the glamour and excitement of the fashion world," another student said. "If we use models who don't look like models, the ads will be dull and boring. No one will think fashion when they hear Parasuco."

"I disagree," a woman said. "I think women would totally love non-modelly ads. They'd be able to picture themselves wearing the product."

"And we'll be seen as different from the competitors," I said, "We'll stand out and the ads will really resonate with our target."

"I'm still not sure," the guy said. "People want to see young, thin, and beautiful. That's fashion."

"Maybe that's what guys want, but not girls. There's so much pressure to look like those stick-thin models and most of us just don't, thanks."

"But you keep buying fashion products advertised using tall, skinny girls. They obviously attract you on some level."

"We wouldn't if we didn't have to. There's no other option. All models look like that."

The professor jumped in: "Wouldn't using models who don't look like regular models position the brand outside the fashion mainstream?"

I countered, "I think the trick is creating ads that look as sexy as regular fashion images. The models will be the only difference. Otherwise, they'll have the same photographers, the same makeup and hair, and the same styling.

People will have to look close to even notice a difference but they'll be excited when they do."

"I don't know," another girl said. "Models are just to look at. People know we're not supposed to be just like them."

"Then why do so many girls feel so much pressure to be skinny?"

"Okay, people, I think we may be getting sidetracked," the prof said. "This is an interesting discussion but time's up. Everybody think about how we should design the ads and we'll talk again next week."

I ran for the door, called the Ottawa office on my cell while devouring a peanut butter sandwich, and rushed to my first women's studies class. The department was in a plain brown brick sixties-style building. The interior was decorated with works by female artists and posters announcing conferences on social issues. Students were curled up on couches, reading books, discussing assignments, and sipping tea and juice from the student-run canteen. I found my lecture hall and grabbed a seat at the front. Glancing behind me, I saw students for the most part in their early twenties, but a few were in their thirties, forties, and up.

It didn't bother me that I was the only guy in the room. I was used to it, having been raised by a single mom, aunt, and grandmother. In fact, I didn't even realize I was the sole male until I noticed everyone looking at me as they walked in, probably wondering how long I would last. I could feel eyes on me now. It wasn't hostility; it was curiosity. I was a distinct minority.

The lecturer entered the room, wearing a dark purple skirt and black hand-knitted sweater with light silver hair to her shoulders. She opened her folder onto the wooden podium (that had a plaque saying it was donated by the class of '87). She took out a few sheets of paper with notes written in blue pen.

"Hello everyone," she began, with a big, warm smile. "This is our third lecture for 'Women's Studies 241: Gender, Race, and Class in the Media.' Yesterday was the final date for new students to enroll so this should be it. I'll begin by introducing myself. My name is Paula Baxter. I am a white, middle-class, straight woman."

Why was she telling me this? So what?

"Those of you who are new to women's studies might be asking yourself why I'm telling you this. It's important to disclose the different identities to which I belong, or what we in women's studies call 'social locations.' These different identities shape my experiences, perspectives, and biases. My hope is that by revealing them, you will be aware of their influence in shaping how I see different issues. It will also keep me open to seeing issues in new ways. I encourage each of you to be aware of your own social locations and also understand how they shape what you see."

Wow. I never thought much about the different identity categories to which I belonged. Sure, I was white, half German Jewish and half Irish Catholic, male, upper middle class, and for all I knew straight (although I suppose tentative would be a more apt way to describe my sexual orientation back then). Never before had I taken into real consideration how much these factors influenced my state of mind.

"As you know from the course syllabus, and the readings that I'm sure you've all dutifully completed, today's topic is 'Advertising and the Cultural Construction of Gender.'"

Professor Baxter revealed that feminists had been busy for a while critiquing the beauty industry—for the way it promulgates an idealized vision of female beauty with disturbingly narrow physical characteristics (young, tall, underweight). But she explained that the feminist critique goes farther than simply *who* is represented. *How* they are represented is also considered problematic.

Our professor explained that models in fashion advertising are usually shown from the "sexual gaze" perspective; in other words, their entire identities are limited to their sexual role. The body is separated from the person, treated as an object that exists for the use and pleasure of others. Diverse voices, ideas, and thoughts aren't featured. Models have no control. They don't take action.

"Models' bodies carry culturally learned meaning," she said. "Every time I open up a women's magazine, my blood pressure soars. If I had it my way, every ad would have a line saying, 'Danger: this model may be hazardous to your health.'"

The professor made a persuasive case that women are defined not by women's own eyes but by those of the heterosexual male. Granted, many photographers, stylists, and image creators aren't straight men. But no matter who they are—straight women, gay men, whatever—they've more often than not internalized this dominant perspective. Art historian John Berger famously explained that men look at women, while women watch themselves being looked at. A female understanding of female sexuality is seldom aired, celebrated, or explored. Understandably, the female body has become the site of a lot of anxiety and insecurity. Knowing they're gazed at, women struggle for ways to transform their bodies to meet the socially accepted standards.

The lecture enthralled me. Never before had I thought about how my identities shaped the way I saw issues. Never had I thought about *how* women were portrayed in addition to *who*. But I'd thought carefully about profit as the driving force behind all this negative energy. After the lecture, as everyone else packed up their books and started leaving, I went to the podium to speak with Professor Baxter.

"Professor, hi. My name is Ben. I just registered for your class. Your lecture was really powerful."

"Thanks. Welcome, Ben," she said with a big smile. "Here's a copy of the syllabus. You can buy the books at the Toronto Women's Bookstore or find copies on reserve at the library."

"Great, thanks." The handout seemed to be at least ten stapled pages.

"The other students have signed up to give presentations at their tutorials. There's still space in Sara's, that's her over there." She pointed to a woman in her mid-twenties with a bright orange and blonde faux-hawk, wearing jeans and a black T-shirt.

"Thanks. Um, I've never taken anything in women's studies before so this is all really new to me."

"Don't worry, Ben. Just ask Sara or me if you have questions about the material. It's all about learning tools to help analyze our world. Each week you'll learn a new set."

I went straight over to Sara. She told me the presentation was supposed to shed extra insight into the latest lecture topic and provoke a lively discussion. She had only one slot left...the next one, the next day. I had no choice but to sign up; either that or skulk back to balance-sheet exercises. The topic was "The Portrayal of Women in Advertising." Hey, I knew a little something about that. Fired up by the lecture, and knowing nothing else about women's studies, I decided to zero in on the idea of sexual gaze.

The tutorial had about twenty students. We sat at tables in a horseshoe. Sara kicked things off with my presentation. The deep end, yet again.

"I've seen ads with women wearing T-shirts that actively assert their sexuality," I began. "And I've seen many young women wearing shirts like that around the city." I showed my tutorial an ad I'd found of a woman wearing a T-shirt that read 'Fit Chick Unbelievable Knockers' from the U.K.–based international chain French Connection. I told the class the tee had actually become a best-selling item for them.

A women in my tutorial jumped in, saying, "I've seen tons of girls on campus wearing shirts with things like 'Babe' or 'Porn Star.'"

Another woman started tittering nervously. We all looked at her, then looked down at her shirt. Embossed in bright pink letters across her chest was 'Squeeze Here.' She laughed. So did everyone else.

"It's that common," I said. "These phrases seem to be asking people to gaze at the wearer and see her as a sex object. Women are paying good money to present themselves in this way. These shirts are $40 or $50." I asked the group, "Is this a step forward in the media's representation of women?"

One woman explained, "Maybe for some women—young, slim, able-bodied women. They do it to incite the desire of men. But older, bigger, disabled women remain sexually invisible. They're never the ones pictured wearing the shirts."

Another woman commented, "One of the problems with a shirt like this is that it creates a need in you for others to validate your self-image. It takes value away from your own opinion of yourself and loads it onto other people's gazes. This makes it scary to gain weight or get wrinkles because if people don't gaze upon you, then they don't value you."

Sara had some thoughts, "These shirts are potentially problematic in another way, too. By presenting herself as an object of desire, the woman wearing the shirt is arguably inviting sexual attention. That provocation can be used to mask sexual violence. The perpetrator can say the woman asked for it."

I ended by saying I thought that as a culture we needed an entirely new way of gazing. Everyone in class agreed.

By the end of my first few weeks at women's studies, I'd made a lot of new friends and spent extra time with Sara and Professor Baxter, catching up on theories and ideas. Everyone was supportive and encouraged me to enrol in the program as one of my majors. I decided to do so. During the first few classes of each course, I would always feel eyes on me. But it was never in an aggressive way. After a few classes, someone would usually jump in and say, "Well, I see the fit, you run a modelling agency representing women, and so this must help you in your work." I would agree that was part of it. But it also had to do with my acknowledgement of my privileges. Due to my own unique combination of identities, I have power in society. By then, I knew I wanted to use the power associated with my position to get rid of whatever oppression I could. Women's studies helped me understand the inequities I wanted to fix.

Trust me, the phrase "tremendous learning experience" is not just a cliché. Women's studies changed the way I see the world and live in it. The minds at work in a women's studies department can deconstruct a society in such a way that you see how every component rubs together until it fits. My classes gave me a new way to see not just advertising but life.

When viewing ads, I learned to ask not only, "Who is included?" but also "Who is not included?" And then find out why. I also learned to explore histories of privilege and systems of oppression. Meanwhile, back at the business school, I was learning how to devise marketing strategies, how to secure financing, and how to hire staff to start a project or a company. Both frameworks were going to help structure the daily operations of my company. I was starting to feel pretty smart.

THEORY BECOMES PRACTICE

Immediately, I began applying my new theories to my own business. I started with our portfolios. Yes, our models were physically very different from other agencies', but we'd been taking the same old approach as everyone else to our shoots. Most fashion images follow a standard formula: the "gaze perspective." The model is sprawled seductively on the floor or against a wall, with her hands floating around her head or breasts. The bending of her body parts suggests submission and passivity. Her legs are usually exposed and open, further conveying that her identity is defined by her sexual function. The angle of the camera places the viewer above the model, inviting us to look down upon her, rendering her powerless. Furthermore, the camera angle often allows the viewer to look at the model without permitting her to realize she's being watched. All this reinforces stereotypes of femininity (and masculinity), race, and class.

Vogue, *Elle*, or *Bazaar*—the images are indistinguishable. It's even almost impossible to tell what spread is from where. The same goes for modelling agency promotional material. Cover up the logo—Ford, Elite, or IMG—and the images look identical.

I wanted our images to be as radical as our models: time to de-gaze everything I could. I hired a variety of female photographers (many of whom weren't trained in fashion photography). We decided to shake up the status quo by altering the angle from which the models were photographed, placing them at the same level as the viewer, allowing them to stare directly and to remain aware of being observed. The equal eye level didn't vary according to age, race, or class. And the models represented diverse "racial locations," for example, one of our Middle Eastern models wore a veil and one didn't. Every one of our images allowed the model to be the subject, not an object. We also included a profile, written by the model, to help bring her to life on her own terms.

I was pretty exhilarated when it came time to send out the new promotional kits to clients. Many called me up right away, curious about what I was up to. Inspiration was striking all around; several asked me to help them style and direct their own shoots. I felt like I was really getting somewhere.

I was exhilarated all over again when I told Professor Baxter and Sara what I was doing. They were completely enthusiastic and asked me to tell the class about my professional breakthrough. I figured I was applying feminist theories to my business and living to tell the tale. Well, I was granted a stitch but not a seam. A lot of my classmates thought that even if the Ben Barry Agency was successful in getting advertisers to employ diverse models to produce equitable images, fashion and beauty advertising would in general remain inherently oppressive and damaging to women. Point blank: ads tell women that their natural beauty is not enough, that makeup and the latest skirt and heel lengths are what you need to be beautiful, and that you need to be beautiful to be a real woman.

In the tutorial, Sara asked how I'd respond to Naomi Wolf's classic feminist analysis in *The Beauty Myth* that the current idealized, unattainable notion of beauty makes it easier to control women:

> Women are in the midst of a violent backlash against feminism that uses images of female beauty as a political weapon against women's advancement: the beauty myth. As women released themselves from the feminine mystique of domesticity, the "beauty myth" took over its lost ground, expanding as it wanted to carry on its work of social control.

This beauty myth is reinforced in advertising, Wolf says, because of "political fear on the part of male-dominated institutions threatened by women's freedom." And because business relies on the beauty myth to make money.

Sure, the beauty myth can be highly oppressive, but I don't think there's anything inherently wrong with fashion and beauty products. In fact, I think they can be a creative and pleasurable way to express oneself. Millions of women enjoy fashion. In any case, most of my female friends do. They derive real pleasure from dressing up, shopping for clothes, getting their hair cut, and putting different outfits together. When they wear clothes they like, they feel strong, confident, and sexy. It's not the clothes alone that make them feel that way, I know that and they know that. Empowerment like that can happen only when a woman's clothing complements her character. "Looking Good, Feeling Gorgeous," as RuPaul so succinctly puts it.

The same goes for men. As you may have noticed, I love fashion (red pants and purple shirts notwithstanding). Trying on clothes, deciding what to wear, having my hair cut—it all makes me feel great. Not all guys admit to enjoying the fashion experience but believe me, it makes them feel good about themselves, too.

I'm a women's studies student; I recognize that the capitalist framework has produced inequities. In an economy organized around the principles of capitalism, the profit motive is the driving force behind the production, distribution, and consumption of goods and services. Advertising legitimizes consumption as a way of life. But even if I had the power to end capitalism and consumption, in particular the beauty industry, there's no way that I would. Absolutely, someone should sell fashion and beauty products: ideally, diverse producers with their own take on beauty developed from their creator's unique experiences and identities. Capitalism can be highly democratic; theoretically, a free market gives everyone the opportunity to profit. Consumption is a way for people to express themselves—their individuality and style as well as their opinions about the behaviour and values of the sellers.

As much harm as business has done in the past, it can be made to do even more good in the future. Imagine a beauty industry made accessible and available to everyone. That would take: one, images of beauty that include a plurality of women (and men); two, products available at every price point; three, products perceived as a means of creative self-expression rather than a rigid requirement; and four, a move away from seeing beauty as purely physical to an understanding of beauty as a product of an individual's moral and emotional qualities.

I was bringing together everything I was learning in business school *and* women's studies in my pitches to clients. I used the language and theories of one department to bolster the other: feminist theories to enrich a company's understanding of their target market—female consumers—and business terms so they'd see how feminist thinking could fine-tune their marketing strategies. I wasn't preaching; I was helping advertisers position themselves.

It was finally reading week. My head was jam packed. Seven days away from the grind was just what the doctor ordered. I headed home to Ottawa to visit Mom. But the moment I plopped down on the sofa, all set to indulge in her meatball spaghetti and season three of *Sex and the City*, I got a call from The Bay (Canada's oldest and most respected department store chain). They wanted a meeting ASAP. As good as dinner smelled, as strung out as Carrie was by Mr. Big's latest brush off, I couldn't say no. I arranged to meet with the marketing director and the fashion director the next morning. Mom covered my plate and stuck it in the fridge while I hit my desk to prepare.

I arrived at The Bay's downtown Ottawa location. My mind was not only filled with which models I was going to pitch but also my new marketing (and feminist) lingo. The marketing director, a middle-aged man, and the fashion coordinator, a full-figured middle-aged woman, arrived at the restaurant. We all stirred our coffee and got busy.

"Ben, we're interested in doing more in-store fashion shows. We want to attract clientele into the store," the marketing director started.

"We like your diverse approach to models," added the fashion coordinator. "How can you help us?"

"What's your target market?" I asked

"Very broad, basically people of all ages, sizes, and origins. But it's primarily females, who buy for the whole family," the marketing director explained.

"Well, one of the things that women don't like about advertising is when models represent a singular idea of beauty that's far removed from how they look."

"That's so true," the fashion coordinator said. "So often, customers tell me they love what I'm wearing. I'm more effective than our ads!"

"And women don't like when they're simply portrayed as passive objects and denied a personality. Forget the standard runway strut. Have them walk with their own unique gait, showing personality and attitude. Some may be sexy, some may be fun, some may be totally quirky. That will position you well to the women making the purchase decisions in your store."

"I'm worried customers won't see our shows as professional."

"I think you'll connect with hearts and minds in a way that will positively differentiate you from your competitors."

"You know, I think it might work. I want to give it a shot," the marketing director said.

"Seconded," the fashion coordinator said.

As we went over model shots to figure out which best reflected The Bay's broad customer base, I realized that "social locations" and the "target market" were essentially the same thing. I kept asking the marketing director and fashion coordinator, "How would this model impact on consumers of different ages? Sizes? Colours? Abilities? Sexualities? Classes?"

The Bay liked my approach. And so did their customers. Sales staff got rave reviews for the fashion shows. People were buying entire outfits right off the models. The Bay eventually asked us to coordinate a model search that would be open to all, no physical requirements. Soon Sears, another national chain, jumped on board and began hiring our models for in-store shows. My new knowledge was earning me marks, and now earning me business.

My ideas about capitalism and beauty and society were totally crystallizing. University was an exciting, intense, intellectually driven time, just like I'd hoped. Both business school and women's studies had something relevant to offer. The two programs didn't see eye to eye; I didn't fit in perfectly with either. So I brought them together, absorbed the best from both worlds, and took it from there.

CHAPTER EIGHT

BUILDING MY WARDROBE

NETWORKING TO
GET WORKING

WHILE I WAS STILL A newbie frosh finding my way around campus, I attended a student organization fair. There were rows and rows of booths, each one with hollering banners and brochure-strewn tables, around 150 groups in all. Talk about diversity—there was everything from ballroom dancing to the United Nations Club to a wine-and-beer society (the free samples were going over well).

One bright red banner caught my eye: the Student Entrepreneurs Club. Their mandate was twofold: to help students become entrepreneurs and to encourage the commercialization of whatever innovations were originating on campus. SEC organized workshops, brought in guest speakers, and was a wing of Advancing Canadian Entrepreneurship (ACE), a national student organization with fifty-three chapters across the country.

I signed up in a flash. The first event was the following week, a workshop on entrepreneurialism in the design field at a design museum downtown. I was in. I even ventured to share some of my experiences with my brand-new ACE mates (fashion is a design business after all). The others were fired up by my story and told me to enter the annual ACE Student Entrepreneur of the Year contest, sponsored by the Canadian Imperial Bank of Commerce (CIBC). I thought hard about it and then I decided against it. The whole point of my freshman year was to be a student first and foremost, not to get dragged back into business.

But by second year I decided to compete.

I was totally missing my business challenges and business persona by then. And I've never been one to turn down a competition; whether a 5K run or a business deal. Not that I always win (actually almost never). But over time I learned to enjoy the feeling of competing: the adrenalin, the roller coasting, and the buzz in the brain. And the figuring out afterward what you learned this time.

The application for the ACE award contest necessitated a five-page business plan. I had to state my company's history to date as well as my goals—an interesting exercise in itself. Whatever I said managed to get me to the finals. That left me with two months of prep before the big coast-to-coast competition.

The climax of the finals was going to be the fifteen-minute presentations in front of a panel of ten judges, prominent business leaders all. Usually, I speak off the cuff because reading from a speech disconnects my mind from my emotions, plus I love going for some serious eye contact. But this time I wasn't taking any chances. I wrote out a speech backed up by a PowerPoint presentation. I edited together a two-and-a-half-minute video montage of my various television appearances (*Oprah* front and centre). I rehearsed in front of my patient friends until I felt comfortable with my material and timing. And I wore my successful businessman look: navy pinstriped suit, crisp white dress shirt, pink tie, and brown dress shoes. Yes, brown shoes are appropriately worn with a blue suit.

I thought my presentation went well but the questions that came afterward were brutal. "How do you make your business sustainable?" "What if someone else copies your model; how will you compete?" "Is this a fad?"

Fine. I'd already asked myself a lot of the same questions. I had answers ready and I thought I articulated them pretty well. But, a first for me, the judges counterattacked my answers. I loved the debate. If I couldn't fully plan out a strategy or think on my feet, now was the time for the judges to find out. It all stimulated me to think a lot more about why I would expand and how.

The judges brought to life the unforeseen in a really useful way. No matter what, I'd won out.

Okay, yes, I was also nervous about the awards dinner that night. The winners would be announced some time between the chicken and the cake. I'd never actively, publicly competed for an award before. I knew how my models stacked up against other agencies but I didn't know how I'd fare competing against other young entrepreneurs. I had good growth and good financials and a sound six-year track record. But I was in a totally different kind of business from the high-tech outfits most of my generation seemed to be delving into. I figured my toughest competition came from a guy who supplied database management systems to Fortune 500 companies, and a young woman whose jewellery company had just broken into the U.S. market.

I also sensed that my emphasis on trying to fix a social problem had puzzled the judges, just like it had unnerved the business experts at the *Teen People* event. Could they accept that I was running a corporation with profit maximization as a main objective? Or would they write me off as an activist who managed to make a few bucks along the way?

I headed home to chill and recharge, then at eight sharp I entered the main banquet room of the Four Seasons Hotel. Solo. My friends had offered to lend moral support, but I told them to come to the after-party, that I'd be calm by then. It was at Amber, a very chic club of the moment, so they were stoked to get on the guest list without having to bribe the doorman.

One hundred round tables were covered with crisp white linen, sparkling china, and shining silverware. At the front of the room was a stage with a lectern and microphone. Behind that was a long table covered with more white linen and several gleaming trophies. ACE banners the size of Times Square billboards covered each wall of the room. Five hundred students, professors, media, and businesspeople milled around looking for their tables. Everyone was dressed in their red carpet finest: long evening gowns, tuxedos, and formal suits. Wanting to round out the successful businessman look I'd opted for earlier, I'd changed into a black suit, black tie, and white dress shoes—professional with a bit of Cary Grant thrown in, I thought. My friends concurred. They'd all selected Grammy-inspired looks for the after-party.

We finalists got to sit at the head table, along with executive sponsors from the CIBC, two business school deans, and various other business leaders. Everyone at my end of the table asked about my agency. The business deans were also interested in my women's studies courses. Finally, the coffee was poured and it was time for the announcements. A short video profile of each finalist was played on screens throughout the room.

Obviously, my firm was too unconventional for a business award, especially one sponsored by a bank. I'd realized and accepted that by the time my montage played to a polite round of applause. I mangled a napkin under the table and smiled back at my tablemates as they tipped their glasses my way. Then I heard my name, my name being announced. My name was being announced? I'd won. The Student Entrepreneur of the Year was Ben Barry.

I sprinted for the stage like I was back on the cross-country team, pumped hands with the presenters like a mayor on amphetamines and clasped the shiniest trophy I had ever seen. As I approached the microphone to express my thanks, the entire room rose to their feet. I quickly switched from stunned to moved. I already know it was a lifetime high; I was humbled. These were my peers—students and businesspeople—and they wanted me to succeed. That generosity felt like the most major thing in the room.

After the award ceremony, several of the judges came up to congratulate me in person. They told me that they had debated long and hard about what type of entrepreneur I was. Was I a social one trying to correct injustices or a profit-driven one trying to make money? In the end, they decided that although working for a good cause was commendable, it wouldn't earn me points on any score sheets. What mattered was whether my business plan was solid and the business profitable—and they believed it was. They defined me as "a renegade profit-driven entrepreneur—a type we have not seen before." I thanked them, solemnly swearing that I'd try to clear a path for a lot more "renegades."

Several business professionals also came up to me to shake my hand. These were legal experts and financial experts—highly skilled and experienced and well disposed toward young entrepreneurs, now offering their support. One of the bank executives urged me to formalize my advisory board. It was informal because I hadn't ever had sufficient contacts for anything else. She now reminded me that a formal board would be a resource when it came to corporate decision making and a sign of credibility when it came to applying for bank loans. I took her advice right away and asked several of the professionals whom I met that night—and at later ACE events—to serve on my board. (Needless to say, this was a lot more effective than searching the yellow pages for contacts.) ACE provided the personal connection as well as the opportunity to meet. It worked: everyone I asked said yes.

The CIBC award and the ACE community made me feel like I had a lot going for me in Toronto. I had help in the big city now and I wasn't going to let that go to waste. Time to set up a real Toronto office.

COMPETITION

I was moving out of residence, I needed to find a location for my new Toronto office, it was mid-term season, and I had a ton of essays due. Time was of the essence. My advisory board suggested I look for an office near to where I'd be living and close to campus, a ten- to fifteen-minute walk max. I decided to move in with Farah, one of my best friends since grade six. We scoured every ad on Craigslist and grabbed the *Toronto Star* hot off the press every morning even before coffee. One afternoon, I got a semi-elated, semi-panicky call from Farah.

"Ben! I found a place! I was just walking down this street, and I saw a "for rent" sign in the window of this house, and I called the number, and the owners were right there, and I took a look, and it's—Ben it's—Ben it's perfect for us." She finally took a breath. "Haaaaaaaaa."

"Farah, that sounds—"

"And there's room for your office!"

"Great—"

"Ben, you have to come down here immediately. You know the Toronto rental scene, Ben. Someone's going to snap this up. I mean, it's right by campus. Ben, you have to get down here right *now*. If we don't grab it someone else will, I just know it."

"I got it, I'm there."

I've never been one to let an opportunity pass me by. Any opportunity counts; I always jump first and fall later. I was working on a women's studies essay for a class called "Gender and Post-Colonialism" that was due the following morning. But I shut down my computer. Hey, only five hundred words to go. Nothing I couldn't pull off in one night. I changed from my pyjama bottoms back into jeans and took off.

The house was a ten-minute walk north on Avenue Road, just off Bloor Street—the Toronto home of Gucci, Chanel, and Louis Vuitton. And cool cafés and clubs, and whatever Hollywood royalty were in town. I started practising giving directions to people. "Oh, we're at Bloor and Avenue, right around the corner from Prada and the Four Seasons." I passed Vidal Sassoon on my right and Vera Wang on my left. I came to a two hundred-year-old church. Farah had told me to hang an immediate left. The side street was filled with old Victorian homes, most of them with gardens that would have given Martha Stewart a run for her money. This was no university residence. I saw Farah. Well, more accurately I heard Farah. She was on her cellphone, talking to her dad about the house. "It's perfect, Dad. Soooo perfect!"

Farah was standing outside a white stucco house. You couldn't miss it on a street otherwise entirely red brick. I imagined my bright orange Ben Barry Agency sign on the white stucco. *Boom*. It would pop. Sold to the man with the orange sign. The owners gave us the grand tour. They'd bought the house nine months before and just completed renovations. In my mind, we'd moved in already. I pictured exactly how we would set things up. The bottom floor would be the agency. There was a long hallway, perfect for runway sessions. Off of it there was a smaller room that would be great for meetings. At the end of the hall was a huge room with a giant window. I'd arrange beech-coloured wooden desks in groups of two, one facing the other. On one wall, I would hang black-framed photos of my models in six rows of ten. The opposite wall would be painted orange, with "Ben Barry" stencilled in huge white letters. Farah and I would call the top floor home. The best part was that the home was zoned residential and commercial. Score. The place was perfect. Farah was right. Perfect.

We told the owners we simply had to have the place and filled out the application form with all the important rental details: social insurance numbers, bank account numbers, and references. Farah called her dad again to get some more info. I heard her saying, "Dad, don't worry. I know I'm living with a boy. But it's not like I'm living with a *boy*. It's Ben." I laughed. "Dad, it's good for safety's sake to live with a man." I laughed louder. While I made deals downstairs, Farah could make toast, or hay, or whatever she wanted, at home upstairs.

The following day, Farah got the call. She text messaged me right away. I was in class, trying hard to keep my eyes open after pulling an all-nighter finishing the essay. "We gt it. Need 2 sign lease 2day. Call me!!!" That evening, the Ben Barry Agency officially changed Toronto addresses from my dorm room to Dupont Street.

THE FOUR-POINT STRATEGY

The ACE award judges had forced me to ask myself seriously how I was going to succeed in Canada's largest fashion and advertising market. I had yet to lose a major contract to anyone but it was bound to happen. And I wouldn't necessarily be up against another young entrepreneur with modest funding; a large, well-financed agency could just as easily decide to play my game my way. The judges had asked one scorching question in particular: what would my competitive advantage be? That remained at the forefront of my mind months after I'd won the award. It inspired six intense months of strategy meetings for my staff and advisory board. Eventually, we devised a four-point strategy to ensure I'd remain competitive.

One, I was the "first mover." That advantage could never be taken away from me as long as I kept moving. First movers were at one time thought to have an unassailable advantage (that's what fuelled a lot of the dot-com frenzy) but research now shows that they're frequently overtaken. Definitely, it helps to be known as the creator of a business category but to sustain an advantage you have to keep working hard and keep changing.

Two, we set up a talent development program. Canada's long history of immigration has resulted in the most multicultural cities in the world. In Toronto, for example, more than 50 per cent of the population is non-white. But people from new immigrant communities often have lower incomes and little exposure to the modelling industry. For many, it's not a job they would naturally consider and, even if they did, they probably wouldn't have the $1,000 to $3,000 required by most other agencies to develop a portfolio. Our recruitment program was established to pay the start-up costs for new models living in poorer areas. That's how we found Jasmine, a Somali woman who worked in a coffee shop in Rexdale. She'd been in Canada for six months when Jen, one of my scouts, and I approached her about a modelling career. It took some convincing, but after Jasmine aced a community fashion show and loved the experience, she signed on.

The community fashion show that Jasmine took part in was another Ben Barry Agency initiative. We've developed relationships with community centres and schools in marginalized communities. We teach them about modelling, fashion careers, and healthy body images, adding to the legitimacy of my agency in those neighbourhoods. My staff and models volunteer their time to conduct workshops in high schools. They organize local fashion shows in community centres. Stars like Jasmine are born. Jasmine ended up modelling in Toronto, New York, Paris, and Milan.

The bottom line is that thanks to my experiences at the ACE competition, and all the contacts I made there, my agency was able to come up with strategies for keeping ahead of potential competitors that were consistent with our mission—to do good while growing profitably. Definitely, our new business plan was more labour intensive than those of most other firms. It entailed a lot of fresh responsibilities for me and my team because now we invested even more in our models, including a lot of time nurturing them emotionally. Since we'd added expenses, we had to save in other areas. Enter technology.

Three, most other agencies were relying on printed photos that they had to mail or courier to each prospective client. Instead, we put all our portfolios online. A client could access the site and within ten minutes of first contact we'd be discussing their needs with regard to specific models, saving on printing and couriering costs and a lot of time. We also added live, remote casting calls. Clients could video-conference with potential models in our office.

Crucially, we also set up an online forum and chat room for the models, so they could support and encourage each other. It fostered a great sense of community and all the peer support helped them sustain confidence and self-esteem. Even though they worked with an agency that appreciated their unique look and didn't want to change them, they still worked in an industry that had primarily one idea of beauty. They posted a lot of comments about uncomfortable castings and the crap things they'd been told at shoots. "You'd be so beautiful if you lost ten pounds, babe." "Sweetie, you could have had this job if you'd tried a little Botox." The forum also shared fun facts and organized get-togethers: the models shared tips and news about skin care, gluten-free recipes, Coldplay concerts, AIDS charity walks (for which they organized a Ben Barry team), and sales at cool stores. And they posted images from their latest shoots so everyone could give them feedback and gush.

Four, probably the most important component of our strategy, was to hire the best possible staff... and to be a kick-ass boss. My staff tends to be young, so it's especially important to know what they're looking for in a job. If I like them, I want to keep them. To do that, I need to keep everyone feeling as sane as possible. The Toronto office was headed up by Erika and Matt. Without them, we never would have taken off in T.O. There would have been a lot of ideas, sure, but Erika and Matt turned those ideas into reality.

Erika became model director, in charge of scouting and developing. She was the one to do the first interviews, to decide who should be signed, to teach runway walking, and to figure out how new models should be marketed. She had previously modelled herself, having been scouted by Elmer, but was unable to get her hips down to thirty-four inches. So she'd trained as a nutritionist and masseuse. Erika has a desire to help people feel confident and healthy in their natural bodies. She'd read in a newspaper that I was opening an office in Toronto and called me to say she wanted to get involved.

Matt had also read about the agency and wanted in. He'd worked as an advertising creative at an ad agency and was now motivated to design images that were a force for social change. He became our creative director. He looked after all of our promotional materials, from our business cards to our website. And Matt designed our pitches to clients.

Erika, Matt, and I routinely went to a twenty-four-hour café frequented by students and artists. We brainstormed, designed pitches for new clients, and devised growth strategies until the early hours of the morning. In between, Erika forced raw-food recipes on us and Matt and I got laryngitis disputing party politics. We were like best friends. The moment we met, we all connected.

As the agency expanded, I needed more and more bookers and scouts. Bookers play a critical role in an agency. They promote models, they negotiate contracts, and they look after scheduling details. It's common practice within the industry to poach bookers from the competition, but I didn't want anyone with a predetermined MO. I was running a new type of modelling agency so I wanted staff with a novel outlook. On the other hand, I wanted people who knew their way around the business.

Jacob had coordinated with modelling agencies in his previous role as the director of marketing for a clothing line. He had plenty of experience procuring models and working out ad schedules. It added up beautifully; the edge of an insider with the perspective of a client. Jacob knew that clothing companies start planning their campaigns nine months before the public sees any ads, and usually book models at about the five- or six-month mark. He pitched our models to clients at the nine-month mark. We got to companies before any of our competition. That way they could work diversity into their basic strategy. Or at least they couldn't give us the excuse that the campaign had already been developed without diversity built into it.

Jacob's tactic worked. After one successful print campaign featuring two Ben Barry models, the head designer called me and said, "I don't need my marketing director anymore because Ben Barry provides the services of a marketing department and model agency." Jacob had pitched her company an ad concept based on real bodies at just the right time and then looked after all the bookings.

Since we were looking for a new type of model, with a special type of beauty, our scouts—the people who find models by approaching them in public—also had to be open-minded. And they needed excellent people skills if they were going to approach people out of the blue, especially those who weren't expecting it. I looked for people with visual arts backgrounds and customer service experience. I also tried to find scouts who were socially diverse themselves. I wanted my scouts to reflect their beats.

I hired Kartick for the financial district. Kartick had completed a business degree in college but sustained a passion for photography. In the evenings, after business classes, he'd taken photography courses and developed his own portfolio of portraits. Kartick worked at my local bank branch and his face lit up when I told him about my business when I first went to open my Toronto account. He loved finding people to photograph, people with unique character and personality. He also had a natural ease when he spoke, making you feel like you knew him already. I knew he'd be a great scout.

Kartick focused on models thirty and over, targeting Toronto's bank tower neighbourhood. He'd stand outside a Starbucks as people rushed in and out for their morning coffee. He'd walk around the popular lunch spots at noon. He checked out the subway entrances and parking lots as people headed home after a long day of work. He'd be in a business suit, looking like he was on break from his finance job, blending in perfectly with the locals. He'd make his pitch quickly; he knew the people he scouted were in a rush. Most people he stopped were surprised but Kartick explained they were perfect for the clients he worked with. "You have nothing to lose," he'd say. "You might end up taking that luxury spa holiday after all, or putting some money aside for your daughter's university fund or for a condo down payment." People laughed but they listened. Seven out of ten people whom Kartick stopped would follow up with an email or a call to arrange a meeting.

High school students Tanika and Mandy worked after classes. Tanika was the little sister of one of my friends from residence and Mandy was her best friend. Both girls had confidence and charm, essential qualities when you're asking strangers to model. Some days, they rode a subway line up and down between four and seven o'clock. The next day they'd switch lines or take a bus route. On weekends they toured shopping malls.

Tanika and Mandy didn't change their clothes after class or leave their backpacks in their locker. Nor did I ask them to speak and act in a certain business-like manner. The point was for them to look and act like regular students heading home after a day of class. An older man might come off as creepy—not the kind of image I wanted for my new Toronto office. Girls they approached could relate to them and guys were thrilled by a compliment from two women (and not freaked that a guy was trying to hit on them—homophobia still runs strong, especially in high schools). Similarly to Kartick, the response rate was fantastic. About nine out of ten kids they approached followed up.

My bookers, my scouts, my models, and my administrators have all responded really well to the Ben Barry goals. Young people want to do something worthwhile. They want an organization they can actually contribute to. They want fulfilling work. Otherwise, they move on ASAP. Every member of my staff has to be valued as a whole person, with a brain, a psyche, and a heart. Otherwise, I'm screwing up.

I also insist that models be part of the decision-making process, not only out at photo shoots but also within the agency. Excluding them makes no sense to me. I give each model my phone number and email address. If they're concerned about not getting enough work, worried about a comment a client made, or have a problem with school or their family, they're welcome to contact me directly. That kind of contact with a CEO is empowering for anyone, especially people who don't even have their driver's licences yet. Once a month many of us go out for a meal or to a movie, and not to just talk business. We focus on getting to know each other. Say what you want about bonding, it's fun.

It's smart to remove the barriers that inhibit people from fully engaging with their workplace. You want them contributing all their insights no matter where they stand in the hierarchy. I regularly put myself in the place of staff members. I think about what might be preventing them from maximizing their talents and fully participating in the company. I ask them what they think about recent decisions and issues. I want to know what they think about how their own talents are being used.

Never underestimate the importance of your workplace decor: it's key in creating a sense of community. Our meeting room is the most frequently used place in my agency. I intentionally avoided any Donald Trump–style mahogany and leather. No chrome art-deco à la Elite either. I opted for a casual living room, with chairs, sofas and pillows, and orange walls decorated with cool posters of our models and bold quotations on beauty:

Beauty? To me it is a word without sense because I do not know where its meaning comes from nor where it leads to.—Pablo Picasso

Ugly is irrelevant. Ugly is an immeasurable insult to a woman, and then supposedly the worst crime you can commit as a woman. But ugly, as beautiful, is an illusion.—Margaret Cho

People often say that beauty is in the eye of the beholder, and I say that the most liberating thing about beauty is realizing that you are the beholder. This empowers us to find beauty in places where others have not dared look, including inside ourselves.—Salma Hayek

I also installed a television and stereo system, chiefly for client presentations, but we watch *Fashion Television* during the morning staff meeting. As usual, I like the discussion that ensues.

It doesn't take my employees five years in a no-brainer job to prove themselves. Basically, I treat all my staff like consultants and remember that they're all ambassadors. You have to pay fairly. You have to compliment. You have to reward both rational and emotional input. The occasional movie or sports ticket never goes astray. Help with paying off student loans strikes a very deep chord. Most importantly, you have to listen.

For me, always, it's about open thought.

So I had my new four-point strategy in place: first mover; talent development; high technology; deeply engaged staff. Time to see how well I could do in Toronto.

CHAPTER NINE

SELLING MY DESIGN

FASHION GRAVITATES

WITH MY TORONTO OFFICE fully open for business, I was ready to pitch diverse models to Canadian fashion powers that be. First and foremost, I needed to approach Toronto Fashion Week—the city's most attended, most visible, and most prestigious fashion event. Ben Barry Agency had to be part of all the action and hype; it would give us immediate credibility, recognition, and force. And my models were dying to see and be seen by the top of the over-the-top: Fashion Week was the best Toronto networking opportunity going. Definitely, I needed a meeting with Robin Kay, president of the Fashion Design Council of Canada (FDCC), the group that organizes the event.

Matt, Erika, and I designed a killer package to send to Robin. It took a full two weeks of midnight brainstorms (coffee *and* chocolate cake), but we came up with a real attention grabber. On four pieces of orange card stock we'd print our history and services, staff bios, and quotes from select clients and media (Oprah included). With these we'd include one hundred model cards; each one featuring a picture on the front and back and a description, written by the model, of at least one of her inner qualities.

We'd put the sheets and cards in rectangular white boxes. On the cover of the box there would be a colour-by-number picture of two women, one rounded and one petite. Little shapes would divide up the women, each shape containing a number. To the right was a box with each number corresponding to a character-istic: 1 equalled humour; 2, confidence; 3, vulnerability; 4, compassion; etcetera. We wanted to send our message loud and clear—that beauty was far more than simply physical. I told Matt and Erika they'd done an amazing job but Matt asked, "What about the four sides of the box? We can't leave them blank, right?"

Thus followed another week of late-night coffee and treats. On one side of the box we'd put a picture of a model walking down a runway, with a question running underneath: "Ever wish you could change the view?" On the other side we'd write "34–24–34 . . . Where am I?" The other two sides would list our contact information.

As soon as all of this arrived from the printers we assembled the boxes, and then all three of us rushed to Robin's office to specially deliver the first one. But when we arrived, Robin and her assistant were out having lunch with a designer so we handed over our genius package to the young guy at the front desk, with a huge navy blue bow around his neck and bright silver highlights.

Next, we invited all our models—who'd been hearing about these "amaz-ing" boxes every day for the past month—to come to the office and celebrate their grand arrival. Our models were thrilled when they saw the packages. Even better, they offered to personally hand out all 250 throughout the city.

This put a huge smile on Mr. Levine's face, who was already concerned about how much I'd spent on production costs. I'd explained that first impres-sions are the ones that last and I needed to make the best first impression humanly possible for my intro to the big city. Having our models courier the boxes would save money and help us stand out even more—who knew whom they might meet that way. Good for business on all fronts.

Two days after delivering Robin's box, I was at my office desk at 7 a.m. I had just come back from a jog and was still a little sweaty, let's say. I was munching away on a piece of toast smothered in peanut butter, Nutella, and sliced banana, and had just finished writing some emails to my models work-ing over in the U.K. I was moving onto footnotes for an essay due later that day when the phone rang. Not the general agency line: my direct line. I fig-ured it was Mom. She was one of the few people who had the number and was the only person I could think of who'd call this early, probably to beg me to go grocery shopping.

"Ben Barry," I answered in my professional tone.

"Halloo," a voice on the line said. There was crackling. Whoever it was had called from a cell and the reception sucked.

"Hi," I said.

"Hallooo, Ben?

"Yes, this is Ben. Hello."

"How are you, honey? Are you there? . . . Honey?"

"Yes. T-h-i-s i-s B-e-n," I responded, trying to articulate each syllable.

"Honey, Robin Kay here. Loved your package. So fabulous. You're doing such fabulous work."

"Robin. Good morning. It's great to hear from you. I'm thrilled you liked my package."

"The package?" The package?" The phone was definitely cutting out.

"I am happy you liked the package. Y-o-u l-i-k-e-d t-h-e p-a-c-k-a-g-e. I a-m h-a-p-p-y," I said.

"Oh, yes. Loved it. LOVED!"

"That's wonderful. I want to arrange a meeting with you."

"Who are you meeting?" she asked.

"I want to arrange a meeting with you." It didn't sound as bold when I had to say it twice.

"You're meeting me? When? Who booked this?"

"No, no. I'm not meeting you. That is, I *want* to arrange a meeting with you. For the future. For maybe later this week?" Explanation was taking away all my dramatic emphasis.

"Fabulous. Yes, let's meet, Ben. Honey, I'm just jetting off to Paris but I'll call you when I return to set up a time."

"That would be wonderful Robin. I would love to have my models be part of Toronto Fashion Week."

"You must. You must."

"Yes."

"No. No. You will, honey. You absolutely will," she said.

"That would be wonderful, Robin. I'm so glad."

"Yes, I'm getting my office to forward your package to Grey Worldwide, our advertising agency. They're putting together the print campaign for Toronto

Fashion Week as we speak. The ads, you know, will be in all the magazines, all the billboards, all over our fabulous city. I want them to use Ben Barry models. Honey, can you do it?"

"Of course, no problem at all.

"What's your problem? You have a problem with that?"

"No. No. I think we have a bad connection. I said NO problem. N-O problem. I would love to work on your print campaign. Thank you for thinking of me for this, Robin."

"Oh good. Fantastic, honey. Okay then, we'll talk when I get back."

"I'm looking forward to it."

"So am I, so am I. Ta-ta. Keep up the fabulous work."

"Bye." I hung up.

WICKED!

We had just scored the print campaign for Toronto Fashion Week! I hadn't even pitched for it! Our boxes were working, that was for sure. I immediately emailed Mr. Levine to tell him that all the expense had been worth it: the amount we'd make from this campaign would more than cover the cost of every single box. Mom called next and I blurted out my exciting news. She didn't ask about groceries. I guess she took the sound of my teeth crunching toast as a good sign.

An account director from Grey Worldwide got in touch later that afternoon. He told me he loved the promotional package that Robin had forwarded over to him. Apparently our boxes—man, he was almost gushing—were so "fresh" and "cool." We arranged a meeting for the following day, and he asked me to bring a portfolio of models who were "suitable" for the Toronto Fashion Week campaign. Suitable, eh? Suitable according to whom? I knew whom I considered *suitable* for Fashion Week: models who represented the city's diverse population.

Toronto Fashion Week was trying to compete with all the glamour of New York and Paris, I understood that. Of course, I didn't think they needed to copy anyone else. But if I didn't show them that I knew what they meant by "suitable," I'd risk not only alienating Toronto Fashion Week but also this top ad agency. I didn't want all Toronto to think I was on some bandwagon and constitutionally unable to stop harping on about truth, justice, and the Canadian way. Well, at least until they got to know me, developed a relationship with my company, and trusted my ideas and advice. Then I'd earn the right to harp all I wanted.

I brought along a portfolio of my Ottawa posse to Grey Worldwide, figuring they'd be fresh faces. The account manager really liked Elena who was close to traditional: five foot nine with long blonde hair but not the perfect model body. She was maybe a size 6 instead of a size 2, with thirty-six-inch hips instead of thirty-four—a total shock horror in some people's books but things were looking good.

The account director overlooked Elena's "imperfection" and hired her anyway. He explained that the ad would focus on her face; the creative concept called for her body to be hidden. He was okay with her being "a bit big" because her strong bones and huge turquoise eyes would be the attention grabbers. "Great," I said. Was this their attempt at diversity? Well, it was a small, small start.

The shoot took place the following week at 6 a.m. It was late August and my summer school class had just finished. No essays or exams to worry about—I could attend. Elena, her mom and her dad drove down from Ottawa, leaving home at 1 a.m. Elena slept the whole way in the backseat. They picked me up from my office/house at 5:30 a.m. Elena was still fast asleep when I hopped in the back. I read directions to the shoot, compliments of MapQuest, to Elena's mom, who translated into Russian for her dad. We all tried to keep our voices as low as possible, not wanting to disturb our sleeping beauty.

Just as Elena woke up we pulled into a street filled with identical brown brick warehouses. I spotted Toronto's waterfront; people were walking their dogs and going on morning runs. We slowly drove past each building, looking for number 62. When we reached the last building the deserted street transformed. About thirty cars and vans were parked bumper to bumper with people rushing around, pushing clothing racks and makeup carts. Everyone was outfitted in their I-just-got-out-of-bed-but-really-spent-one-hour-getting-ready look: hair perfectly dishevelled, bright eye shadow with smudged dark liner, tight denim paired with equally tight tank tops. And then there were the shoes. Some wore sneakers and some wore heels with clicks that could be heard at five hundred paces. My distressed denim, vintage Pet Shop Boys tee, and retro Adidas would do fine.

Elena and I headed in while her parents went to get breakfast. The warehouse was buzzing with people setting up lights, photography equipment, and the hair and makeup station. A tall, slim man with a faux-hawk and jeans so tight I questioned why he was wearing them at all, tossed an arm around Elena's shoulders. "Sweetie, you must be our girl. Come with me and we'll fix everything!" Elena smiled and introduced herself. I did the same. "You're the agent?" he said to me. "I thought you were her little brother."

"Ben just looks young," Elena said.

As he dragged Elena off, I heard him say, "Sweetie, we'll need to cover up that nasty big zit on your left check, oh my." I hadn't noticed a thing.

I went to sit on a sofa with a bunch of exhausted people. "Espresso?" one woman offered.

"He's way too young for espresso," another person said.

"Orange juice?" she tried.

"An espresso would be great, thank you," I said, trying to keep smiling. I was handed a little cup full which I quickly belted back. I listened in as the ladies discussed the fact that they hadn't been up this early in "like, oh my God, ten years," and how eager they were for the new Gucci collection to arrive. I realized they both worked with Robin at the FDCC office.

The account director come over, "Ben, I'm so happy you could make it. Elena looks great. Have you met everyone?" He introduced me as Elena's agent.

"You're her *agent*?" one of the women said, mouth wide open.

"No way," the other said. "How old are you?"

"Ben's been an agent for five years now," the ad guy laughed. "He runs a very successful company with a new office in Toronto. He's even been a guest on *Oprah*."

"*Oprah*?!" they shrieked simultaneously. "You've been on *Oprah*. Like, oh my God, I love, love her. I watch every day."

"That's nice," I said.

While I was explaining how I'd started up a modelling agency, a group of people gathered around. "That's so cool," one woman said. "You have to meet with Robin as soon as she gets back from Paris and get involved in the shows." Then people started giving me their business cards, telling me to call so we could do lunch. I was meeting stylists, designers, agents, advertising people, hairdressers. By 10 a.m., I had over forty business cards from the Toronto fashion who's who stuffed in my back pocket.

Elena was now out of hair and makeup and had been ushered on set. The photographer was explaining the concept of the shoot: Cool Fashion from a Cold Country. Elena needed to look "frozen," to be a "beautiful ice sculpture." She was pretty well there. Her eyes and checks were white and sparkly as if she was covered in snowflakes. Right at that moment, someone turned on Madonna's "Frozen" track. Elena and I started to laugh but we quickly stopped when we realized no one else found anything funny. Elena assumed her best "ice beauty queen" attitude and the photographer started shooting. The account director, the two women, and I looked on. After the shoot the photographer let us watch the retouching. This time blemishes were subtracted and icicles added. It looked amazing.

Finally, we said our goodbyes. Elena's face was still frosted over. We found her parents parked down the street, fast asleep. We decided to walk to a nearby café and celebrate with blueberry muffins. As we walked down the block, Elena and I sang: "You're frozen/When you're heart's not open...If I could melt your heart/we'd never be apart."

MY TORONTO FASHION WEEK FINALE

Robin had promised we'd meet as soon as she returned from Paris, but arranging that was another story. I left message after message, email after email. I was starting to consider carrier pigeons until one day at 8 a.m. she called my private line again. She apologized for the delay in getting back to me; she'd had a lot of catching up to do after her trip. She suggested we do lunch at my place the next day. I said that was fine by me. I hung up, then I freaked out. We had to get the office ready. Pronto.

By the time Erika and Matt got to work, I had Ajax, Pine-Sol, and Windex lined up, and sponges, mops and, the Swiffer ready to go. We dusted and polished until we could see our anxious mugs reflected back from every desk, computer screen, and picture frame. We sorted and re-sorted the shots in each model's portfolio. We strategically arranged letters on our desks to make sure the ones from the biggest fashion names were visible, letterhead and logos clearly peeking out. We hung up posters of major campaigns featuring our models, especially Elena's Toronto Fashion Week shoot. By the time we were through, the office looked like it was ready for a close-up on *The Apprentice*.

The following morning, Erika stopped at an organic food shop to pick up lunch. We had discussed what we should serve while we'd toiled the day before, probably spending more time on that decision than most people do on their wedding dinner. We'd settled on grain-fed chicken, spinach, heirloom tomatoes, orange peppers, and cucumber, all stuffed inside a whole grain pita with hummus. A gluten-free chocolate cheesecake would satisfy the sweet teeth Erika and I shared (Robin, too, we hoped!). We arranged each pita on a plate with a few spinach leaves as garnish and did the same with the cheesecake, trailing circles of chocolate sauce around the plate and adding some fresh strawberries to the mix. Erika and I cued up the DVD player with the agency promo video. I checked my hair in the bathroom mirror, Erika reapplied mascara and fixed my collar. It would just be the two of us; Matt was tied up in meetings. We had our nerves in check. We were ready.

Noon came and no Robin. We waited. The phone rang—we were told she'd arrive shortly. We waited some more. At around quarter to one Robin swept up the stairs to our office. She was what you call a "presence": five foot two, Mariah Carey curvy, perhaps in her fifties, dark chocolate hair to her chin with a dense vanilla chunk swept through it. She was wearing a jacket with a train that trailed four or five feet behind her; it looked like something you'd see at Paris Fashion Week but would never dream of wearing yourself. Robin was engrossed in a cellphone call as she entered. Her assistant followed, chatting on her own cell while carrying various gizmos and papers and trying to make sure Robin's coat didn't get caught in the door.

Erika tried to look busy, too, although clearly no one could be as busy as our guests. Once they were both off the phone I greeted them cordially with an air kiss on each check, and showed them to the meeting room. I could see their eyes taking in everything—Erika, framed pictures and posters, lamps, and couches, and our strategically decorated desks.

After we were all settled in orange chairs, we started off in the same way that all my first meetings did—with my age. Robin explained that there were a lot of young designers working in the industry but I was the first young modelling agent she'd met. How old was I again exactly, twenty-six or twenty-seven?

"I'm twenty."

Robin was stunned but very encouraging. Her assistant immediately blurted, "You know he's been on *Oprah*, right?" Erika and I smiled. This was one name that never failed to impress.

Robin said yes, she already knew that. "It's so fabulous!" she allowed.

A perfect cue to show off our media montage. Robin and her assistant watched my company's five-year history in five minutes while I brought out lunch. As we crunched on our organic greens, Robin was generous.

"I'm just thrilled you're now in Toronto, honey. You have to meet Elmer Olsen: He is the best of the best, the top of the top, the crème de la crème."

"I agree, Elmer is legendary. His eye has defined an era of modelling and he's extremely savvy. Actually, he was my chief mentor. I met him when I was fourteen years old. He taught me all about the business."

Now Robin was even more impressed: "If you apprenticed under Elmer, you obviously know exactly what you're doing, honey."

We dished a bit about Elmer's latest news. He had recently left Elite to begin his own agency, Elmer Olsen Models. Robin said most of his Elite models had followed him, leaving Elite's roster almost dry. "Even the *New York Post* reported on it." Robin took in the billboard-sized poster for Fashion Week featuring Elena that took up an entire wall. "I've received such positive feedback on that campaign," she said. "Everyone tells me your model is fabulous. She has such an elegant look. I'm sure she'll go very far."

"She's also a grounded person and really fun to work with," I said. "We've gotten some serious interest from Paris and Tokyo." Erika handed Robin Elena's promo card with the Fashion Week image front and centre. Elena was now staring at us from every direction.

"This is fabulous!" Robin said, putting down her pita. "Canadian girls are doing so well internationally. They're our best fashion ambassadors. In Paris, everyone said that they want Canadian girls."

Sensing an opening, I pounced.

"Canada has an important contribution to offer, I agree. Our unique understanding of diversity could really take the industry to the next level."

Erika jumped in. "It's so great to scout here because people are from so many cultures," she said. "We're constantly finding models from diverse backgrounds. And many of mixed ancestry, too."

"We always have diverse models in the shows, honey, always." Robin sounded a bit defensive now.

"I know," I said. "It's so great. But I'm thinking about more than just cultural diversity. We need to show human diversity at its fullest: all ages, sizes, and abilities. I can't think of a better way to position Canadian fashion than to reflect the core Canadian values of acceptance and diversity on the runway."

Branding would be a key selling point when it came to convincing Robin and the FDCC to use my diverse models. Robin was intrigued, I could tell.

"Branding Canadian fashion is our raison d'être, honey. It's true, diversity and acceptance are part of what people think of when they think of Canada."

"International surveys would totally back you up," Erika added. "Our politicians talk about Canada's leadership regarding issues of tolerance all the time."

"But it all comes back to business," I said, sensing we needed to get away from fluffy "values" chatter. "No other Fashion Week uses older and larger models as well as being ethnically representative. Think about how much media attention you could generate for the designers. You'd grab attention from all over the world."

"But we also need some of the usual models, hons. You can't be inclusive by being exclusive," she warned.

"Totally. That's why we represent traditional models as well. Literally, we span all ages, sizes, and colours." I spread our pictures across the table.

Robin ended up asking the agency to supply the models for the big closing show at Toronto Fashion Week. I was on cloud nine, or maybe nineteen. Right away, I urged her to consider working with me on an ongoing basis. "We should form a partnership. We'll be one of your exclusive suppliers of models, and I'll offer you a discount," I suggested.

"I believe in partnerships," Robin said. She told me to send a proposal.

Over chocolate, we chatted more about what could be done to brand Canadian fashion—in between what seemed like a hundred cellphone calls. Robin's assistant was also constantly taking her own calls, running out the door and back. It made for a frenetic hour. At the end, Robin, her assistant, Erika, and I each exchanged another round of double air kisses (and I handed Robin a thank-you note from Elena for the opportunity to do the Fashion Week promotional campaign). "Ta-ta, hons, ta-ta," Robin said as she strutted down the hallway and out the door, shutting it on her fabulous coat. Her assistant quickly reopened the door, bundled whatever fabric still remained in our office out the door, and shut it again. While Erika and I waved goodbye out the window, I quoted Christian Lacroix like a mantra: "Haute couture should be fun, foolish, and almost unwearable."

A TALE OF TWO AUDIENCES

Robin was true to her word. Ben Barry models were slated to strut down the runway for the grand finale of Fashion Week 2002. Shortly after our meeting, one of the show producers called me. Right away I emphasized to her that Robin and I wanted to incorporate all different shaped models into the show. She was agreeable to that. "Sure, all types of girls are fine," I remember her saying. "Just make sure they all have strong walks." We selected fifteen models for the show: five traditional and ten non-traditional. We faxed the producer a list with all their sizes. Everything seemed to be running smoothly.

The day before the show we sent our models to meet the designers and get fitted for their outfits. Everything fit the traditional models like gloves. Nothing fit anyone else. The producer was infuriated. "The show is in less than twenty-four hours. Nothing fits the big and short ones. Nothing, Ben."

"I'm sorry," I said, "but we gave you a list of sizes over a month ago."

"I have over forty shows to oversee. Do you think I have time to remember your particularities?"

"I believe you agreed to those *particularities*. And so did Robin." I didn't want to be blamed for this.

"I have over *forty* shows to oversee," she restated. "I work with *hundreds* of designers. I don't have time to relay different sizes to *each one* and they *certainly* don't have time to hand tailor each outfit."

"I don't see why not. That's what the designers have to do for customers. Who, by the way, probably have bodies a lot like the larger and shorter models."

"I know how fashion works, Ben. I've been producing shows for the last twenty-five years." She took a deep breath. "Why can't you give us normal models like everyone else? You've made this so much more complicated than it needs to be."

Looking back, I should have been more diplomatic. And I should have foreseen this problem. I should have recognized that this was the first time the producer and designers had put on a show with models of varying sizes. I should have routinely verified things with the designers, personally, especially since it was our first time working with Fashion Week. Better to come off as a perfectionist and a worrywart. But all that was hindsight. Now I needed to fix things.

The producer and the designers scrambled for the next twenty-four hours: cutting clothes, adding fabric, making adjustments. Erika and I apologized frequently and spent the night doing coffee runs. I offered to sponsor the models for an upcoming charity show the producer was doing. Right up to show time, everyone was busy. The show started two hours late. Fortunately, in the fashion industry a late start isn't frowned on in the same way as arriving late to your third-year biology final. It's actually seen in an optimistic light; everyone assumes extra time is being spent on hair and makeup so that the result will be all the more glamorous. This time, however, we were fighting to make sure all the clothes covered everyone's T&A.

The other Fashion Week shows weren't open to the public; most of them are invitation-only for media, buyers, industry folk, celebutantes, and glitterati. But tickets for the final show had been made available to the public. The audience was divided in two: a section next to the runway for those who had been coming all week, and an outlying space for the masses.

It was fascinating to watch the mixed reaction when our models emerged. The insiders in the front rows kept looking at each other and whispering. No sneers, but no smiles either. Their hands remained clasped tightly together on top of their tightly crossed legs. The general-admission seats, however, were on fire. When a woman in her forties came out a lot of them cheered. They also wildly put their hands together for a full-figured woman, this time hollering in support. When two women in their sixties, one with long, beautiful grey hair and the other with a huge white afro emerged, they jumped up and applauded in a frenzy, screaming "You go, girl," and "Work it!" Meanwhile, the traditional models received polite applause and far fewer flashbulbs.

I felt the show had gone well considering the panic beforehand. The Fashion Week authorities didn't agree. They were in tune with the front rows only. Robin was in damage control mode for days and not one bit pleased. We chatted about two weeks later. She'd been swamped, and I was pretty sure Ben Barry wasn't at the top of the list of people she wanted to speak to. I repeated my offer to supply models for the finale annually, but Robin declined. She had nothing against my mandate; *au contraire*, she was entirely in favour of diversity. But it just wasn't the way the industry wanted to work and there was nothing she could do about it. The designers were the ones making the clothes. Her job was to supply them with what they needed: 34–24–34, end of story.

You understand me well enough by now to know that I staged something of a fight. I talked up the general public's reaction and the excellent media coverage. Apparently, none of that counted for much. Robin reminded me that the press for the final show was from mainstream newspapers, not the fashion industry. She finished off by telling me that the whole experience had simply been too much work. If Toronto was going to compete with New York, London, Paris, and Milan, it had to present shows the way they did. This show hadn't had a "high-fashion" feel. The models hadn't looked "right."

So not only had we lost out on the big annual contract I was hoping for, but my ideas were being crushed as well—and by somebody who said that she personally agreed with me. I found it ridiculous that the designers couldn't or wouldn't make clothes for my models. Weren't they trying to sell clothes to the people who'd been cheering in the balcony? The logic seemed tangible to me, but no one else wanted to reach out and hold on to it.

FIVE NEW YORK MINUTES

My first few trips to New York had convinced me to start visiting once a year, preferably more. I had relationships that I needed to cultivate, plus I could always use new contacts. I wanted to meet with different magazines, design houses, and modelling agencies—to promote my models for sure, but most of all to touch base with fashion mecca.

During my second year of university, after dozens of calls, faxes, and emails to numerous Manhattan-based firms, I scored meetings at *Elle* magazine and Tommy Hilfiger—two extremely high-profile potential clients. In fact, it was weird, if not insane, that a university student from Toronto had managed to secure the meetings. Normally, modelling agents from Canada have to arrange for a New York agency to promote their models. But I wanted to do business with clients directly and found that by calling often and sending many, many faxes and emails, meetings could eventually be arranged.

I always asked for just five minutes. I told them my age and that I was running an agency in Canada. I tried to sound different and interesting. Most people are willing to commit to five minutes, after which a secretary knocks on the door and says, "You have another appointment." This is the moment of truth. If the session is going well, you get the time you need to explain yourself in full. If the fish isn't biting, you get, "Excuse me, please. My assistant will take it from here."

THE FASHION BIBLE

Elle is one of the world's premier fashion magazines, published in nine languages in fifteen countries. I was to meet with *Elle*'s booking editor, responsible for hiring some of the models for the magazine. She worked with the fashion director, the beauty editor, and ultimately the editor-in-chief, to refine the theme for each issue. The *Elle* offices were in a soaring Manhattan skyscraper. I waited about thirty minutes for my five-minute appointment. Not bad.

When an assistant showed me to the booking editor's office, I understood right away that this was one of those busy people. She had piles of model photos covering her entire desk, floor, and walls. There was also a big calendar hanging on one wall for organizing shoots. She quickly took hold of my portfolio and started flipping through it, pausing at some of my traditional models and flying past the rest. She smiled occasionally, saying, "She has a pretty face," or, "She looks sweet," but otherwise fled along at shutter speed.

Apparently, I had an interesting collection of models but most weren't appropriate for *Elle*. Maybe a few of them would work. Many, she suggested helpfully, would work better in soap or toothpaste commercials. I pressed her as to whether she would ever consider some of our non-traditional models like full-figured Elizabeth or white-haired Kosa. I said models like Elizabeth and Kosa would reflect her readers. She said she occasionally did special spreads with plus-size or older models but couldn't attempt that routinely—largely because she had no control over what clothes the designers sent out to her magazine. Another of the fashion powerful hamstrung by sample sizes.

I had assumed this woman was as stratospheric as her tower office—that she called the shots from on high. But here she was telling me she was a prisoner of the system. Every shoot depended on the "creative vision" of the editors. She was constrained by the storyboard. Every concept needed to fit with *Elle*'s brand: the allure, prestige, and fantasy of fashion.

"Why can't you change the brand image?" I asked.

She explained that *Elle*'s advertisers would get angry if a shoot violated the magazine's image. They were buying space based on what the *Elle* brand consistently represented. If *Elle* changed the brand, advertisers might pull out of the magazine. *Elle* (as do 99 per cent of magazines) depends on advertisers' dollars to stay in business.

I was confused. I thought she was constrained by the designer's sample sizes. But no, she was constrained by the other editors' "creative visions" for the shoot. No. Wait a minute. The editors were constrained by the omnipresent and omnipotent brand image, some higher power that dedicated that only young, tall, skinny models could be featured in the magazine. No. No. Hold on a minute again. The editors were constrained by the advertisers. Everyone was blaming someone else for not having the power to change the industry standard.

"You know, Ben, fashion isn't about reality anyway," the booking editor said. "It's about ideas, creativity, and vision."

"But your creative vision is having a negative impact on your readers psychologically," I said.

"Please! Don't give me that old argument that skinny models create eating disorders. I've heard it a million times. We've had groups of women protesting outside our office building for years. It's just way too simplistic. Eating disorders are caused by psychological triggers like family trauma or sexual abuse."

"I agree many factors go into creating eating disorders. But showing only young, thin, tall, mostly white models in the fashion media doesn't help. I know for a fact it makes things worse."

"Come on, a girl doesn't get a body issue simply by looking at a picture in *Elle*."

"Not only because of looking at a picture in *Elle*, but there's the cumulative impact of living in a culture where every fashion media image shows only one skinny version of beauty."

She laughed. "Why can't people just get it through their heads that these are just models?" She laughed again. "It's just fashion, darling. Nothing to get all politically steamed up about."

Why was she laughing? This was serious. This was very political.

"If it's so ridiculous that an ordinary girl would think she needs to look like a model, then why do you publish so many features telling ordinary girls how try to do their wardrobes, hair, and makeup like models?"

"So they can be inspired by models, not copy them literally. You're making too big a deal about this. Look, think of the magazine as an art gallery. We arrange visual elements based on a standard blank canvas."

I wasn't even going to start ripping apart that metaphor. (Many artists don't even use canvases, hadn't she ever heard of modern art?!) Einstein said that the solution to a problem would never come from the same minds that created the problem. So why was I expecting fashion-industry insiders to see and solve the very problem they had created? I was making some progress on the periphery of the industry but it seemed like the closer I got to its heart, the less open its ears.

At the end of the day, I was a businessman; I wanted contacts and contracts. Coming off as a political activist would scare away decision-makers. My responsibility to my non-traditional models would always haunt me but if I wasn't careful I'd jeopardize the careers of my traditional models.

"Fine," I said.

"If you put this much energy into your business, you must be a great agent, really fighting for your models!" the editor said.

"Thank you," I said. "I try."

"If I'd known you were going to debate me about body image, I would have asked security to keep you outside with the protesters," she said, smiling.

I smiled back. "Hey, it made for a lively meeting."

"Definitely a memorable one. And I think I have a project coming up that's perfect for you. I'll be doing a shoot with mature models. Send me whomever you suggest. But promise me one thing—no more debates!"

She did keep my card at the top of her older and plus-size piles, as promised. When *Elle* published a spread on women in their fifties, we supplied two of the models. And I kept my promise and didn't debate with her during the whole process. Okay, I guess that depends on how you define "debate." I didn't argue about the media and body image. I just offered constructive advice on how to represent the women in the shoot. I hadn't changed *Elle*, but I had secured some non-traditional work. Planting seeds—it never really stops.

TOMMY HILFIGER

At *Elle*, I was told that designers ultimately dictate model sizes with their sample sizes. Now I was going straight to the designer.

It was late afternoon when my yellow cab pulled up outside a massive warehouse, supposedly the headquarters of international design house Tommy Hilfiger. But the place looked totally deserted. I walked into a stark white room with concrete floors. A security guard at the desk stared at me. I gave him my name, showed him my ID, and he checked me off on a list. He directed me to an elevator and told me to go up one floor. As soon the doors opened, I was transported to another world. People buzzed around what resembled a Southern mansion: mouldings, plush sofas, and mahogany galore.

I had a meeting lined up with a marketing manager. Naturally, I was wearing Tommy Hilfiger clothes: loose dark jeans, a red tee with the Tommy Hilfiger crest embossed on the front in silver, a white dress shirt with a small red and blue Tommy logo on the pocket, sneakers with red and blue laces, and a red baseball cap with a small Hilfiger logo on the back. Maybe this was overkill, but at least it showed I was a big fan of the brand. I sat on one of the plush sofas directly across from the reception desk. The words "Tommy Hilfiger. How may I direct your call?" hummed in the air.

It's important to keep busy when you're waiting for a meeting but you also have to avoid getting distracted. I stay away from checking my BlackBerry or working on another project. Instead, I review notes for the upcoming meeting or read whatever company literature I can find. In this case, I grabbed a book from the coffee table. It was Hilfiger's "look book" for the latest collection: an assortment of photographs, like a magazine spread, showcasing the different items from the season and how they could be put together. As I flipped pages, I saw lots of young models with rock-hard bodies. But I noticed something special: white models and coloured models had equal billing. In fact, there were even more coloured models than white.

"Ben Barry?" a man asked. I looked up from my magazine. A tall Latino guy stood in front of me.

"Hi, yes, I'm Ben." I stood up, we shook hands, and he led me to another elevator. I was heading upward again, to meet his boss, a marketing manager. En route, I told him that I liked the look book and had noticed the unusual degree of racial diversity. He said he also liked it a lot and told me that Hilfiger had a diverse consumer base, "From prep to hip hop and everything in between."

We entered an office where a black man sat behind a huge mahogany desk. Hilfiger ads from the past ten years were framed on every wall. He was on the phone and motioned for me to grab a seat. "Tommy thinks Julie is fantastic," he said. "Absolutely, we want to book her again. Great. Later, man." He hung up the phone.

Our meeting began with the usual conversation about my age. I repeated how much I liked the look book and complimented him on his use of models. I explained how much I appreciated the fact that no one group was in a minority position. He thanked me and said Tommy Hilfiger consumers were smart enough to see any token efforts as insulting and condescending. He said his target market was racially very broad and he always looked for diverse models to reflect that: "It's not a special effort, it's an entrenched policy dictated by our brand values."

He flipped through my portfolio of models. As he turned the pages, I talked about my philosophy of promoting models of all kinds, size and age included. "You already reflect your customers racially. Would you also consider reflecting their diverse sizes and ages?" I asked. He wasn't necessarily opposed to the idea but he voiced some concern over sample sizes. I pointed out that his company produced clothes in all sizes. Surely extra sizes could be made available for his ads? Evidently not. He explained most sizes were shipped directly to the stores, not used for shows or given to magazines or ad directors. Only sample sizes went out to the latter.

"Couldn't you make samples in different sizes?"

It would be a disaster, he explained. "No models would fit them. Then no magazines would include our clothing in their spreads."

"I offer models in different sizes 2 to 18," I countered.

"But you're just one agency. No one else does." He added, "Magazine editors don't want diverse models. It doesn't jibe with their image and perspective."

"Why not?"

"It's just not fashion. Fashion isn't supposed to be real," he said.

I was in a Catch-22. The magazines said they couldn't do anything because designers wouldn't budge, and the designers said they couldn't do anything because the magazines wouldn't budge. Then, to top it off, this guy was blaming the modelling agencies for having only one type of model, and then saying I couldn't make a change myself by representing diverse models. Was I frustrated? To my core. But considering the *Elle* meeting had become a little tense, I didn't want to push too hard this time.

"I'd love to get more information about your needs so we can send you appropriate models," I said.

Before we said our goodbyes, he told me that Tommy Hilfiger would be doing a major show in Canada in the next few months and he wanted to use some of our models. The show would take place during Toronto's annual

Caribana festival, a summertime celebration of Caribbean culture. It was going to be invitation only: to Toronto's trend-setters and fashion press. They needed fifteen models to reflect the cultural diversity of Tommy's consumers and show off the latest collection. When I got back to Toronto I requested the marketing fact sheet. The Hilfiger demographic starts at age fourteen and goes up to fifty-something. The sizes go up to 16 for women and XXL for men. There's diversity there, that's for sure.

I did my best to squeeze some size and age diversity into my suggestions for models. When I sent in my picks, I made sure to quote the Hilfiger demographics and size ranges. Okay, the manager said. He'd check on what other sizes he could possibly secure. Fantastic, right? Well, that turned out to be one item in size 12. All the other models had to fit into samples.

The marketing manager also explained that the new collection was sexy and hot and he wanted none of the models to be older than twenty-five. Did sexiness expire after twenty-six? I was especially frustrated because I had one feisty model named Angie who was a fifty-year-old size 4 woman from Trinidad. I knew she'd be amazing in the show—she was a dancer and had strong posture and a fierce walk. I pushed and pushed to get her in the show: "I know the audience will go nuts over her. You should have seen how they all screamed when she came out during Toronto Fashion Week." The marketing manager was hesitant but finally agreed. Angie was in. Two out of fifteen models were non-traditional, a token effort but a start.

The Tommy show was a huge success, despite one potential disaster. Two of the models were in a car accident the evening before the show and were in the hospital. (They ended up recovering just fine.) I needed replacements fast. I asked two of my other models with killer walks. The "problem" was that Rachel was a size 8 and Michelle was a size 10. Not wanting to create an issue for the show producer, stylists, and head office, I called to explain the situation. Well, I explained that two models had been in an accident but that I had replacements already lined up. Then I casually inquired what outfits the two models were wearing. Right away I found them in the Tommy look book. I jumped on the subway and rushed to the Hilfiger store in downtown T.O. I explained the situation to the sales staff, who were all very excited about the show and happy to help. We found similar outfits on the racks to those in the look book, some pieces exactly the same. I rushed them to the stylist just as the models were arriving for hair and makeup. She was extremely pleased that I had foreseen a problem and thanked me for my initiative. The fact that the models were larger didn't even cross her mind.

The show started right on time. All the clothes fit perfectly. The audience snacked on roti with curried chickpeas and sipped on rum cocktails as the models stalked the runway and paraded through the crowd. Everyone was dancing and cheering to the hip hop and reggae and fashion. After the show, the producer and stylists told me the models were outstanding, thanked me again for getting the replacement clothes, and invited me to grab some friends and come dance the night away.

RETHINKING MEN

Most of my work was female focused but I didn't completely neglect the other half of the population. In my third year of women's studies, I found an opportunity to learn more about the representation of men in the media and since then I've been applying that knowledge to my business, particularly in relation to the fashion shows we do with Harry Rosen.

The course was called "Women and Health." For our term paper, we could choose any topic covered in class. Naturally, I wanted to do mine on body image. When I suggested that to the professor, she was skeptical. She was concerned that I might not fully grasp women's body image issues because I was, well, male. As much as I loved the inclusive and open environment of the women's studies program, I had experienced this syndrome a few times: I was a guy, and so I just wouldn't get it. While I didn't necessarily agree, I proposed that instead my paper could explore how men's relationships with their bodies developed by viewing images of men in fashion and beauty advertising. She loved the idea and thought I would really understand and connect to the issue since I was, well, male.

I interviewed ten of my guy friends. I got them to flip through four men's fashion magazines, asking them to stop at any images of men that jumped out at them and describe their reaction. I followed up with further questions in response to their comments. I noticed that for the first half hour most guys were reluctant to talk about how the images affected them personally and only discussed them objectively: "This guy has a nice shirt" or "I like the lighting in the picture." But as we started talking and they felt more comfortable (and forgot about the tape recorder), they began to make more personal comments, saying things like, "He's so fit. Man, I've tried to get a body like that but I don't know how anyone has the time. You need to spend, like, three hours every day in the gym and watch every single thing you eat." Another would say, "I don't think I could ever pull off this guy's look. You know, I never really cared before but now I feel there's more pressure. You need to be in shape to get chicks and a good job. You have to look good to compete for everything nowadays." Evidently, media images of men do affect men's body image. Many feel the need to have a body that's simply unattainable.

More and more of my male friends have become active fashionistas. And not just the ones who enjoy arts and aesthetics. Many of my jock and geek friends have now begun to study the fashion pages of the newspaper and spend a Saturday afternoon at the mall updating their gear. They've stopped going to the local barber and instead visit "hair stylists," paying triple the cost to get their hair cut, and sometimes coloured. And they're starting to talk openly about fashion: discussing the coolest shoes, jackets, and hairstyles with each other. An interest in style has become part of masculinity.

Product lines have certainly tapped into this developing male interest in grooming. I've noticed a huge increase in the number of fashion and beauty products and services targeting men. There are specific men's moisturizers, hair creams, high-fashion lines, and even a new male edition of *Vogue*.

I also began making a concerted effort to convince advertisers to use diverse male models. In general, men's fashion and beauty advertisers are much more open than women's advertisers to using men of different ages and ethnicities. The bigger stumbling block has been body size—the men need to be tall, toned, and thin. I've worked hard to get larger men and shorter men into fashion and I've had some success.

My agency now supplies models for an annual fashion show at the National Arts Centre in Ottawa. It's a big event on the Ottawa social calendar, attended by politicians and the city's top business and cultural leaders. The menswear comes from Harry Rosen, a Canadian-based men's fashion clothing retailer that carries the top European designers as well as its own high-end in-house label.

When I was approached for the contract, I said that the use of diverse male models had to be a given. At this point, I had run my company in Ottawa for seven years; locally, my opinion carried weight. The fashion show coordinator and the manager of the local Harry Rosen store were sold on the spot.

Andrew, the store manager, explained that very few of his customers had body shapes like typical male models. "No one comes into the store and buys a suit off the rack. We always have to make adjustments. When was the last time you saw a politician with a body like Brad Pitt?" he joked.

Exactly.

The show featured some of my professional models, traditional and diverse, plus some members of the orchestra. All the guys were well received, but the warmest response was for a five-foot-six, sixty-year-old male violinist with greying hair who looked absolutely elegant in his clothes and whose smile was more infectious than the common cold. The event raised money to fund scholarships for young musicians and boosted Harry Rosen's sales locally.

BURSTING THE FASHION BUBBLE

My agency was getting by on small shows for the most part—shopping mall shows or charity events. Unfortunately, we had no big Fashion Week shows that might be televised around the globe and spread the word about our models. Marketing managers in small centres were willing to take a risk on me (for instance, word of the Caribana runway show got out to local Tommy Hilfiger managers and department store reps and they were now all over our MO). Of course, I knew the Ben Barry method wasn't really a risk. Audiences were always excited to see themselves in fashion shows, and stores like Harry Rosen always reaped the rewards. But New York wasn't buying my message: major campaigns weren't willing to be diverse.

My tactics probably made sense to local marketing managers because they were closer to the actual consumers. They weren't locked into the prevailing mythologies of the larger industry. It was also less work for them—after all, the clothes were sitting right in their stores. The Madison and Fifth Avenue crowds—and their equivalents in Paris, London, and Toronto—work in a bubble. They're not in stores seeing consumers' reactions or in malls overhearing their conversations. Instead, they're seeing and listening only to each other. I guess focusing so much time and attention on an unrealistic body type gives it the authority of reality. At *Vogue*, *Bazaar*, and *Allure*, the exceptional has become the truth.

I realized that I couldn't take on New York alone. I needed local managers and customers to convince decision-makers that my approach worked. They needed to share what happened on the ground with the tall towers. After all, I was trying to profit from diverse models so of course I was going to argue in their favour. Persuasion needed to come from people within the firm invested in its success. And customers—the people who'd determine whether the business flew or flopped.

I worked to usher these voices together. Every time a manager used diverse models and received enthusiastic customer support, I told her to write to head office and tell them. Every time a customer cheered during a fashion show, I asked her to write to the chief marketing director at the company's head office and tell him. Every time someone related to one of my models in an ad or a magazine, I asked her to write to the ad agency or the editor-in-chief. I also asked people to write to editors and corporate head offices that weren't using diverse models to explain that they were unhappy as consumers. Wanting to practise what I was preached, I had to do so myself.

One of my favourite magazines, especially when I was coming to terms with my sexuality, was *fab Magazine*, a Toronto-based gay publication. It was empowering for me to read about the gay world—issues ranging from politics to profiles to music. For the first time, I realized that there was an entire gay community filled with diverse people of all ages and backgrounds living active and out lives. I realized that being gay wouldn't prevent me from doing anything I wanted to do: I still had the choice of getting married, having children, and running an international business or not. Being gay was just one part of me. And if I faced discrimination, I would fight it.

While I enjoyed many of the *fab* political articles and profiles, the cover images always disappointed. They followed the same narrow ideal of beauty that plagued media images of women. All the men were young, hairless, ripped, and primarily white. It was so hypocritical. For a community that prides itself on being inclusive the publication was erecting one set of discriminatory barriers at the same time as it fought another.

I sent off this letter to the editor of *fab*:

Dear Editor,

The latest issue of *fab* hits the magazine stand. Readers sit along shop steps reading the buzz from their gay scene magazine. Next time this happens, I want you, editor, to try something: Look at your cover model and then look at the people reading it.

Notice anything? Yup, I thought so. The cover models and readers look nothing alike. And please, don't tell me you just put a man of colour on your last issue (who also just happens to be ripped and young). Wow. First one of the year. No wait. Second or third. You produce one issue every two weeks. That's not inclusion. That's tokenism.

Why are your covers so predictable? Could you be more formulaic? I'm rarely surprised by your creative vision. It's cookie-cutter creativity: primarily white, young, toned, lean, and able-bodied models (with women, politicians, or famous people thrown into the mix once in a while). Where are the models who are over twenty-five; have beards and hairy chests; are South Asian, East Asian, Aboriginal; have disabilities; or are trans? Is this the limited notion of beauty you think your readers want to see on your covers?

Well, this reader certainly wants more from you.

Your selection of models reinforces a view of beauty based on a single ideal, one that the vast majority of us don't conform to. Your selection of models reinforces the stereotype that gay men have to spend all their time plucking, toning, and dieting in order to be attractive to others and be accepted in the queer clubhouse. Your selection of models reinforces the idea that beauty is solely physical; that personality, compassion, and character are irrelevant in defining beauty.

If *fab* hopes to actually live up to its supposedly progressive and inclusive editorial policy, I suggest you start by reflecting your readers, not some ridiculous, outdated ideal. Keep the sexy stares, the detailed art direction, the intense lighting, and, please, the skin. A magazine using models of all ages, sizes, colours, gender identities, and abilities doesn't have to look like a Sears catalogue. Just change the people being photographed.

I also recommend you include more than just the model's name: maybe have them write something about themselves. Let their beauty be about more than just their face and body.

Anyone who has been in a relationship knows that a typical pretty face and body get dull very quickly. It's character that makes and keeps people beautiful.

This is your opportunity to fashion reality. Represent us, your readers.

Ben Barry

My letter was never printed. Nor did I ever hear back from the editor, nor did any of the friends whom I asked to write in. I guess it's a struggle to shift the standards of beauty no matter how liberated the social group.

LIZ JONES

Once in a while on Madison Avenue you'll find someone who understands the problem with fashion imagery well enough to want to make changes. Liz Jones was the editor of *Marie Claire* during 2000. She tried to encourage her editors to feature a greater diversity of women: models of different sizes and more black and Asian women. She suggested a voluntary code across the industry— a group of fashion-industry professionals could review all fashion editorials prior to print to ensure that the models looked healthy, without bones showing. Part of the code would entail setting consequences for models who had eating problems: fashion editors would dismiss them from the shoot, notify the model's agency of the issue, and inform other fashion editors of the model's situation. The fashion editors would all voluntarily agree to not hire the model until she became well.

Genius, right?

Liz had struggled personally with anorexia so she intimately understood the impact of media images on women. Her suggestions, however, were completely rejected. Not one single magazine wanted to adopt Liz's code. Consequently, she resigned as editor of *Marie Claire* in April 2001, explaining, "I had simply had enough of working in an industry that pretends to support women while it bombards them with impossible images of perfection day after day, undermining their self-confidence, their health, and hard-earned cash."

Here's to you, Liz. You are a true leader.

CHAPTER TEN

CAMPAIGNING FOR REAL BEAUTY

MY LOVE FOR DOVE

WORD ABOUT THE BEN BARRY method was finally spreading throughout the industry. Fashion and beauty executives began not only hiring my models but also asking me to consult on marketing strategies. They'd call and say, "Our district manager says the customers love your models and we want to know more," or "We've heard about your work and we're interested in what you can do for us." I was happy to help. It's great to see a client switch over to a more realistic depiction of beauty. It's even greater to watch the dividends add up for them as a result. Things began to get really exciting when I finally started helping multinational brands adopt diversity strategies for their advertising campaigns worldwide.

My contribution to the Dove Campaign for Real Beauty is definitely one of the proudest accomplishments of my life. The Dove ads appear all over the globe—from the U.S. to Russia to Japan. They generate an enormous amount of attention, from the public and the industry both.

THE DOVE STORY

I first met Erin Iles from Dove when she came up to me after a talk I'd given at a forum called "Jeans or Genes," sponsored by Sheena's Place. It was early 2003; I was in my second year at university. Three speakers—a medical doctor, a women's studies professor, and I—were asked to talk about the various factors that contribute to eating disorders. Erin was there because she wanted to learn more about body issues. Right away, she and I clicked, over (surprise, surprise) an intense impromptu discussion about beauty industry advertising.

A few months later Erin told me the big news—that she was spearheading the Campaign for Real Beauty, a big new Dove initiative. Dove was expanding from its solid base of soap into a whole array of beauty products. Erin wanted to develop marketing that treated Dove customers with renewed respect by breaking from tradition. She was competing against seriously well-established brands; stealing market share wasn't going to be a stroll down Madison Avenue.

It didn't take Erin and me long to merge our teams. Dove wanted help exploding all the tired old beauty clichés—our mission for years now. Dove had a vision of something a lot lovelier and far more compelling. Dove wanted to build a sound, sane new view of beauty—methodically and undeniably. The campaign was going to take about two-and-a-half years to pull together. Dove decided on a four-phase approach.

Phase One: The Survey

Dove began by eradicating all its assumptions when it came to what women think about beauty. Instead of telling women how they should think, Dove decided to ask women exactly what was in their heads and in their hearts. The company commissioned a study to explore how women define beauty; how they feel about the portrayal of beauty in society; how satisfied they are with their own beauty; and how beauty affects their well-being. There was concern that the limited portrayal of beauty in the media was preventing women from recognizing and enjoying beauty in themselves and others.

The study was based on a survey of 3,200 women, aged eighteen to sixty-four, in ten countries: the U.S., Canada, Great Britain, Italy, France, Portugal, Netherlands, Brazil, Argentina, and Japan.

Some might argue that a survey designed by a for-profit company will inevitably be biased. True, Dove was seeking answers for marketing problems. But the company followed a rigorously academic approach to its research. Dr. Nancy Etcoff of Harvard University and Dr. Suzie Orbach of the London School of Economics designed the study, and an independent research firm was hired to manage it. Eventually, answers were limited to a scale (i.e., rate your response from strongly agree to strongly disagree). Initially, however, Dove conducted a pilot study in which two hundred women were interviewed in their homes, individually, or with friends and family. They were taken to shopping malls and makeup counters. They were asked to keep journals, take photographs, and gaze in the mirror. Findings from this first qualitative study provided the questions that made it to the final questionnaire, which Dove was then able to write in language that captures the way women really talk about beauty.

Dove didn't confine itself to Western notions of beauty. The company investigated what had been researched and written about beauty, appearance, and self-worth in 118 countries. The Dove survey itself was translated into seven languages with local researchers reviewing the translations in detail. Incidentally, no reference whatsoever to Dove or its parent company, Unilever, showed up on any of the pages.

The final survey didn't hold back. It asked women to rate their comfort level when it came to describing themselves as beautiful. It asked women what makes them feel beautiful and what attributes make a woman beautiful. It asked if they thought that the media sets up an unrealistic standard of beauty. Finally, the questions that excited me the most asked if women wished the media did a better job of portraying diverse physical attributes as beautiful, and if the media should define beauty as more than just physical. The results made for fascinating, if not joyful, reading.

First, the study found that beauty is a vital issue to women but one that is layered with discomfort and tension. Most women didn't feel like they could take ownership of beauty as it's currently understood and represented. Only 2 per cent of women around the world felt comfortable calling themselves beautiful.

Second, physical appearance is a key aspect of beauty for women today. Women rated overall physical appearance (64 per cent), skin (67 per cent), and hair (54 per cent) as important components of beauty. Sixty-one per cent feel beautiful when they like how they look in the mirror, 55 per cent when they get complimented on their appearance. But beauty is nonetheless understood to be more than skin deep. In fact, inner qualities and personal experiences rated far ahead of physical attributes. Women consider beauty the result of kindness (89 per cent), being loved (88 per cent), happiness (86 per cent), being engaged in a favourite activity (86 per cent), confidence (83 per cent), dignity (81 per cent), a close relationship (81 per cent), humour (78 per cent), and wisdom (72 per cent). The majority believe that a woman can be beautiful at any age (89 per cent), that every woman has something about her that is beautiful (85 per cent), and that beauty comes not from looks but from spirit, attitude, and joie de vivre (77 per cent). Obviously, women understand beauty as rich and complex, not rigid and limited.

Third, women around the world would indeed like to see the media change the way it represents beauty. A majority wants to see beauty portrayed as more than simply physical. Seventy-five per cent want to see diverse features, varying sizes, and a broad range of ages defining beauty in the media.

Even Erin was shocked by the survey, and she'd had her doubts about the way beauty products were typically advertised. "Before, we used to sit in our boardroom, saying, 'We don't want to show real women because people want to see supermodels.' We were wrong and now we have proof. Women want us to show women of different body weights, different ages—everyday women."

Dove published the final survey results in *The Real Truth about Beauty: A Global Report*. It began with an open letter to women:

At Dove, we think differently about beauty. Our point of view is optimistic and realistic. We embrace the philosophy that each woman's looks, shape, size, and spirit are what create her own unique beauty. We believe that a wider definition of beauty is possible—one that is multi-dimensional and defined by women themselves. Dove wants to be a part of making this definition a reality.... We believe, and the findings of our study reinforce, that a cultural shift can take place. Our vision is that a new definition of beauty will free women from self-doubt and encourage them to embrace their true beauty.

I was thrilled by what Dove was up to. Dove had distinguished itself from every other beauty company by painstakingly positioning the company according to women's deepest ideas and needs. The vast majority of the fashion industry supports the supermodel theory—which is supported by a mere 25 per cent of their consumers. Dove was determined to advertise to the other 75 per cent.

Phase Two: The Exhibit

The second stage of Dove's four-phase approach was a photography exhibit. Not an exclusive affair at a ritzy gallery—this show toured North American malls. Dove asked a hundred famous women photographers from around the world (luminaries such as Annie Leibovitz and Peggy Sirota) to shoot their personal take on *real beauty*. Dove curated all these images together and called the show Beyond Compare.

I went to the launch of Beyond Compare at Toronto's BCE Place and also visited when it hit Toronto's Eaton Centre and Ottawa's St. Laurent Shopping Centre. In the middle of the mall thoroughfares, in between clothing stores facing off against shoe stores, stood a large regular white box. At one end was an opening. You'd walk through and step onto a white floor. Inside, white walls faced off at different angles. Big, black-framed photographs hung below spotlights. The photo's title, the photographer's name, the country she was from, and her thoughts about beauty were printed in black font on a white card beside each image. I wandered in a fascinated trance.

One picture was of three teenage girls biking down a hill. Their mouths were wide open as they screamed with excitement, wind rushing into their faces and throwing their hair all around. The image was by U.K. photographer Elaine Constantine, who wrote: "Beauty means confidence in yourself and not worrying what other people think." These three girls couldn't care less what anyone thought of them; they were way too exhilarated.

Another picture was of two black girls, named Tori and Ti, who looked about eight and eleven years old. They stood side by side. Each girl held up half of a picture of Naomi Campbell's face against her own. I could see half of the girl's face and half of Naomi's. Photographer Aura Rosenberg explained that the image explores the relationship between beauty and ideal proportions.

Naomi's face looked like an ice sculpture, static and lifeless, against the sparkle and vivacity of Tori and Ti.

Another picture was of a grandmother and little granddaughter. These were actually two separate images but placed right beside each other. Each person was captured from her bare shoulder upwards, on a forty-five-degree angle against a white background. The granddaughter's face was covered in freckles while her grandmother's was covered in lines and creases. I was agog; I wasn't used to seeing nearly that much character in portraits. In fashion photography, skin is normally covered up with heavy foundation and other cosmetics, rendering complexions perfectly even and therefore utterly identical.

One of the final images was of Dixie Evans, photographed by Kate Murray. Dixie stands at ninety degrees to the viewer but has turned her head so your eyes meet hers. She is standing in a desert with white sand all around her. She has bright red lipstick shining from her lips, wispy bone-white hair down to her shoulders, and an ivory silk dress that flows to the ground. Beside the image it said that Dixie was a famous entertainer in her time and currently lives in Las Vegas. The photographer chose the picture because beauty isn't often associated with age. I stared at this picture the longest. I loved everything about it—the contrast between the scarlet lipstick and the white hair, the loose curves beneath the dress, the droop, the hunch, all of it. No loose "old lady" clothing for Dixie.

There was an amazing reaction to Beyond Compare. I listened in on as much as I could. "She's so beautiful!" some would whisper, and some would gasp. One woman's eyes started to well up. I heard her say to a friend, "I feel joy but I also feel sad that I never see anything else like this in public." Another woman whispered to a friend, "I feel stronger just looking at them." A daughter kept tugging a mother's sleeve so she'd come see the picture of a teenager in a prom dress fixing her eye shadow, with a football on her dresser. One man had come with his son. He told me, "All he knows about women is from *Maxim* magazine. Hopefully, this will enrich his understanding of women, and his relationships."

On average, people spent thirty minutes at the exhibit. Remember that companies spend millions of dollars to get people to glance at a magazine ad or to pay attention to a thirty-second television commercial. Dove got its potential customers sharing an unforgettable experience for half an hour. What a stupendous way to build customer relationships and loyalty.

On leaving the exhibit, visitors were asked whether the exhibit had changed their feelings about beauty. Half the people said it did. They were then asked if they had changed their views on Dove. Half the people were a lot more positive about the brand and a further third were "somewhat more positive." Before seeing the exhibit, most people had just thought of Dove as a company that makes good affordable soap. Now they were starting to make a connection between Dove and the idea of inclusive, diverse beauty. Dove was making people think and feel in a way that interested them—great brand repositioning and a great start for a lasting and trusting relationship.

Backed up by both the survey results and the stellar response to the photography exhibit, Erin was able to move past any worries her bosses might have had about cutting loose from the old business model. Goodbye, ideal beauty. Hello, Real Beauty.

Phase Three: The Campaign

Phase Three was an international advertising campaign designed to build on the results of the survey and exhibit. As Erin put it, Dove "embarked on a real commitment to showing what I call 'real women.' I don't want to say that models aren't real women, but we've made a commitment to showing diverse, real women in our advertising."

I was ecstatic. Finally, after five years of pitching diversity, an international brand was putting real money behind using real women in a campaign. And this was no mall fashion show or local catalogue—this was international print, television, and web advertising buys. Unilever invested more in the Campaign for Real Beauty than any other advertising effort in Dove's history, or for that matter in company history. And these were no half diversity measures—a couple of real women mixed in with traditional models, all in typical poses. And it wasn't a one-shot deal, a "let's try it once and see what happens" approach. Dove had committed to use real women in their ads from now on. Everything I had been advocating was coming to life in a gigantic way.

Dove decided to hit the streets and approach females who displayed confidence and spark. My scouts and I embarked on our most intense recruiting mission ever: to find women of all ages, sizes, and backgrounds with character and a love of life. Hey, we'd been doing this for more than five years—radiant spirit and sparkling character was our specialty. We searched the usual hotspots: campuses, Starbucks lineups, business districts, malls, protests, the subway and buses during rush hour. We approached women with no modelling experience whatsoever, asking, "Do you want to be in a Dove ad?" As usual, most were skeptical at first, laughing and saying that there was no way. But we explained that Dove was challenging the beauty status quo and actually wanted women just like them. The vast majority become delighted with the idea and signed up.

I approached Heather in a suburban Ottawa supermarket while I was grocery shopping with Mom on a visit back home. Heather was wheeling a cart packed high with groceries, with three children fetching hot dogs, ketchup, and ice cream cones. She was forty-three years old, white, size 8, with brown hair just past her shoulders. She jumped out at me because of the way she interacted with her kids. The minute they'd run up to her she'd glow and sparkle. Not from bronzer and shadow—from pride and joy. Heather radiated beauty from the fruit-and-veg aisle.

I asked Mom to come with me when I approached Heather because I knew it would make her more comfortable. Mom was reluctant but I put the screws to her. We walked up to Heather while she was in the middle of asking her son to go pick out some soap.

"Excuse me," I said. "Sorry to interrupt you, but we work with a modelling agency and we're currently looking for new models for a Dove ad. We think you'd be great!"

Mom smiled and nodded.

"Wow, thank you!" She laughed. "I'm flattered, but I'm not a model in the slightest."

"You could be. Dove wants to feature beautiful *real* women in their ads."

"I don't know if I'd have time, not with three kids, and I teach part-time."

"Just one or two days, all expenses taken care of, and you'd also be paid."

"It's a really fun experience," Mom chipped in.

"This is just, well, to be honest so...random." Heather's son came back with some Dove. I smiled and so did she. "It's great soap," she said. She sent him off to pick out some oatmeal. "I better hurry," she said. "The kids will be wanting dinner soon."

"Us too," Mom said. "We have people coming over and I have a lot of cooking to do."

"And I have cleaning," I said.

"Yes he does," said Mom.

Heather ended up calling me the next day. I soon met with her, took a few Polaroids, and sent them off to Dove. They loved her. Heather was used on their website and in a commercial. She had to leave Ottawa for only four days in total. Once her ads were released, she told me that her kids showed them to all their friends and teachers, saying, "My mom is a model. She's beautiful!"

Dove held open calls for real women in cities all across North America. Women of all ages, backgrounds, and sizes turned up in the hundreds. At one of the castings, in Halifax, Nova Scotia, one woman told me, "I don't care if I'm not picked, I just love being here with all these babes; it makes me feel so confident and beautiful!" The same thing happened in Montreal. I heard equally touching stories about castings around the world. And I heard some hilarious ones, too. (One woman who was scouted in England thought the smiling stranger who followed her into a computer store was angling for a saucy lesbian encounter.)

Designing the ads was a tougher assignment. How do you represent *real* women in advertising? How do you avoid photography that presents women as objects rather than subjects? How do you make the women appear equally stylish and strong? Dove brought together a team of in-house experts, academic brains, advertising execs, and potential customers to figure it out. I was part of this answer-questing team.

At one point, I took Erika and Matt to meet with Erin, her team, and a contingent from Ogilvy & Mather, at Unilever's Canadian head office in Toronto. Dove's boardroom didn't look like any other I'd ever visited; I felt like I was back in the lounge at the women's studies department. One of the largest consumer goods manufacturers in the world was playing things very low key with red overstuffed sofas and armchairs, and coffee tables covered with mugs and snacks. There was a flip chart for notes and a small kitchen to make coffee, tea, and sandwiches. We all dove into the comfy seats.

We spent the afternoon brainstorming empowering ways to depict women without sacrificing the glamour that makes beauty products so enticing. I explained the theory of the sexual gaze that I'd learned in women's studies and stressed that we had to ensure that Dove's images didn't play into that kind of oppression. (Thereby proving wrong whoever said a liberal arts education can't be applied to business.) I reviewed the Ben Barry Agency guidelines for portraying women aptly and soundly.

I explained that changing the visual codes of the photographs was just as important as showing diverse women rather than status-quo models. The subjects needed to be accessible and therefore empowering, not detached and therefore oppressive. A model's facial expression and body language in combination with camera angle convey key messages as to the power of women in society, and what's considered beautiful. We needed to focus on those visual codes.

First I asked, "Ever notice how the model is never smiling or standing up straight in most fashion ads?" Everyone nodded. In most fashion ads, I explained, the model's body is tangled and twisted, and her facial expression is one of shock. Her mouth is wide open. Her stare is blank. It's alienating. It's a reminder to women that they need to look blasé and submissive in order to be seen as beautiful. A smile, on the other hand, conveys warmth and fun. A smile brings vitality and energy to the face. A smile is inviting. "Think how you feel when someone smiles at you," I said. "You smile back, right?" The models in the Dove ads needed to smile for sure. And they needed to stand tall.

As for camera angle, typically that's high or low in fashion, to make sure one person is looking down on another. I thought the Dove models should be photographed at exactly eye level to the viewer. This would convey an equal power relationship between the viewer and the model. But I knew Dove needed more than that. "Don't hire the usual photographers," I urged. "A fresh eye really helps."

I proved my point with pictures of Alex: a traditional model in every sense: five foot ten, size 4, eighteen years old, and white. But she wasn't on display; she was in control. Her body wasn't twisted or tangled, rather alert and strong. Even in when she was sitting on a chair in the middle of a room in boy's underwear, legs pressed to her chest, arms outstretched, her head back and her eyes closed, she was in control of the image. Sarah-Monica wasn't making eye contact, but she was obviously aware she was getting her picture taken.

Erin was emphatic that the Dove images needed to be extremely professional, to stay consistent with the quality of the brand and the competition.

I agreed wholeheartedly. The *real* women had to convey plenty of sophistication or Dove would be sending a message that real beauty was lesser. "Absolutely, we need great lighting, spot-on art direction, and fabulous stylists. Forget amateur, forget lacklustre." I passed around Kosa's portfolio (the winner of the Billings Bridge model search). Kosa was far from a traditional model, yet she had the sizzle of fashion.

"What I love about these is that they don't look like the photographer just took a snapshot of his mother," an ad rep said.

"We definitely don't want to go discount catalogue."

"Isn't using makeup and lighting going to contradict the real beauty message? Isn't it hypocritical?" one of the Unilever woman asked.

"The key is using lighting or makeup to enhance, not hide," I insisted. "We'll show women achievable glamour."

"Normally when I see older women modelling they have no wrinkles. They look like twenty-five-year-old women with white hair," she said.

"That's so true," I replied. "It's a thoughtless move because it makes models look thoughtless. You need lines on your face to think. But who wants women to think, right?"

"Okay, we need wrinkles," Erin said.

And that's exactly what Dove did, right from the very first batch of ads. It was the Check Box series. None of these ads promoted a specific product; they were more about introducing Dove's new values and philosophy, the new rebranded Dove. They were on billboards beside freeways or posted downtown. All the ads were shot against a white background and featured an image of one woman. To the side were two checkboxes, each with an opposing trait. A question on beauty followed.

One ad showed an elderly woman, crow's feet and laugh lines aplenty, wearing a headscarf. The checkboxes asked, "Wrinkled" or "Wonderful," with the question, "Will society ever accept old can be beautiful?"

Another featured a young woman showing off her curves—the adjacent boxes read, "Oversized" or "Outstanding," and the viewers were asked, "Does true beauty only squeeze into a size 6?"

Another had a beaming woman with dreadlocks. Beside her was "44 and hot" and "44 and not," and the question was, "Can women be hotter at 40 than 20?"

Every ad had the Dove logo at the bottom directing readers to "Join the Beauty Debate" by logging onto the campaign's website. They could check the boxes they wanted. They could also see the grand tally beside each box, which changed as people voted.

The next ad series was for Dove Body Firming Lotion. It featured six women of all sizes and colours in their white underwear. The copy read, "New Dove Firming. As tested on real curves."

Another ad was for a body lotion with a self-tanner. It featured four women, again of a variety of sizes and colours, in black underwear. The copy said, "Who would have thought getting a tan could be good for your skin?"

It was such a trip seeing giant Dove billboards unveiled as I booted around town. When I went to class, people were buzzing about them. But the most exciting moment came when I was flipping through October 2005 *Vogue*. Smack in the middle was an eight-page spread of Dove ads back to back. They didn't jump out, they bounced out. How could they not? Beauty brands generally advertise indistinguishably; if you cover up the logo, you don't know who's selling what. As far as I was concerned, the Dove ads were infinitely better than that. They had vital signs.

I'm one of the biggest fans of the Dove campaign; I promote it everywhere I go. But women's studies has taught me always to step back, analyze, and critique. Especially my own work. Sometimes, my friends help me with that.

I bonded with Amitha and Jean in a third-year women's studies class. We three formed a study groups for tests. Our connection was based on a vital trait we all shared: the need to talk pretty well every political issue we encountered deep into the ground. One evening both women rode their bikes over to my place for an organic stir-fry. As I chopped the broccoli, I let it slip that the Dove campaign had just won a big advertising award.

"It's really great, Ben," Jean said. "You must be happy."

"Obviously you think the Dove campaign rocks," said Amitha.

"For sure I think it rocks. But I know it's not perfect."

"Yeah right. You're so brainwashed, just admit it." Amitha was attacking the carrots with a little too much relish.

"Why don't you two tell me what *you* think is wrong?"

"Those check boxes for one thing," said Jean. "By telling us to pick just one, Dove is saying the model can be wrinkled or wonderful but not both."

"Those bug me, too, Ben!" Obviously, the ladies had been talking between themselves. "There's an assumption that wrinkled isn't wonderful. Or that the woman in the ad is wonderful despite her wrinkles. Or that she's so wonderful we have to forgive her for the wrinkles. Screw that."

"I think Dove is playing on our assumptions in order to expose them." I was going heavy on the chili oil. "Dove never said you couldn't pick both. Look at the question at the bottom: 'Will society ever accept old can be beautiful?' They're saying you *should* have picked both."

"Okay then," said Amitha. "What's with the underwear?"

"Women on display yet again." Jean was snatching veggie bits right out of the wok.

I pointed to the cutlery drawer; she knew her way around that.

"You're both equating being on display with being objectified. But the models look like they're truly having fun. The visual codes are all empowering."

"Gee, I guess I need new underwear. Mine's not very empowering," Amitha said.

"They're in underwear to prove that you don't have to cover yourself up if you're bigger than a size 2. Who wants brown rice and who wants white?"

I don't think Jean and Amitha both sat across from me on purpose, but in any case, the table talk remained them against me for a while.

"I just wish I knew *who* these models are," Jean said once she was ready to pass the soya sauce. "Why don't I know anything about them?"

"Because they don't have a voice," said Amitha.

"I agree, there's a problem there," I said. "Future ads have to show more soul. Some of the incredible stuff we heard from the survey. Check out some of the profiles on the website."

"Seriously, Ben." Jean paused long enough for her brow to furrow. "Don't you think Dove exploits women's more personal experiences just to promote themselves?"

"Body image issues are deeply personal. Beauty is personal. So are racism, sexism, and homophobia. I think way too much gets kept in the closet. We need to publicly share issues that are seen as personal. Otherwise, it's easy to keep oppression hidden. Exposing it educates people about the issue so they become aware and can create change. As the classic feminist mantra goes, 'the personal is political!'"

"My major beef is with the firming lotion," Amitha said. "I think it's hypocritical for Dove to say women are beautiful just the way they are and then tell them to buy something to dejellify their thighs."

"Possibly not the best choice of product," I conceded. "But Dove never lied about being in business. I mean, they're traded on the New York Stock Exchange. Obviously, they want to make a profit. By encouraging people to enhance what they have, not change it. By going to a lot of trouble to find out what women really want and then providing it for them."

"Ben, good old Ben. What a relief," Amitha said. Now it was time to crack open some beers. "We thought you'd been co-opted by the corporate world forever."

"They didn't take the feminist out of the businessman," said Jean.

"It's the feminist that makes this businessman," I said.

We all toasted to that.

Our debate over dinner was exactly what Dove wants to happen. The company intends to stimulate dialogue. And these first ads are the baby steps of a project that intends to mature beautifully over the years. To me, that's what's most exciting about the Real Beauty campaign; it's not one stop on a train, it's around the world by jet, glider, and submarine. I encourage everyone to write to Dove. The company deserves it. No other international company has so boldly denounced the restrictive old standards of the modelling world and turned beauty into such an interesting conversation. Dove understands that beauty ignites a lot of burning feelings.

Phase Four: The Dove Self-Esteem Fund

The Campaign for Real Beauty was designed from the start to give rise to action. Beyond its financial objectives, Dove supports a social objective.

Money raised from the Beyond Compare exhibition has gone into the Dove Self-Esteem Fund. Essentially, the fund supports educational programs and organizations that seek to raise self-esteem and positive body image in young people. Its goal is actually fairly basic: to touch a million lives through its programs and to foster an international discussion on beauty that will alter the entire fashion industry.

The Dove Self-Esteem Fund supports the National Eating Disorder Information Centre (NEDIC) in Canada, Girl Scouts of the U.S., and the Eating Disorder Association in the U.K. The organizations teach teens, for example, what I first learned in New York: that the pictures we see in magazines are the result of hours of prep by a team of fifteen specialists followed by computer enhancement, and that not even Naomi Campbell and Paris Hilton can achieve this look on their own—the look that the rest of us are supposedly going to acquire by buying hair gel or the right moisturizer. Fundamentally, these programs remind girls that their best attributes aren't physical.

REACTION AND IMPACT

While the ads were an inspiration to many, the big question for Dove's shareholders and executives (and my nosier business friends) was whether listening to real women increased the brand's sales. Check out Erin's response:

> I can't tell you how nervous I was, how much time, how much debate, how much effort went into convincing people, much more senior than me, that we could run these ads and be inspirational for women. The fear, the worry was intense. We decided one ad was not going to ruin the brand (but it might ruin *my* reputation). So we ran these ads—outdoors, on billboards. The amount of press coverage was outstanding. It went all over Europe. We got on the cover of the *London Times Sunday* magazine. We experienced a 700 per cent increase in sales in the countries where the ads appeared. We have never, ever in the history of Dove had a campaign as successful as this.

Erin doesn't like to go into a lot of detail about the huge boost the Real Women campaign had on sales and profit. But I can tell you that the call centre at Unilever received more calls than from any other campaign or issue in its history—and 83 per cent were positive. The campaign got a lot of great media attention, including an *Oprah* appearance by the real women in the ads. Unilever reported that sales were up for the fourth quarter in a row in November 2005. Earnings per share were up 25 per cent. The personal-care section of products drove this surge.

Nonetheless, Erin doesn't see society dramatically altering its attitude to beauty any time soon:

> There are many cultural influences at work, momentum is building but it's not a groundswell yet. . . . In the inner circle of the fashion industry, change is still seen as too risky. And advertisers are conservative: this would be a marked shift in their business model and they don't believe it's credible, yet. . . . Many people fear that if they don't show the stereotypical ideal then they are taking a risk economically that they can't afford to take. But we have found there is tremendous success in showing alternative views of beauty.

Dove top management realizes the popular definition of beauty likely won't evolve for another generation, yes, but they're committed to the long haul; changing their advertising cost them millions. Meanwhile, I asked Erin to sum up her advice to the industry: "Treat women intelligently. Talk with them; listen to them, without assumptions. Give up on 'we've always done it this way.'"

CHAPTER ELEVEN

THE REAL WOMEN BANDWAGON

OTHER BEAUTY BREAKOUTS

THE DOVE TEAM HAS been a total trailblazer but it's not alone. A growing number of brands are recognizing that real women bring in real profits. I'd like to introduce you to a few in the fashion industry. I've worked with several of them; I admire all of them. I'm definitely not the only beauty-in-diversity, diversity-in-beauty expert hard at work.

THE BODY SHOP

The Body Shop was issue driven long before I was born. The company's motto is "Profits with principles" and it's seen thirty years of ups and ups—from a single shop in rural England to more than two thousand stores worldwide. Since the beginning, founder Anita Roddick has seen to it that The Body Shop is an activist-oriented, environmentally friendly, socially responsible, and profitable business. Broadly, the five key Body Shop values are to activate self-esteem, defend human rights, oppose product testing on animals, support community/fair trade, and protect the planet. It was Anita's idea to divert the money that would have gone into traditional advertising toward community projects and grassroots activism instead.

Also, Anita has always been realistic when it comes to touting what her products can do: "Our products care for your skin and your hair. That's all.... We sell moisturizers that help prevent loss of moisture. What they don't do is make you look younger."

The Body Shop never uses models. Correction: once it used Rubenesque Ruby. She's a computer-generated, Barbie-type character, albeit full-figured, reclining on a couch. Below her runs this caption: "There are three billion women who don't look like supermodels and only eight who do."

In contrast to Dove's multi-millions, The Body Shop spends very little on advertising; they concentrate on in-store promotions. The approach is that "the product is the hero," and that promotion works best by word of mouth. Each country directs its own campaigns. Activate Self-Esteem, an Australian campaign, is worth taking a look at. Anita explains that Activate Self-Esteem "challenges the cultural conceptions of femininity as portrayed in the beauty industry...promotes self-esteem, [and] cultural and physical diversity," concluding on a cautionary note: "The next generation will base who they are on what we tell them. Don't betray that trust."

I'd call that right on target.

A booklet supporting the campaign points out that "if shop mannequins were real women, they'd be too thin to menstruate. Slim, tall, young, cellulite-free.... The world doesn't see beauty that way, marketers see beauty that way. Hey media, where we come from cultural and physical diversity is the norm. It's called Planet Earth."

The booklet gets even more political:

Could it be that these over-thin girls are actually there to inspire insecurity and vulnerability...by showing only these women, magazines can create a fantasy atmosphere. One we can envy. One for us to aspire to. "If I looked like her, everything would be all right." "If I were that slim, I'd be happy." Advertisers want us to believe that happiness does come from within their products. And that waif of a model, with

the perfect hair, in that gorgeous setting, holding their product, is tes-
timony to that fact.

Manjit Basi owns and operates three Body Shop franchises in Ottawa.
Manjit regularly gives her staff paid time off to do volunteer work (tied into
the company but otherwise the employee's choice). At one store, for example,
the employees support a women's centre. At other times they've assisted at a
home for single mothers, taught healthy eating and cooking, given personal
hygiene and makeup lessons, and helped children learn to read. One store ran
a "makeover marathon" benefit. Manjit donated products and staff time to do
makeovers in exchange for donations to a local women's foundation. Body
Shop staff members are what you'd call energized. They want to be contribu-
tors and they're given that opportunity.

Manjit puts it this way:

We are in the beauty industry, an industry that can be pretty horrific.
We want to do something positive, to help women celebrate themselves. Cosmetics and body-care products do not make you beautiful,
but can bring out your inner beauty through caring for your physical
and emotional needs. It's about your inner beauty and your inner
voice. I put lipstick on this morning not because I'm ugly but because
it makes me feel damn good. Our approach is to be a contributor to
society, to encourage people to focus on what they are good at. Our
goal is to create a fun, inspirational, feel-good approach to taking care
of yourself. To focus on what's right, not what's wrong.

Through various community groups, Manjit gives self-esteem workshops
for girls and teens. She understands that no matter how many times Mom says
"You're gorgeous!" 1,500 ad images out there are bombarding females with
another opinion entirely. Manjit teaches that real beauty is about positive
energy, not C-cups, teensy hips, and pouty lips.

The Body Shop pioneered a new approach to making and marketing beauty
products and perpetuated it for thirty profitable years. Then, in March 2006,

cosmetic powerhouse L'Oréal—owner of Maybelline, Lancôme, Garnier, and L'Oréal Paris—bought The Body Shop.

Many Body Shop supporters were alarmed by the takeover, given that the two companies have such a different approach to beauty: L'Oréal is about being the most beautiful person in the room and The Body Shop is about everyone in the room being beautiful. Trying to assuage such fears, L'Oréal chairperson and CEO Lindsay Owen-Jones commented in the *Guardian* on March 18, 2006, "I can't overnight use The Body Shop approach in all of the L'Oréal companies, but our long-term commitment is to join Body Shop. I cannot be clearer than that."

Anita Roddick has a blog on her personal website; on March 21, 2006, she wrote: "I do not believe that L'Oréal will compromise the ethics of The Body Shop. That is after all what they are paying for and they are too intelligent to mess with our DNA." I agree with her. L'Oréal is too trend sensitive not to notice what's happening to beauty. No doubt that's why the company bought The Body Shop in the first place—a brand that's renowned for working inclusively and environmentally sensitively. L'Oréal is going to learn a lot by being privy to The Body Shop's daily decisions. Of course, L'Oréal could end up transforming The Body Shop into yet another Milla-in-the-ads brand with some "You're Not Beautiful Without Us" slogan. Only time will tell.

MODE MAGAZINE

Mode was established in 1997 as a monthly, high-fashion magazine targeting "plus-size women." It built a subscriber base of 600,000 readers. *Mode*'s guiding philosophy was reflected in an interview it ran with comedienne Margaret Cho in which she said, "Unnaturally thin isn't beautiful and it certainly isn't right for me. I'm not going to die because I failed to be someone else. I'm going to succeed as myself."

It would be a great world if every good cause led automatically to business success. *Mode* folded in 2001. The magazine had, by its owners' admission, failed to attract the cosmetics and perfume advertisers it needed to make a profit. Several other magazines that welcome curves have started up in the past and most have folded. There's subscriber interest on the one hand, but fashion companies just don't seem interested. As Angell Kasparian, whose magazine *Grand* folded, notes, "The issue is whether or not they feel the plus-size woman is a market for them." Evidently not.

As far as I'm concerned, the lesson the magazine industry learned was the wrong one. The lesson should be "Don't carve off a section of the market and label it as outside the norm." These magazines have to stop marginalizing the women they want to target. Frankly, I've often heard readers of "plus-size" magazines say they feel worse about their bodies when they have to buy a special magazine. It reinforces their feelings of being disqualified.

"Plus": a term that is positive in pretty well every context except fashion. Let's take a close look at Emme. Perhaps unique in the business, she's a supermodel who wears a size 16. She's been picked by *People* magazine as "one of the fifty most beautiful people in the world" and by *Glamour* magazine as "woman of the year." Despite all that recognition, however, Emme is never just referred to as a "model" but always as "a plus-size model." It reminds me of the way supermodel Tyra Banks is always referred to as a "black" model. All you have to do is add a qualifier in front of the word "model" and presto: the beauty status quo remains intact.

One new effort, a website called Beautiful, hopes to launch a magazine. When it emailed its target audience to suss out the degree of interest, the editors got an unheard-of 250 per cent response rate (women completed the survey then passed it along). Beautiful's marketing kit says, "You are looking at a publication that gives your brand a new opportunity to present a powerful message of acceptance, embrace and caring for all women regardless of size, colour, political or religious conviction." I just hope they remember to have some fun while doing so.

GLAMOUR MAGAZINE

Glamour is an industry leader, with more awards than any other women's magazine (in 2005, it won the General Excellence award from the American Society of Magazine Editors). With 2.3 million regular subscribers and twelve million readers, *Glamour* is what you'd call a powerhouse. One of *Glamour*'s core messages is self-acceptance. Bit by bit, the magazine has pushed the envelope, nudging fashion and beauty closer to reality.

Glamour was the first fashion magazine to feature a black woman, alone, on the cover (the August 1968 issue, Best-Dressed College Girls). In 2005, in a truly groundbreaking move, *Glamour* showed actress Aisha Tyler's *before* shots—with computer-enhancement notes scribbled all over her beautiful features as to how they should be upgraded. Also in 2005, *Glamour* named twelve Women of the Year, including top model Petra Nemcova for her role in supporting victims of the Asian tsunami. The list also named acclaimed international correspondent Christiane Amanpour, and Pakistan's Mukhtar Mai, a woman who was gang-raped on order of a tribal council in retaliation for an alleged offence by her brother. Mukhtar took her case to court, the offenders were sentenced, and she received a sizable award that she immediately used to build two schools in her hometown. In a BBC interview, she said, "School is the first step to change the world. It is always the first step that causes the most trouble, but it is the start of progress."

The April 2006 *Glamour* Reality issue was billed as the magazine version of truth serum and it delivered. TV star Teri Hatcher was on the cover along with her makeup artist, the stylist, the hair guy, and the lighting assistant. The message was "relax, no one looks this good outside the studio." Inside, non-waif Kate Winslet said, "After *Titanic* I thought, I'm not going to not eat. I'm going to say, 'Listen, I was in the highest-grossing movie ever made and I'm not a stick!'" Another feature, "Models Take off Their Makeup" showed what models look like on their own time.

Glamour deputy health editor Wendy Naugle is responsible for all the food, fitness, cancer, heart disease, and sexuality stories. She confesses, "Early on, we did what many companies still do, and we fell into the pitfall of saying 'real women have curves.' But we can't ignore thin women, because they are real too—as readers quickly pointed out to us. We shouldn't talk only about 'plus' size women and 'fat acceptance.' What we should be doing is celebrating women in all of their diversity, from petite 2 to plus 20. We try to have boy shapes, curvy women, all the body types, in our magazine."

Wendy senses that women aren't as misled by photo retouching nowadays as they used to be, thanks to widespread tech savvy. "People at home are using their computers to enhance their pictures; wedding photographers are asked to make changes." One possible obstacle to diversity she notes is the current obsession with celebrity culture: "Celebs sell everything from phones to body wash. If they continue to have only a very narrow body type, that could be a roadblock. The celebrity culture may evolve, but that's hard to tell."

Every few years, *Glamour* does a survey on body image. In 1984, 41 per cent of its readers were unhappy with their bodies. By 1998, that had risen to 53 per cent, with some readers admitting to throwing up and starving themselves. The last survey, however, was down near 1984 levels, with fewer women reporting dangerous dieting regimes. Wendy noticed a big jump in the number of women saying they would rather be healthy, happy, and a little overweight than very thin and not healthy and happy.

> There is a movement toward realizing that health is more important than size. I think that's a wonderful place for us to be going. Women are asking more questions about their health. And that's just one reason why we continue to be very aware of the message we're sending. Occasionally, after a photo shoot, the pictures of a model may look frighteningly skinny. Perhaps, without our knowing, she lost weight before the shoot. So we retouch them to look less thin. If you can see someone's bones sticking out, that's not acceptable, that's not healthy; nothing you should aspire to.

I asked Wendy about *Glamour*'s approach to representing differing ethnicities and she responded affirmatively: "We have a real commitment [to that] on every level.... For example, interracial-dating stats reminded us that when photographing couples we should reflect those trends." Unfortunately, *Glamour* can't control its advertisers. Some *Glamour* ads feature ethnically diverse models but most are 100 per cent Caucasian. At $160,000 and up a page, advertisers feel they can't afford to take a tumble. Based on cover sales, using models of colour is still perceived as a big risk; sad but true, which hampers progress.

A forward-thinking editorial policy might not be having a dramatic effect on *Glamour*'s bottom line but it sure isn't hurting anything. Ad pages were up 19 per cent last year. Subscriptions were up 3 per cent. Though not at liberty to talk about profit margins, Wendy was able to describe reader response. "Overwhelmingly positive," she says:

> The Queen Latifah [cover] issue sold extraordinarily well and the response to Mukhtar was overwhelming. As an editor, it is so rewarding to get the mail. People tell us how thought-provoking and re-affirming it is to have alternative views of beauty. It is clear the kind of impact we are having on women and the effect on their conversations. We can have a ripple effect in their environment.... What we are seeing now are the early entrants. Others will follow; what we need is for women to raise their voices directly to those companies that need to change.

Glamour is leading fashion-industry changes, albeit cautiously. Traditional models and skinny white celebrities still grace most of its covers, articles, and ads. But as the indomitable Mukhtar Mai said, the first steps always cause the most trouble.

O MAGAZINE

O, The Oprah Magazine is another extension of the influential Oprah Winfrey brand. *O* aims to embrace all women and promote bona fide self-awareness and lasting self-empowerment. The magazine's editorial policy protects its ideals: fashion spreads by necessity contain women of all ages, sizes, and backgrounds, some of them models and some of them *real*.

One thing is for sure: traditional models are *never* on the cover of *O*. Oprah herself graces every single one. You can't help but notice the contrast to all the other covers that nuzzle her shoulders month in, month out as they sit side-by-side on the magazine racks: a black, early fifty-something, dress size 8 but sometimes 12, smiling out from a crowd of young, thin, white girls. Everyone knows Oprah; she's the heart and soul of candid. She's so much more than just a face; she stands for struggle and triumph in a constant, human cycle. Oprah is always shot at eye level, she always holds her body with pride, and she always smiles. I guess she's having a lot of fun defying expectations. No one thinks black will sell over white, ever. But *O* magazine has some of the highest newsstand sales and ad revenues of all the Hearst magazines, and that includes *Cosmopolitan, Marie Claire, Bazaar,* and *Seventeen.*

O magazine will do a spread on fashion tips from real women, not snooty fashion editors currying favour with advertisers. Articles feature friendly info about the models: their names, ages, occupations, and thoughts. In *O*, there is no one look that's in style above all others; rather, many different looks in style for many different women, with many different body shapes and very different budgets. *O* is willing to admit that most of its readers can't afford Chanel and Dior. Still, beauty has its standards. *O* uses completely professional hair, makeup, photography, and art direction. Take that, *Vogue*—glamour and accessibility *do* go together if you're enlightened about it. And *O* has definitely had an impact on its advertisers. I counted ads in a recent issue: seven out of ten used diverse models.

NIKE

While not strictly a fashion company, Nike customers want to look fashionable on the courts and at the gym. Clearly, the company has been trying to recruit new customers through new models. "Active women come in a lot of sizes and shapes," says Nancy Monsarrat, director of marketing for the Nike Thunder Thighs campaign of 2005. Each Thunder Thighs ad shows a body part with copy beside it. One ad says, "Ten thousand lunges have made my butt rounder, but not smaller." Another proclaims, "I have thunder thighs. And that's a compliment because they are strong and toned and muscular and though they are unwelcome in the petite section they are cheered on in marathons."

The Thunder Thighs campaign is nothing new on Nike's part. For the past ten years, the "This is Not a Goddess" and "Move to the Pulse of Your

Soul" campaigns have been broadcasting Nike's message that beauty is individual, not universal.

Significantly, Nike is also making progress correcting the sweatshop injustices that came to public attention in the 1990s. The company now involves outside stakeholders in audits of its seven hundred offshore contract production factories. It's working with the Fair Labour Association to set, measure, and enforce standards in the factories.

Has Thunder Thighs been commercially viable? It's difficult to discern the contribution of one advertising campaign to a $2 billion company with several big campaigns going on simultaneously. In any case, Nike stock was up 17 per cent in 2005 and it was a record year for sales and profitability. I hope Nike will keep asking its customers, rather than its advertising executives, what they want. "Change the question and you change the answer," says Monsarrat proudly.

AMERICAN APPAREL

American Apparel is a clothing manufacturer that's growing at techno beat speed by defying the so-called wisdom of the clothing industry. The company makes fitted tees, shorts, jogging pants, zip-up hoodies, boy briefs, and other basics—in every colour. American Apparel also pays double the minimum wage, plus health benefits, and has five masseuses roaming its factory floor to knead tight shoulders back into shape. Production is by team rather than assembly line. There are no logos. Needless to say, the firm uses diverse models.

In fact, long before the Dove campaign, American Apparel was using real people in its advertising. "Even in our earliest catalogues," Alex Spunt, advertising director for American Apparel, told me. "We're more interested in showing something that people can relate to, an attainable experience as opposed to something impossible, like a fashion model who's also been retouched."

Most ads feature employees, friends of employees, and customers. They're usually twenty-something (the primary target market). Many are of mixed race, have asymmetrical features, relaxed bodies, blemished skin, and even vis-

Intellectual Chic
Sitting on the steps of Trinity College,
University of Toronto, at age eighteen.

"So, What's Her Favourite Ice Cream?"
(Cue Bewildered Looks!)
Judging at the Ben Barry Agency, Ottawa Sun,
and Sears Model Search in November 2002.

Cheers
Erika and me at a party for Toronto Fashion Week.

We're Worth It
Kenda and me in Ottawa about to go to fashion show.

So Chic at Fashion Week
Me, Chris, Farah, and Stephen (the guys from *So Chic*) at Toronto Fashion Week, 2004.

Model Moms
Mom with some of my models at a garden fashion show in Ottawa.

Personality and Perseverance
Model-search winner Joey works the camera like he works the track.

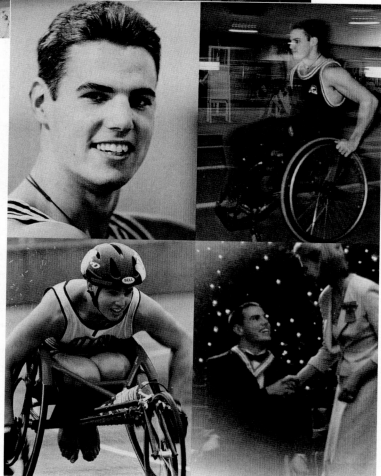

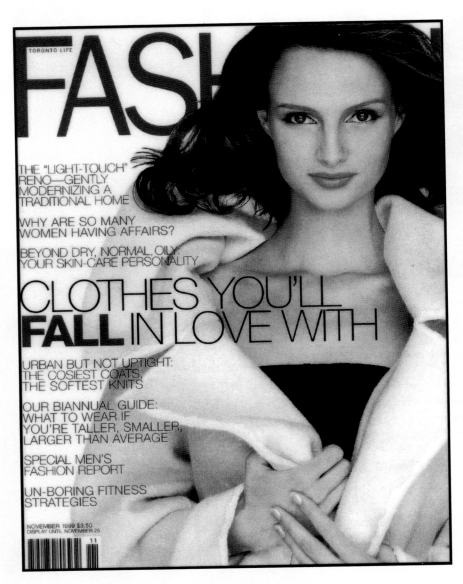

Vous Êtes un Mannequin?
Élodie on the cover of *Fashion* Magazine.

☐ wrinkled?
☐ wonderful?

Will society ever accept 'old' can be beautiful? Join the beauty debate.

campaignforrealbeauty.co.uk 🕊 | *Dove*

☐ fat?
☐ fit?

Does true beauty only squeeze into size 8? Join the beauty debate.

campaignforrealbeauty.co.uk 🕊 | *Dove*

Don't Forget to Double-Check Your Answers
Irene, ninety-five and retired; and Tabatha, thirty-four and an international
account coordinator, letting their real beauty shine through.

Let's face it, firming the thighs of a size 2 supermodel is no challenge.

Real women have real curves. And according to women who tried our new Dove Firming lotion, it left their skin noticeably firmer in just two weeks. What better way to celebrate the curves you were born with? New Dove Firming. For beautifully firm skin.

I HAVE
THUNDER THIGHS.
AND THAT'S A COMPLIMENT
BECAUSE THEY ARE STRONG

AND TONED
AND MUSCULAR

AND THOUGH THEY ARE UNWELCOME
IN THE PETITE SECTION

THEY ARE CHEERED ON IN MARATHONS.

FIFTY YEARS FROM NOW
I'LL BOUNCE A GRANDCHILD ON MY THUNDER THIGHS
AND THEN I'LL GO OUT FOR A RUN.

JUST DO IT.

NIKEWOMEN.COM ✔

Real Curves Come in All Sizes
Dove and Nike show that we can and should be proud of our body's natural curves. (For the record, I think the Dove ad should have stuck to moisturizer and not firming lotion.)

MY BUTT IS BIG
AND ROUND LIKE THE LETTER C
AND TEN THOUSAND LUNGES
HAVE MADE IT ROUNDER
BUT NOT SMALLER
AND THAT'S JUST FINE.
IT'S A SPACE HEATER
FOR MY SIDE OF THE BED
IT'S MY AMBASSADOR
TO THOSE WHO WALK BEHIND ME
IT'S A BORDER COLLIE
THAT HERDS SKINNY WOMEN
AWAY FROM THE BEST DEALS
AT CLOTHING SALES.
MY BUTT IS BIG
AND THAT'S JUST FINE
AND THOSE WHO MIGHT SCORN IT
ARE INVITED TO KISS IT.
JUST DO IT.

NIKEWOMEN.COM ✔

Quick on Her Feet
Sarah Monica

**Move Over, Tyra:
Ben Barry's Next Top Model**
Kosa

Full of Fire from Her Head to Her Heart
Elizabeth

ible sweat stains on their outfits. "What we're looking for is intuitive . . . it's not a certain set of features," Alex emphasizes. The models seem like the kind of artsy, indie-minded young adults that shop in the neighbourhoods where American Apparel stores are found.

American Apparel photo shoots are different from the typical twenty-people-plus, seven-hour-hair-and-makeup, day-long extravaganzas. "Our shoots are not very long and they're really relaxed and much more personal than the typical fashion shoot," Alex reveals. "Often it's just the photographer and model, maybe one other person. Given that we don't use makeup, lighting, etcetera, there are less variables to consider."

Most American Apparel ads give the model's name and a brief descrip-tion—usually where they're from and what they do for the company. For example, "Chanaye, an 18-year-old self-professed hippie of Afro-Cuban descent is taking a year off school to work, travel, and experience everything that she would not have had time for." Alex explains, "The biographical ele-ment was just something we started doing for fun, and to engage people, but I suppose it drives home the point that these are people with lives and jobs, and not just models. In some cases, when they're employees, it also illustrates the fact that vertical integration extends to all aspects of the company." (By vertical integration, Alex means that American Apparel manufactures all their clothing so there are no separate factories or wholesalers; the company's tees and hoodies go straight from the American Apparel factory to the stores.) As we all know by now, any information about a model is a welcome anom-aly in fashion advertising.

Some find American Apparel ads too racy for comfort, for reasons that go well beyond all the flirty knickers and clingy knits. The ads depict young men and women in bed or in the shower, or lounging on a sofa with their legs spread. Frequently, they're wearing just the item of clothing being advertised. A couple of young women appear to be in a heightened state of pleasure. And the camera angle is never at eye level. Let's face it, these images are porn inspired. (It doesn't help that there have been media reports that the co-owner enjoys a lifestyle that's a lot more Hugh Hefner than archbishop. Several sexual harassment lawsuits have originated from employees, and he's admitted to masturbating in front of a reporter during an interview.)

I asked Alex whether she finds the ads overtly sexualized. "The manner in which the models are shown is no more overtly sexual than many other ads and magazines," she told me. "I think it's just more intimate and raw. It's a much less plasticized sexy."

I agree with Alex. I have a hard time seeing the American Apparel ads as simply oppressive. The images are seductive and submissive, but the text is empowering and gives a sense of personhood. Obviously, American Apparel is trying to get me to rethink by placing two contradictory codes beside each other. I visited a Toronto American Apparel store recently to parse the political environment (while also trying on some tees). As I changed into a bright red rugby shirt, I had to wonder why the company would provide personhood on one hand and deny it on the other.

My conclusion is that American Apparel is challenging the idea that being seductive precludes having a powerful voice. It's debunking the binary notion that people can either be seen as objects or subjects. Instead they're establishing a continuum of what it means to be human. A real person has both a brain and a libido.

The target market loves the merchandise; shots of real twenty-somethings flirting away in their skivvies are definitely driving sales. American Apparel has over 110 stores worldwide and employs over 3,500 people. Between 2004 and 2005, sales jumped from $140 to $250 million. One customer wrote in to say, "Thank you for having Asian models. They seem so comfortable with themselves." Another said: "My boyfriend saw one of your ads, tore it out of the magazine and told me to check out your website. I love it! The women look so real to me, unlike the pencil-thin, extremely tall models most ads show. I immediately got a boost of confidence just by the women on your site. Thanks for keeping it real. I will definitely support your business. I also love that you are sweatshop-free."

"We've had so much positive feedback from showing unconventional models and it's something that's really come to distinguish us," Alex says. "Has it created brand loyalty? I think it *definitely* has."

LEVI'S

Denim went ballistic in the nineties. Suddenly, it was all about hip-hugging, whiskering, stretch, distressing, bell bottoms, and then drainpipes again. Jean makers spent the last decade scrambling and Levi's was no exception. The creators of that quintessentially American icon, the 501, shifted the bulk of their marketing budget to promote trendy cuts and finishes. But Levi's couldn't compete with all the new hipsters, and the trendy looks were too radical for faithful Levi's wearers. The result was six years of declining sales. (They fell from a peak of $7.1 billion in 1996 to $4.1 billion in 2003.)

Levi's decided to re-brand itself as cool while at the same time taking pride in its long history. Amy Jasmer, Director of Presence and Publicity for Levi's, told me that the company's ad agency searched deep into the extensive archive of letters from Levi's customers over the years in order to generate the new campaign. "We literally have hundreds of letters in our archives, some of which date back to the end of last century, of people telling the story of their Levi's Jeans," she says.

After much reading, sorting, and re-reading, a theme emerged: everyone's Levi's suit their lifestyle. Hence, "A Style for Every Story": the largest advertising effort Levi's had undertaken in its 131-year history. According to Amy, the campaign was meant to "celebrate the bond that wearers have with their Levi's while showcasing the broad range of styles." Everyday people from a wide variety of professions and trades replaced professional fashion models in full-body black-and-white images. Beside each model are their name, age, occupation, and a quote about why they like the particular style of jeans they're wearing. The campaign offers appropriate reach and diversity for a brand that's worn by people from all walks of life and sold for $45 to $500 in over 110 countries. The models are never detached or alienating. We're talking a very wide range of lifestyles and personalities here, from an aircraft mechanic to a rancher.

In the October 18, 2004, edition of the *New York Observer*, the advertising executive who spearheaded Levi's campaign, Thomas Hayo, explained how Levi's wanted to select people with jobs that others can aspire to, yet relate to at the same time. "Going with people on top of their field would be a mistake.

Then it becomes an endorsement campaign." Amy told me that Levi's found models by sending emails to workplaces like newspapers, restaurants, and art galleries, and posting messages on websites asking for people to submit their photos. The casting message read as follows: "Females, 24–55, all ethnicities. Real looking, beautiful women with good bodies. No professional models. Males, 18–55, all ethnicities. Real looking, rugged, lean, not buff. No professional models." Hayo is quoted as saying he found the casting process difficult: "Once all candidates had come in, we had to find who has an interesting look; who has a certain pair of jeans they like; and who looks good in certain jeans."

Erik Rasmussen, a twenty-six-year-old journalist, was picked for the campaign. He explained to the *New York Observer* that he was working as a photo assistant in New York when a stylist who also worked with Levi's approached him for a Polaroid. Rasmussen agreed, then forgot all about it and moved to the U.K. A few months later, the ad agency contacted him to say he was in. He earned $10,000. He was more excited about the money than the modelling. "I needed a new car. And I needed my wisdom teeth pulled. I'm one of those forty-three million Americans without health insurance. I'm twenty-six."

Consumers appreciated the new Levi's campaign. Amy couldn't share brand equity information or any related data but she did tell me that people responded "very positively" to the campaign because "they were able to identify with the diversity of Levi's jeans wearers." Ad Track, a *USA TODAY* poll, found that 25 per cent of people surveyed liked the ads "a lot" (the Ad Track average for that is 21 per cent). They appealed equally to men and women. Unsurprisingly, Levi Strauss is showing signs of a significant financial recovery. In September 2006, it reported a profit of $46.6 million in the third quarter versus a $4.3 million loss the year before.

My only complaint with "A Style for Every Story" is the lack of body diversity. The models came from a whole range of ages and races but Levi's only wanted people who were lean and long. Hopefully, the next series will feature models of all different sizes as well.

MADRID FASHION WEEK

The star attractions on high fashion runways are human beanpoles. Not, however, in Madrid. Not any longer. For the Madrid Fashion Week of September 2006, the organizers and the city's local government imposed the world's first ban on overly thin models. If any emaciated models do turn up, they will be classified as in need of medical help.

The Madrid city council, which sponsors Madrid Fashion Week, and the Spanish Association of Fashion Designers, which organizes the shows, put the ban in place after fielding one too many complaints that young women were contracting eating disorders by trying to copy rail-thin models. Organizers say they want to project an image of beauty and health, not waifs on heroin.

The Madrid shows use body mass index, or BMI—based on both weight and height—to measure models. The Madrid city council has ordered that every model in the shows must have a BMI of at least 18. According to the World Health Organization, a woman is underweight if her BMI is less than 18.5. The council has a nutritional expert on hand to check every model taking part in the shows. Any woman found to have a BMI of below 16 is offered medical treatment. Almost 40 per cent of the models slated to appear in September 2006 were subsequently barred. Esther Canadas, Spain's best-known model, didn't qualify under the new rule.

Spanish government officials say they don't blame models and designers for eating disorders. But they believe that the fashion industry has a responsibility to portray healthy bodies. "Many teenagers imitate what they see on the catwalk," said regional official Concha Guerra.

Some people are critical of Madrid's bold move. Cathy Gould, of Elite Model Management in New York, for one. She complained on the Yahoo News website that the fashion industry was being used as a scapegoat for weight-related illnesses. "I understand they want to set this tone of healthy, beautiful women but what about discrimination against the model and what about the freedom of the designer?" she asked, adding that the careers of naturally "gazelle-like" models could be damaged.

On a similar note, Stan Herman, designer and president of the Council of Fashion Designers of America, said that if it had happened in the U.S., the ban was discriminatory enough to result in likely legal action. "It would be the same as banning somebody who's too fat," he told ABC News Online. "Those people could sue. In America, they could sue everywhere for prejudice or discrimination. I wouldn't touch it with a 10-foot pole."

Sorry, Cathy and Stan, but you're missing the point. Hate-speech laws limit freedom of expression in order to prevent harm. Similarly, banning ultra-thin models prevents harm (to the public and to the models). It's not like the ban outlaws slender models altogether. Designers can still book whichever models they want as long as they're healthy according to medically approved standards. I believe that a day will come when a ban like this will be unnecessary because no one will want to see unhealthy girls anyway—they'll become too hard on the bottom line. But for now, I'm happy to see a government step in and overturn a stereotype that's become ingrained into the culture.

Madrid Fashion Week is a minnow among sharks but Madrid's move is having a ripple effect on fashion capitals around the world. In London, British Culture Secretary Tessa Jowell told BBC Online, "The fashion industry is hugely powerful in shaping the attitude of teenage girls and their feelings about themselves. The industry's promotion of beauty as meaning stick thin is damaging to young girls' self-image and to their health." Jowell urged the London Fashion Week to follow Madrid's example for their shows. "I applaud the decision taken by Madrid to ban super-thin models, and urge the organizers of London Fashion Week to do the same," she said.

But the British Fashion Council (BFC), which runs the London Fashion Week, said it wouldn't tell designers how to run their shows. In a statement to the BBC, the BFC said that it "does not comment or interfere in the aesthetic of any designer's show."

Nonetheless, a consortium of retailers from Birmingham, England, announced that it would prohibit extremely thin models from participating in Clothes Show Live in December, a major fashion event that's kicked off the careers of many famous models.

As for Italy, the mayor of Milan told the *Times* that she'd seek a similar ban for the Milan shows unless a cure could be found for "sick"-looking models. The organizers of Milan Fashion Week 2006 said that it was too late to impose new guidelines since models had all been selected and clothing tailored for the shows. But they were open to discuss the idea for the next season.

FASHION FORWARD

These companies (and others) have had a lot of success using diverse models. Cosmetics, magazines, clothing: it's a winning strategy. Customers are empowered; productive relationships are forged. Fashion and beauty executives are extremely observant; they're watching closely to see who says thanks at the cash desk. Watching so closely, in fact, that Ogilvy & Mather, Dove's advertising agency of over thirty years, hooked up with me, via Cambridge University, to fund extensive research on diversity in fashion. I'll be sharing those results far and wide the minute they become available.

Every significant change requires leaders. Once they demonstrate success, others follow, then more, then more. Only sad stragglers stick with tired approaches. Ten years from now I'm planning on taking a nice hard look at every billboard I can see, every magazine I can get my hands on, every fashion editorial and beauty ad out there, and breathing a sigh of relief. We will have fashioned a new reality by then. I mean it.

Okay, we fashion types aren't known for our patience. How do we move as fast as we can? I'd say the answer lies in the hands of entrepreneurs. Business changes society incisively; that's been the underlying theme of my own story. For business to work at its best, we have to get rid of the things that hold people down when they're envisioning and re-envisioning. Industry experts get entangled in their own feedback loops. They listen to each other "blah, blah, blah," too scared to hear out their customers. What we need to do now is remove the risks attached, rightly or wrongly, to the diversity process. (Bad memories of Toronto Fashion Week intrude here.) Using diverse models in empowering images is a complicated thing to do right now. It takes more work, done by specialists who know how to ask not just *who* is represented but *how*. But the change is going to be worth it.

CHAPTER TWELVE

A NEW SEASON, A NEW LOOK

RESEARCH AND CONSULTING

INTERNATIONAL BRANDS WERE edging toward adopting my goals as their own—but gingerly. Most execs worried that Dove's triumph was an aberration. Marketing directors asked whether the same strategy would work for their brand and, if so, how to make the transition. For example, should their company proceed cautiously, like Panda Plus, with one normal-looking model in five? Or should they really go for it, like Dove, with the potential advantage of catching a bigger market share? Multiple questions with different answers for each brand. My strategies had to evolve to keep up. Simply offering a diverse roster of models and a few success stories wasn't going to cut it with a fashion multinational. I had to develop powerful research mechanisms to provide rigorous, empirical evidence tailored to individual firms. I needed new tools.

CAMBRIDGE, TAKE 2

My last undergrad semester was coming to a close, I was a month away from graduation, and here came history. Once again, I had to choose between staying in school and focusing on the agency. To make the decision that much harder, I'd just been accepted into the master's program in innovation and strategy at the Judge Business School, at Cambridge University in England.

School versus business was an easier decision to make this time around. Now I knew the university experience inside out and I knew how classes and assignments could spark business ideas. I also knew that at Cambridge I'd conduct highly targeted studies supervised by world experts. I'd cultivate the top-of-the-line research tools I'd been coveting. Cambridge seemed like the way to go.

Not that grad school would to be a stroll down the catwalk. Cambridge is one of the most selective, competitive schools in the world. And the Ben Barry Agency was bigger and more complex than when I'd left high school. I had two offices now and over twice the clients and staff. I'd be a whole ocean and half a continent away from my office. (On top of all that I had crazily decided to write this book.)

But I was up for all of it. I'm an opportunity fanatic after all. Being away would give me perspective on the business and the industry. That in turn would help me to evaluate where the Ben Barry Agency had been and where it was headed. On a personal level, I was keen to do the same; I was twenty-three years old. Escaping the daily buzz of the office would help me get to know Ben, not just Ben Barry.

Everything would run as usual, but with two changes. The agency wouldn't expand (i.e., take on new clients) until I returned. And some of my duties (acting as the lead contact on specific accounts, and handling human resources issues and crisis management) were delegated to my core management team. I'd remain an active CEO, however. No relinquishing listening, problem solving, emails, phone calls, online conferences, and trips back to Canada.

I guess I'm lucky because if there's one thing I like to do, it's take a plunge and dive down deep.

BIG-TIME SUPPORT

Cambridge was a far cry from BlackBerry-flavoured *fabulous*, although secluded academic life felt like just as much of a fantasy as fashion. It was

Harry Potter meets Cinderella at the ball. All of Cambridge revolved around the university; it filled the town centre. Every building was more beautiful and historic than the next—stone, stained glass, and turrets divided by vast velvety lawns. The roads were mostly cobblestone, filled with students and professors, walking and biking, books in hand. There were twenty people in my program, each one representing a different country. We were all immediately busy—debating with our supervisors in their studies and with each other in cozy cafés. Or reading by the river as rowers heaved past. (And some of us were busy answering business emails.) At dinnertime we sat in black robes at long tables, in rooms lit by candlelight, eating six-course meals during which we'd talk for hours about politics, scientific discovery, literature, philosophy. And—now that *I* was a member of Cambridge—fashion.

To be honest, my academic life could have easily become pompous and precious. I could have nestled up inside the Cambridge bubble—where the latest news involved a breakthrough theory, where major freak-outs were caused by an inability to debunk someone's argument or find a book in the library. It would have been easy to mistake lab observation as human experience. Sometimes I needed out. Nearly every weekend, I took the forty-five-minute train ride to London and stayed with my University of Toronto friend, Lindsay, who was now studying sociology at LSE. I'd go to London galleries, theatres, and concerts. I'd scope out the latest billboard ads. Mostly, I'd take in a big dose of the street and ride the Tube to people-watch, just as I had done during my summer in London five years before.

By the end of my first semester at Cambridge, I needed to submit a thesis proposal to the academic committee. We all had to get our topics officially approved by the business school and board of graduate studies. When I proposed my goal—to research the impact on consumer loyalty and purchase intentions of using diverse models in fashion and beauty advertisements—my profs weren't sold. Models and fashion were shallow stuff at an eight-hundred-year-old university that's been home to eighty-one Nobel Prize winners, numerous prime ministers, royalty, Charles Darwin, Isaac Newton, and Stephen Hawking. My professors weren't convinced I was referring to a legitimate business or strategic concern, let alone exploring a sufficiently academic research area. Executives had to be facing more pressing decisions than *that*.

So I had my work cut out for me from the start. To persuade my teachers that selecting models for advertisements was indeed a critical management move, I crafted a proposal with research culled from a selection of disciplines: business, sociology, women's studies, health studies, and economics. I argued that in today's competitive marketplace, brand identity is a firm's main advantage. Advertisements, and therefore the models depicted in them, contribute in numerous ways to the dynamics of a brand—and hence the overall mission of the firm. The use of models in advertising is actually a huge business decision. Yet no academic research had been done to explain whether traditional models have a greater influence on purchase intentions and buying behaviour than diverse models (when it comes to fashion and beauty advertising). That was where I was going to come in.

I found a supervisor, Simon Bell, who was as excited about the research as I was. He was a thirty-something senior marketing lecturer from Austria. What drew me to Simon was that he had a very practical way of working; he was all about setting up schedules and actually getting things done, not just talking about it. At our very first meeting we set up a timeline of what needed to be done and when. I'd heard horror stories about people who'd spent years working on their thesis, some of them never finishing. There was no way that was going to be me. Cambridge was formal but Simon was down-to-earth and funny. We debated business theory but we also chatted about our lives. With Simon, I never felt there was a hierarchy at work; I valued his experience and knowledge in marketing theory and conducting academic research, and he valued my expertise in the modelling industry, fashion advertising, and feminism. In fact, he had been using Dove ads in lectures to his MBA marketing students.

But what utterly drew me to Simon from the start was an email he sent me the second week of classes. I'd approached him about supervising my dissertation and had followed up by emailing him a draft proposal. In his response, he said there were two types of dissertations: "theory research" that contributes to the academic dialogue, and "impact research" that contributes to changing people's everyday lives. He said my project was definitely the latter. Simon felt passionately that research should have a positive impact on the world. On that note, he'd be personally delighted to supervise me. Fantastic, we were on the same page.

Much to my relief, the academic committee approved my research topic. Shortly thereafter, Simon was at a meeting of the school's advisory board, where he found himself in conversation with Shelly Lazarus, CEO of Ogilvy & Mather. The Ogilvy & Mather advertising agency is one of the largest in the world, with over 500 offices in 125 countries and a client list that includes American Express, Sears, Ford, IBM, Kodak, and Dove. Simon learned from Shelly that the Ogilvy Foundation (the agency's not-for-profit organization that funds academic research) was looking to fund advertising-related research coming out of Judge. Simon mentioned my project to her. Later that night, he sent me a cryptic email: "I have surprisingly good news for you. Come to my office in the morning to discuss."

The following morning, I rolled out of bed, showered, grabbed a freshly brewed coffee thanks to my neighbour Jean, and hustled over to Judge. The business school was housed in the city's old hospital: a stone building with tall pillars holding up vast balconies, albeit modernized with new multicoloured windows. I hurried up to Simon's second-floor office. His head popped up from his computer.

"Ben!" he said. "Come in, come in."

"I got your email. I was in suspense all night. What's up?"

"The Ogilvy Foundation wants to support your research. They think the issue is 'topical' and 'emotive.'"

"Holy—!" Let's imagine I said something polite.

Simon and I got right to work on the proposal I had to submit ASAP to Shelly and Eleanor Mascheroni, Ogilvy's chief marketing officer, responsible for the Ogilvy Foundation's activities. I promised Simon I'd have a draft ready first thing the next morning. Drafting a proposal was simply a matter of writing down and refining what was so clear in my head. I went back to my dorm room, skipped class for the day, and rewrote my thesis proposal with Ogilvy now in mind.

First I summarized all the existing research. Past studies had found that using traditional models didn't always lead to increased "purchase intentions." Instead, typical models were shown to make women feel bad about their bodies and themselves, leading to negative feelings about the brand. Previous research had also shown that the more physically similar a viewer of an ad and the model, the more likely the viewer was to feel positively about the brand and purchase it.

As far as I was concerned, all the existing literature suggested that real women would work well in ads. Anecdotally, I could totally support that. Officially, I made plans to compare "reality-reflecting" models with "ideally attractive" ones. I'd find out exactly which type of model leads to a favourable perception of a brand and increases those almighty purchase intentions.

But I soon clued in that my task was more complicated than simply finding out if one type of model was more effective than the other. Clients also need to know *when* one type of model is more effective. There are many different fashion and beauty products, at many price points and with various promoted purposes. And there are many different ways for beauty to be realistic: age, body, ethnicity. My study would need to address all these differences.

My revised research agenda went as follows: will reality-reflecting models (where age and size reflect average consumers) or ideally attractive models (who follow the traditional young and skinny formula) work better for a luxury brand like Christian Dior or for a consumer brand like Wal-Mart? Do realistic models or ideally attractive models work better when a product is promoted as enhancing or promoted as problem solving? (Mascara, for instance, can be used to enhance gorgeous eyes or to thicken thin lashes.) Which beauty characteristics such as body type or age, resonate the most with consumers?

I proposed starting with a series of focus groups and interviews to accumulate some qualitative data. I wanted to get people talking by showing them a series of mock-up ads with different models and differing products. Then I'd conduct some quantitative research in the form of a controlled experiment. The participants would be shown ads and then would complete a questionnaire that measured which models had improved their brand attitudes and increased purchase intentions. I would conduct an initial study in Canada, the U.S., and England. Then I'd replicate the experiment and test the results from the first study in China, the United Arab Emirates, and Brazil.

I knew the international element would add a fascinating cultural dimension to my study, especially given the widespread proliferation of Western media (and therefore Western beauty ideals) that's resulted from globalization.

Ogilvy had an office in every one of the countries I wanted to study; Cambridge had students from all over the world. I'd get my peers to administer the interviews and surveys in all the relevant languages.

By 5 a.m., the proposal was done. I emailed it to Simon with a muffled hoot. Thankfully, Jean had brought over fruit, yogurt, and tea. At 7 a.m., Simon emailed back with a few edits. The final proposal was emailed to Shelly and Eleanor by 9 a.m., at which point, my adrenalin levels were churning and there was no way I was going to sleep. Simon and some classmates decided to join me in the traditional Cambridge ritual after pulling an all-nighter (Nobel Prize winners no doubt included): we hit the pub.

I soon went up to London to present my proposal to Eleanor in person, and also to Mike Hemingway, who spearheads the Dove account. Once Mike found out that I'd been involved in the front end of the Dove campaign in North America, and I found out that he'd managed the international campaign, our mutual respect ballooned.

Mike knew that the issues I'd be researching are among the trickiest facing the industry. Other companies eager to repeat Dove's success had approached Ogilvy. Dove had charged ahead on faith but the bandwagon wanted more data before proceeding. Mike said I was going to answer questions clients had been asking ever since Dove changed all the rules of the game. Will real beauty work for other brands? In which situations? What messages need to be tied to the model? "These are the sort of questions we don't have answers for yet," Mike said.

The Ogilvy Foundation officially decided to fund the research, which will become my doctoral thesis over the next three years. We signed an agreement in which I have full ownership of the research. I can make it available to all interested parties at a standardized cost (including to Ogilvy), and Ogilvy can't have any influence in guiding the study. I hope my study will draw other interested researchers into the field; I say the more fact finding, the better.

This is a lot more than I hoped for when I decided to go back to school. Ogilvy's support gives me a chance to work with the advertising industry up close. I get to blend academic research with practical experience. And my research will get funnelled directly to people creating ads. Eleanor says this is the empirical evidence Ogilvy has been waiting for to make decisions about new models. I went to Cambridge because I wanted to conduct research that would one day persuade fashion advertising firms to hire diverse models. Now the industry had come on board from the start.

And things got even better.

Business schools often have executives in residence: high-profile business people who take a few weeks or months out of their schedules to share their knowledge with students on campus. When I was at Cambridge, Judge recruited Kevin Roberts, the CEO of Saatchi & Saatchi (a creative advertising firm with a team of seven thousand working in eighty-two countries). Kevin is the author of the bestselling book, *Lovemarks: The Future Beyond Brands*. Imagine you're a singer dropping by Pavarotti's dressing room for some vocal coaching—that was basically me, hitting up Kevin for feedback as often as I could.

I met Kevin after a speech he gave on creativity in business thinking to the MBA group at Judge. After the talk, Dr. Allègre Hadida, the professor who organized the talk and also taught my strategy class, took him to her study so he could check his email and have a bite (he had just arrived that morning from New York and had spent the past four hours lecturing and answering questions). Dr. Hadida knew of my research and had emailed me earlier in the week asking me to wait outside her office after his talk—she'd make a personal introduction. My classmates were a fashionable shade of green. I put on my Cambridge tweed coat and striped scarf and waited nervously. I felt like I was about to meet a movie star.

I got an hour of Kevin's time. Kevin was interested in the way I combined academic research and real-world application. He was especially interested to hear how women's studies had impacted on my study of management and my business. I left the meeting with twenty-five scrawled pages: ideas, questions, and resources. And the buzz I acquire in my head, and my heart, when I've found a new mentor.

Kevin thought my research study was "necessary and timely." High praise from someone who got his start working with fashion designer Mary Quant—credited with inventing the miniskirt and hot pants. "Letting consumers participate in the brand is very powerful," he told me. "The ultimate objective of every brand is to have consumers develop a kind of loving, emotional relationship with them. Models play an essential role in that. If the consumers identify with the model—feel included in the ad and feel beautiful by looking at it—they're going to feel more connected to whatever brand is being advertised. It's the right time and the right environment to start using diverse models. Your research would persuade firms to do so."

MACY'S HAPPY ACCIDENT

Right when Simon and I secured the research funding from Ogilvy, I got an email from New York. It was from the vice-president of marketing for Macy's, the legendary American department store chain. She'd found out about the benefits of using diverse models completely by chance. Macy's had wanted to put on a high-profile fundraiser fashion show that happened to coincide with New York's Fashion Week. The planning had started late and most professional models were already booked. In desperation, the organizers decided to use their own staff. They discovered—just as I had at local malls and high-end shows—that the crowd (members of the media, industry players, and celebrities) not only roared approval for the real models but were inspired to buy more products.

The VP had been sharing her accidental success story over dinner with a colleague who, by chance, had just been to one of my talks. This woman said, "It's not a fluke. There's a business model to explain it. And there's a modelling agent who specializes in it. Call Ben Barry." So she called me right up. She liked what she heard, and now we're working together to find models for Macy's fashion shows that reflect Macy's wide-ranging clientele.

I couldn't say no to a new business opportunity that huge. Luckily, most of the work would begin when classes were over and I'd headed back home.

This much support—from Cambridge, Ogilvy, Kevin Roberts, and Macy's—makes a guy feel pretty validated. I'd been working toward change pretty painstakingly for ten years and I was finally feeling things pick up. The industry was getting the message I had really wanted to send and acting on it. Not exactly a good time to kick back and take a break.

EXPANDING

My course work at Cambridge was all done by May 2006. I headed home to start my research (Cambridge allows its students to live anywhere while working on their dissertation) and get back to the office. My head was full of branding theories, consumer behaviour, and business strategy expertise—from long conversations with Simon, Mike, and Kevin; from the thousands of pages of reading I'd done; and from some very heavy-duty term papers. No keeping those ideas up in the air. In the same way that a lot of designers' brains go right from illustration to garment, my mind went straight from theory to application.

And I had a dynamically emerging business environment to profit from. It was time to change my business model again. My agency's advantage was our understanding that every brand needs its own approach to diversity and our ability to finesse that. I'd evolved from a model agency into a model *consultancy* and it was time to start selling myself that way. Basically, we offer custom model scouting and sourcing. We find, train, develop, and manage models specific to our clients' needs.

To compare—most agencies send photos of every single one of their models to clients. There's no taking into consideration the history and nature of the product and the brand. The client has usually asked five or six agencies to submit models, so it has to go through multiple portfolios, pick a short list, and hold a big casting call for one and all. Once the client finally selects the models it wants, it has to coordinate scheduling details with separate agencies. Moreover, a client is at risk of booking a model who has already been used by a competitor. Guaranteeing exclusivity means paying extra fees.

We streamline the process. Once a client signs a contract, we meet with the company frequently to develop a complete understanding of its brand—its history, objectives, and upcoming projects. Instead of showing the client our entire group of models, my team can curate a selection of models who specifically meet its needs and let the client make a final decision.

The benefits for clients are clear. They work with a team who understands their brand exceptionally well—something that doesn't happen when they deal with five different agencies. They're guaranteed that competitors won't hire the same models. Furthermore, our models perform energetically during shoots.

The truth about full-time traditional models is that a lot of them get jaded and cynical. Their appearance is under constant focus, discussed during almost every work interaction. Meanwhile, their personalities almost never come into play, not unless they're making the cover of *Vogue* or strutting for Jean Paul Gaultier. I'd find a work environment like that exhausting, draining, and dehumanizing myself. The unfortunate result is sometimes dull, lacklustre shots.

My custom-scouting approach eliminates full-time models. All of our models work part-time, scouted for a specific client. They have careers and lives outside modelling. Balancing a regular life with their modelling guarantees that photo shoots and fashion shows remain exciting and fresh, for the models and for the audience. We encourage our models to exude energy and uniqueness at every show and shoot (instead of detached and stale poses). We also train them out of defining themselves solely based on their appearance. We hire people with a multi-faceted sense of self, an understanding that they are whole people.

Sheila, for instance, arrived at her shoot after seeing her daughter off to college. She was radiant from having just experienced such a significant moment, and now her eyes were sparkling at the excitement of being in her first fashion photo shoot.

Freda, a medical student, rushed to a shoot right after the final exam of her second year. Her excitement and pleasure at finishing school made for a peerless glow.

Amuro came to her photo shoot after finishing her shift at the grocery store, and picking up her granddaughter en route. As Amuro stood behind the lights, her granddaughter clapped and cheered at Granny's antics. Amuro's warmth and joy couldn't have been more real.

GOING INTERNATIONAL

We couldn't operate as an effective consultancy for the global fashion and beauty industry by simply remaining in Toronto. We could manage all the research out of Canada, and take meetings, but we couldn't scout the U.S. or U.K. markets without teams in place. It was time to embark on the first phase of that international business plan I'd developed during my summer at LSE. Ever since my last year of high school, it had been waiting in my top desk drawer.

First, I set up satellite offices in New York and London. I needed a base for the Ben Barry scouts I'd already been working with there and the new ones I brought on board—mostly people I'd met at young entrepreneurs' conferences and former classmates from Cambridge. But finding offices isn't easy. My scouts don't sit at a desk, Monday to Friday nine to five. They work on the subway on Tuesday from 5 a.m. until 2 p.m., in the mall on Saturday from noon until 5 p.m., at a hot concert on Saturday night, and then in the office on Monday from 1 p.m. until 9 p.m. meeting prospective models. Nonetheless, I needed someone to answer the phone and return emails so no one who got in touch went unanswered. Furthermore, I didn't want a small room with one lonely person in it. I needed a cool space bustling with action to keep everyone pumped when they walked in the door.

My New York friend Tina (whom you'll meet in Part Two) told me about a downtown office compound offering space to companies in the creative fields. Her company had one. She was right; it was totally going to work for me. The office sizes are flexible—they can be upgraded on demand—and there are communal facilities such as meeting rooms and reception areas (with receptionists) to rival the big company on the forty-fourth floor. Even Mr. Levine agreed. Eventually, the Ben Barry Agency will need a five-thousand-square-foot loft all to itself in New York and London. In any case, my first choice for a meeting is always a coffee shop. A grande, no foam, extra hot, tazo chai latte definitely makes up for those square feet right now.

How exactly am I swinging all this? Welcome to one of my typical Toronto days...

September 20, 2006
8 a.m.
I wake up. Usually I'd have been out of bed for an hour by now, but I was up late last night enjoying a steak dinner with Mom. She's in Toronto for a visit. I bring my banana and yogurt breakfast bowl over to the computer where I scan a few newspapers just to wake up my brain. Then I click open the first draft of

my dissertation and stick with it for a solid three hours. Good: I've got something ready to email off to Simon for notes.

Noon

I'm on a red Toronto streetcar heading to the office and listening to Fergie on my iPod while returning messages on my BlackBerry and eating a leftover fully loaded baked potato. There's no need for me to own a car; I don't want to contribute to the smog burden nor do I want to be distracted by city driving. The agency is abuzz when I arrive. The Toronto International Film Festival was on last week. Marketing mavens from every major fashion and beauty brand in the world were in town; I ate more lunches per day than most people eat in a week. Thanks to a recent contract I signed on a trip to L.A., I'm now promoting diverse celebrities—seeking "brand synergies" for Demi, Madonna, and others. Madonna and her dancers and crew from the Confessions world tour just starred in an H&M campaign; I want to suss out opportunities like that. My staff is following up on my film fest lunches with pitch packages and in some cases already negotiating deals.

1 p.m.

Matt and I have been working for an hour on a pitch to an upscale fashion chain that I plan on cold calling later in the afternoon. We know that as soon as I get the marketing director on the phone, she's going to say that she loved the Dove campaign but can't see diverse models working for a luxury brand. Naturally, I'll disagree. I'll say that effectiveness depends on execution. To practise what we preach, Matt is overseeing a stylish design for a package to send her way.

1:20 p.m.

I say hello to two best friends whom I'd scouted at a shopping mall the month before. Both are sweet sixteen. One is Latina with short spiky black hair, a size 6. The other has red hair down to her shoulders and is more like a 12. I'm working on a campaign for a brand that's featuring real-life best friends as models and I'm convinced these gals will be a perfect fit. They're excited at the thought of modelling. One of them keeps saying, "I still can't believe you want *me* to be a model! I never thought I was pretty enough." "This is way cool," says the other.

1:40 p.m.
I walk in on a meeting of my scouting team. They're discussing Macy's scouting profile for some in-store fashion shows: the ages, sizes, and cultural backgrounds of the models we need to find in order to match the Macy's target market. I suggest that we need to develop a different profile for each U.S. region based on its ethnic composition. I ask my scouts to research where we can find potential models in seven northeastern U.S. cities. I want to see a timeline for the scouting project, from when the scouting would begin to when we would have models ready to present to Macy's.

2:15 p.m.
As I walk back into my office, the phone rings. It's the marketing director of an international denim brand targeting young adults. He's rebranding and wants to follow a philosophy similar to Dove's. He's going to hire us to manage the models and consult on the entire campaign. I arrange a meeting with him in New York for later in the week. As soon as we say our goodbyes, I email my assistant and ask him to book me a flight returning that same day, but late enough so that I can have dinner with lovely Tina.

2:50 p.m.
Time to make the cold call Matt and I have been preparing for. I get the luxury goods marketing director on the line. I remind her that women come in all shapes, ages, and colours, regardless of their budget and tastes. They all want to wear the same clothes as models in ads. As soon as I hang up, I email over Matt's stylish package.

3:05 p.m.
I read through my to-do list. Number 1 is finishing this chapter and sending it off to my publisher by today—the deadline. I crank out ten good pages, look them over, rewrite a bit, then email it off.

6:45 p.m.

I need a five-minute break. I make some tea and open the latest *Vogue* and *Glamour*, both on my desk. I flip through the pages and check out the ads. Ninety per cent of them feature traditional models. Henry Ford produced only one model of car in only one colour at first. He told a reporter, "People can have a car in any colour they want, as long as it's black." For too long the modelling industry has been operating in the same reduced way. Agencies recruit and train one type of model, offer only that type of model, and invite clients to "pick" from that one single choice. Not me, never again, not now, not ever.

7:15 p.m.

I head out and meet my boyfriend for dinner and a movie. It's a toss-up between sushi and Italian, and *Little Miss Sunshine* and *Snakes on a Plane*. Sushi and *Little Miss Sunshine* win. I'm glad. I need to eat light and laugh hard.

I strive toward the day—and I can feel it coming—when models in the fashion industry will no longer be recruited according to a narrow definition of beauty; when they will not be treated as products with shelf lives of five years; when their characters and personalities will be properly celebrated and when their presence on runways and in print will make their audience feel better about themselves than ever. Until then, my fight in the fashion world goes on.

"Hello, my name is Ben Barry from the Ben Barry Agency and I have an idea for you."

PART TWO

BUSINESS CAN CHANGE THE WORLD

THE PURSUIT OF PROFIT AND A BETTER SOCIETY

CHAPTER THIRTEEN

ENTREPRENEURSHIP'S NEXT TOP MODEL

THE BALANCED CONTRACT

I STARTED MY BUSINESS IN an attempt to right a wrong. I wanted my friend Lauren to be able to get modelling jobs without having to give up pie forever and fork over a lot of dough. The more I learned about the modelling business, however, the more my motivations took shape. My ultimate goal evolved; I became determined to see to it that my friends—and everyone like them— would feel empowered, not discouraged, by the media's narrow, pervasive definition of beauty.

But like any entrepreneur, I've always wanted to make money. No profit, no business. Profit allows me the freedom to continue to work for social change. Furthermore, winning clients demonstrates support for my cause and my solutions. I love that my life's work isn't split between doing a job that pays the rent and then spending my leftover energy helping out. Instead, I devote all my time to my cause—my cause pays the bills.

Creating inclusive media images and making money—these two aims continue to guide my work. The combination often puzzles businesspeople and it puzzles activists, too. Historically, there's a tendency to think of the two objectives as oil and water. Activists protest that capitalism harms society by privileging profits at the expense of people and the environment. Business executives complain that social movements stir up noise and unrest that hampers the marketplace.

In building the Ben Barry Agency, I made up a method of entrepreneurship for myself as I went along. I had no idea what I was up to when I was fourteen, sixteen, or eighteen. I was chasing my instincts rather than any mapped-out strategy. It was only after I learned more about both social movements and business that I came to understand how differently I did things. Really, why not combine knowledge, objectives, and experiences from both camps?

I'm not alone. Other young entrepreneurs whom I've met as I've gone along have had the same idea and are now running businesses that are doing well by doing good.

What's with the long-standing opposition between activism and business, anyway? The divide is artificial. Not only do activism and business hold mutually compatible objectives, but also their objectives are best achieved by working together. Activists understand the social, political, and environmental world; business can provide the means to change it.

In her book *No Logo*, Naomi Klein talks about the way that protests, spray painting, culture jamming, and other activist activities are challenging exploitative business practices. I've been a social activist myself, as a member of the Toronto Youth Cabinet, fighting against potential funding cuts to the city's youth programming. Our team got significant media attention and influenced the public to write in protest to city council. We won a meeting with the mayor and in the end youth programs were spared funding cuts.

Hurrah, right? But as protesters, we could only call attention to the problem. We relied almost exclusively on others to take corrective action. We could pressure the decision-makers but they got to make the changes. We could propose innovations but we were missing the tools to implement them. That kind of power remains in the hands of government or business. Activists are well symbolized by the events at the World Trade Summit in Seattle: the protests made world headlines while a barbed-wire fence separated the protestors from the decision-makers.

My point is that as long as activists remain outside the fence, so will their ideas. Generally, activists are seen as naggers and complainers. The business attitude toward them seems to be contain them rather than listen to them. They're dismissed by politicians when they seek changes that require government legislation and they're dismissed by businesspeople when they seek changes that require new corporate policy. Executives aren't inclined to listen to anyone who doesn't speak fluent business talk.

But the marketplace today (and tomorrow) is full of activism. No business can afford to go on ignoring that. Technology is so innovative and accessible that most products are made, and services delivered, by multiple companies within nearly identical quality and price ranges. To get an edge, companies have to differentiate themselves with distinct brand identities. We live in an era of relationships; modern consumers are attracted to brands that connect with their lives, values, and identities.

Kevin Roberts, the top global brand expert whom I was fortunate to meet in Cambridge, says the best way to market is to create products and experiences that have the power to foster long-term, emotional connections. Businesses wanting to make those connections need to understand that today's buyers are brand-savvy and increasingly socially conscious. We live in a society in which we have access to multiple forms of media: the five-hundred-channel universe, newspapers, and blogs, all updated by the minute. And I'm not just talking about people lucky enough to have a laptop. Free newspapers are handed out on the subway and the twenty-four-hour news station plays while you wait for the next train. We hear about issues way beyond our own borders. We want problems rectified and we want to play a part in the solution.

The Canadian Centre for Social Entrepreneurship conducted a study in 2001 called "Strengthening the Generational Chain." It interviewed Canadians between the ages of eighteen and thirty-four. The respondents want to see the creation and growth of socially responsible business. They want a socially engaged private sector. They want the private sector giving back to the communities from which it makes a profit. Those are the kinds of businesses the respondents will support (if their social commitments don't affect the cost or availability of their products).

Real social responsibility, however, involves more than just the notion of corporate social responsibility (CSR) that developed in response to the activist-led anti-globalization movement. CSR calls for fairness to employees and contributions to charities. But it can't give a soul to the soulless. A lot of times, CSR is carried out as a defensive reaction in order to appease activists—to build goodwill without really fixing any problems. It's isolated within public relations departments rather than embedded in every aspect of corporate strategy. Goods get produced exploitatively, then a percentage of the profit gets donated. In return, the corporation gets its logo on a charity's list of supporters or gets a community event named after it.

This may give off a warm and fuzzy feeling, but the hug is loose and fleeting. Slim-Fast gives money to support positive body image yet sells and markets a product promoting thinness as the ideal. Wal-Mart gave money for a breakfast program yet continued to sell products produced by child labour. Ironic, don't you think?

Respondents to the "Strengthening the Generational Chain" study expressed cynicism about companies that use social issues as a marketing tool without also making a genuine commitment to improve society. A majority of respondents said they wouldn't support organizations that offer band-aid efforts to social problems. The damage control mindset of CSR blinds managers—to doing real social good and to the corporate benefits of doing social good.

Previously, the socially driven had few options: they could join the Peace Corps, do volunteer work, work for a non-profit, or enter the public service (or politics). They had the satisfaction of contributing, but at a likely loss of income. And for the most part they were outside an arena where important social changes get initiated: business. But people with altruistic motives can now choose to be on the inside, making decisions that lead to change while still making money.

My understanding that business can do well and do good came to me intuitively—seeing the impact of my own business on friends and the public. It also took shape intellectually, through my joint major in women's studies and business. My feminist profs had a thorough understanding of society, while their counterparts in business had access to the tools that best affect change. The two fields obviously needed to be bridged.

THE BALANCED CONTRACT

I call the bridge that links social thinkers with business minds the Balanced Contract. The Balanced Contract calls for a profit-driven yet socially oriented entrepreneurial model, for a business that incorporates socially responsible practices into the delivery of services, production of goods, and day-to-day operations. The Balanced Contract recognizes that while making a profit is the rightful goal of business, creating a better world is a rightful end. The Balanced Contract is a moral agreement between entrepreneurs and society. In exchange for profit, the business venture will provide products and services to help resolve a social problem.

Three factors combine to make the Balanced Contract relevant and feasible:

1. Social Issues Influence Purchase Choices
    Social issues aren't a barrier to the bottom line; instead they can drive it. Granted, most consumers make their purchases on a simple need-to-get-it-done basis, but a growing number are insisting that companies embed socially responsible intentions into their operations. These consumers won't compromise on quality but they will go out of their way to support firms that operate with integrity.

2. Business Can Be a Vehicle for Social Change
    Governments and social agencies have a key role to play in making the world better. But most administrations operate on limited funds according to competing priorities; they can't and shouldn't be doing everything. Hybrid businesses, with both for-profit and not-for-profit initiatives, offer new approaches to old problems. Dove's Real Beauty campaign, for instance, has stimulated a society-wide dialogue on the perception of beauty. As I travel around the world, I hear a lot more people saying, "Wow, those Dove ads are great" than "Hey, that pamphlet from the health department really got me thinking."

3. Young People Are in a Great Position to Initiate the
   Balanced Contract

My generation is inclined to make contributions in ways that fall outside the traditional. We've grown up with multiple means of communication at our fingertips. We know that a kid working out of her basement in a small town can build a website to rival a multinational. We've grown up aware of the whole world. If there's a particular issue we're concerned about, we'll read about it in newspapers from the countries where it's taking place, from various international perspectives, and from personal blogs. Meanwhile, we've been the target of marketers since we were born. We know how marketing works. And thanks to technology providing us with communication and transactions that are immediate, we hate delay. We want things done and done now.

THE BALANCED CONTRACT GENERATION

I asked my friend Tina Wells of Buzz Marketing Group (whom you'll get to know better in the next chapter) to conduct a study especially for this book, specifically for this chapter. Were other young people ready to bridge the gap between profit and social change? Was I writing about theory or reality? Was I just living my own dream?

First, I did a review of similar studies, to get an idea of how to ask my questions. Then—with some help from Simon and a dip back into my Cambridge research methods course notes—I drafted a questionnaire. What vehicles do young people feel are best for creating social change? Which are they most inclined to participate in? I showed my survey to a business prof, I got his approval, and then Tina got it out there. She distributed the survey online in the winter of 2006 to six hundred people between the ages of eighteen and twenty-five, in the U.S., U.K., and Finland.

It took four months to get the results. Remember the part about how much our generation hates to wait for things? Basically, I was finding out if I had any street cred at all or was twisted up in Cambridge ivy. Finally, in April, Tina emailed me: "You're no alien on Mars...LOL...you're right on, Ben."

Eighteen per cent of the survey respondents thought that public protests and demonstrations were an "effective means of achieving social change" and would choose those methods to advance their own causes. Meanwhile, more than 50 per cent thought that starting their own business venture would be an effective means of achieving social change. Clearly, my generation is open to and for a new way of business. I'm not the only one who's about sector blending.

Meanwhile, the "Strengthening the Generational Chain" study performed in Canada further proved my point—that young people want to contribute to society the Balanced Contract way. The majority who answered said that they want to be more socially and civically active but feel frustrated by constraints in the voluntary sector (they find decision making slow and use of volunteer time inefficient). They're interested in politics but think mainstream political parties are ineffective in creating change. Most want to be involved with organizations that combine social and economic goals. They're very receptive to blurring the traditional boundaries between public, private, and voluntary.

The Balanced Contract was a global movement. I was so not alone.

THINKING AGAIN

The Balanced Contract takes some rethinking on everyone's part. No one likes to have to pull a 180. I have activist friends who take part in protests as regularly as fashion editors shop for shoes. We get into, ahem, heated debates about the Balanced Contract. They think business is inherently oppressive because it's driven by profit. The way they put it, profit motivation is an evil force and nothing will ever happen to change that. They just assume that since profit is the bottom line of business, its efforts to better society are always limited.

But when you think about it, we all have bottom lines. Politicians want to win elections. Professors want to get tenure. Students want to pass. Well, politicians can win elections by proposing fair policies. Professors can get tenure by conducting research that advances social good. Students can pass by being honest. Businesses can make a profit by doing good. There's more than one route to a bottom line.

So then my activist friends say businesses that do good appropriate activist ideas and turn them into market opportunities. Yes, they do. But what's the point of developing theories of objectification and the sexual gaze if they're used only as answers to exam questions?

My business friends need to think again as well. Corporations need to remind themselves that consumers are their real bosses. Maybe a company has a massive worth, a huge headquarters, and a fleet of jets. But it may well be customers who take the subway and rent studio apartments that keep the company in business. Yes, businesses are on a path toward profit, but consumers operate the traffic signals, voting with their shopping carts. Those consumers have concerns, some of them personal, some of them social. It's only good business to pay attention to the things that really matter to people.

I work toward getting the fashion industry to rethink its traditional models. With vision and ingenuity, other young entrepreneurs are getting industries and activists to rethink other mantras. Eventually, anyone who resists the Balanced Contract is going to look pretty outdated.

Really, none of us can do enough rethinking.

CHAPTER FOURTEEN

CUTTING-EDGE DESIGNERS

YOUNG ENTREPRENEURS FOLLOWING THE BALANCED CONTRACT

THE YOUNG ENTREPRENEURS TO whom I'm about to introduce you all have something in common. Some dropped out of school to focus on their companies, others kept studying. Some operate local businesses, others have gone global. But they're all creative, intelligent, and diligent. And they're all determined to use business as a vehicle for social change.

Many of them epitomize an approach that a lot of protesters ignore and that Naomi Klein missed in *No Logo*. They're addressing issues that are usually taken up by protesters, but they're not on the sidelines throwing stones at some big scary monster called "capitalism." They're inside the system. They're tackling social issues as businesspeople.

There are a lot more problems in the world than non-profits can tackle. Some of the business owners you'll read about in this chapter apply themselves to issues not typically seen as social causes. To me, a social issue is anything that has an impact on our lives as citizens—local or global citizens. Taking any steps at all toward solving these issues is going to make the world better, point blank. More equitable, just, and sustainable.

Meet the problems—meet the problem solvers.

THE MEDIA MAKER

"It's another crazy day," explains twenty-six-year-old Ben Goldhirsh, in his trademark khakis and button-down, today some stubble, and trainers that look like they've seen hard times on a court. Something tells me this is a guy whose just-got-out-of-bed hair has nothing to do with product. Especially when I hear about his schedule.

"I get caught up with so much in terms of running the business day to day that it's hard to find time to get my work done," Ben admits. "I usually read and write at home starting at 7 a.m. until about nine, but this morning I had to go to the animal hospital at six to see my dog. He got bitten by a rattlesnake last night. He's in some serious pain." Ben then headed to work in West Hollywood to start his business day. "At 9 a.m., I had to follow up on a meeting I had in New York last week with MTV. I had lunch at eleven with a movie financier. He did *Crash*. At noon, I had my interview with you," he says laughing.

"Worst part of the day," I say.

"Just terrible," he says laughing. "No, no, it's cool, man," he covers. "I like to share what I'm doing. Let me check my schedule for this afternoon." Ben takes a second to scroll down his BlackBerry. "At 3 p.m. I have a meeting with Worldchanging.com, and then one with a reality-show producer. I have a dinner with the Foundation for Teaching Entrepreneurship and then I'm back at the vet by about 9 p.m. to visit my dog. After that, I hope I'll be able to get in a few more hours of reading and writing without interruption." He takes a long breath.

Jam-packed eighteen-hour days are routine for the founder and CEO of Reason Pictures and *Good* magazine–his two-year-old media empire. "I thought the media was dominating social change," Ben says. "But there was a hole in terms of meaningful content. So much of that is locked in classrooms and books that aren't available to a larger market. I became frustrated."

In 2005, Ben decided to put his frustration to an end and found Reason Pictures. Reason currently has six projects in production. "We make films that have a commercial element to put people in the theatre, but content that gets them to really think," Ben specifies.

Bernard Goldhirsh, Ben's dad, was the founder and CEO of *Inc.* magazine. Bernard grew up in a tiny Brooklyn apartment, intent on becoming a scientist. In his free time he started a sailing newsletter driven by his passion for the sport, which grew into *Sail* magazine, and he sold it for $10 million in 1980. Bernard invested most of the proceeds in a new magazine called *Inc.*—for and about entrepreneurs. In 2004, he sold *Inc.* for $200 million. "My dad was a big head on a little body," says Ben of five-foot-five-inch Bernard. "But I never saw him stand up on his toes."

Even though Bernard was a millionaire, he hated to watch his kids grow up in a privileged environment. He gave Ben hardly any spending money. But he wasn't hypocritical; he bought his own clothing at a discount and ate at diners. "My dad really taught me about investing," Ben recalls. "I learned how to take money from one company and put it into another, instead of spending it on expensive disposable things."

Ben's teenage life was turned upside down. While he was a junior in high school, his mother was diagnosed with stomach cancer and passed on in eight months. A little over a year later, during his first year at Brown University, Ben found out his father had brain cancer. Bernard had lessons he badly wanted to teach his son before it was too late. He told Ben about his failed investments over the years and why they'd run aground. He had Ben come along to meetings with his lawyers, financial advisers, and business colleagues. When Bernard became too ill to run *Inc.*, he suggested that Ben take over. "The idea of *inheriting* a magazine about entrepreneurship seemed pretty hypocritical," Ben remembers. "How could I defend it in my editor's letter?" His answer to his father was simple, "I couldn't do it. It was his thing, not mine."

Bernard gave away $20 million from the sale of *Inc.* to his employees (he made Ben listen to every grateful voicemail). He gave some to a foundation, to support charities and research. He gave the rest to Ben and his sister. Ben would be allowed to access the cash to start companies or make investments, but he would have to make a pitch to a board of his father's close friends and financial advisers in order to do so.

After his dad died, Ben moved from Boston to Los Angeles to enrol in the film and television program at the University of Southern California (USC). Since Brown, he'd thought about making movies that ask hard questions about society without missing out on any of the sex, comedy, and action that make movies fun. Now he was finally studying production. But he dropped out after only one semester. "I was dealing with lots of stuff because of my dad's death...I couldn't balance it all." And Ben found film school frustrating. He wanted to go out and make movies, not just read about how to do it: "I was fortunate. I could afford the opportunity to learn through action."

Ben inherited the cash he needed to get started and keep going, but he's still faced his fair share of challenges, decisions, and setbacks. Starting up wasn't simply a matter of sticking a bank card into an ATM. Like most entrepreneurs, Ben had to write a business plan and, in his case, sell his venture to his trustees. "They wanted to see a sensible business plan. I'd never written one before. I had lots of learning to do."

Once Ben dropped out of USC, he hired a classmate and began reviewing scripts. They read hundreds of pitches, plot summaries, and drafts, but none of them were delving into the issues that mattered; fourteen-hour days of reading and rereading—but nothing. One night Ben was at home organizing some old papers. He found a political science essay on globalization he'd written at Brown. Inspiration struck. He commissioned a film based on his term paper. With that, production started on *The World 2006*.

"We use soccer as a platform to look at what's going on in the world. We follow six stories in six countries. Each story is emblematic of an issue in that country, and relevant to what's going on in the world, and they all revolve around the World Cup tournament. It's kind of like a state of the world address using soccer. Here's a set of rules for a game that's endorsed or adhered to all around the world, right? Things are so divisive, and you wonder if it's possible to find some kind of common denominator of values. Soccer turned out to be a nice example."

Ben likes to consult with the academic community in order to refine his themes. For *World 2006*, he sat down and made a list of the major theoretical issues that he wanted to examine—the exportation of Western culture, the tension between Islam and the West, developing nations and developing markets, the emergence of a superpower, America's relationship with the international community, and the environment.

"Certainly, we have an agenda to instigate change but that doesn't land us on one side or the other in a partisan debate. Our goal is to pose interesting questions but we don't want to give any answers. I want our movies to be made for people who want to go see a good movie. And then make them care."

Americas, another Reason Pictures project, is definitely a case in point. It's about a Salvadorian gang near Los Angeles. According to Ben, "At face value it's a kick-ass gang movie, but it allows us to look at the issues of the Latino population in America, to look at the issues of border policy, of immigration. All these issues that are on the periphery of public debate but are heading toward the forefront."

Ben also works within the communities affected by the issues he documents. For *Americas,* they reached out to an organization at work in gang-heavy neighbourhoods: "They were skeptical of us at first. They were like 'Hollywood has basically screwed us every time they've ever done a movie about any sort of gang activity. We don't want to help.' And I was like, 'Well, if you don't help, I'm just going to fail and everyone loses again.' I'd said I'd help their organization at a financial level if I believed in what they were doing. Maybe then they would teach us how to tell their story."

Ben, his writer, and his director spent a month in East L.A. "It's a different world. The people there have never been to the beach. They've never been to Beverly Hills. The lack of a transportation system just keeps these communities so isolated."

Ben is making exactly the kind of films he wants to, but it can take years for a movie to evolve from idea to production to screen. His big dream lacked traction; he'd wanted to create continuous, not sporadic, dialogue. Instead of backtracking, Ben decided to fast-forward. He widened his reach by founding a magazine called *Good.*

Ben asked his college roommate and his best friend from high school to act as *Good's* editors. He hired a designer and some young writers. Launched in September 2006, *Good* is about moving things forward—renewable energy, organic food, sweatshop-free fashion, politics, socially responsible businesses, and green living. As Ben puts it, "like what *Wired* did for technology, taking it from the esoteric and nerdy and giving it pop and sex, we're trying to do for goodness. Rebrand it, take it from the fringe, make it more in your face. Like, *good is where it's at.*"

By September 2006, *Good* had raised $122,860 from 6,143 subscribers. But Ben's not keeping the cash. Instead, he's created an innovative subscription policy whereby all the fees go to one of twelve non-profits (the subscriber gets to choose which). These include Ashoka, which gives micro-grants to promote social entrepreneurs around the world, the World Wildlife Fund, and UNICEF. The goal is to have fifty thousand subscribers supplying $1 million by mid-2007.

Ben says his subscription policy is good business—allowing him to build a solid and committed list of subscribers. The money most magazines make from subscriptions and newsstand sales is actually negligible compared to advertising revenues. But by seeding more and more subscribers, a magazine can then charge more and more to advertisers. Traditionally, magazines attract new subscribers by sending out junk mail to people who might have some interest. Ben likes his tactic more: "No one responds to unsolicited mail, especially not our generation. So we decided to partner with organizations that our consumers respect. This way, we can activate their mailing lists—which we could never have afforded to purchase—through their newsletters and websites. If this works, we'll actually spend less than half of what it traditionally costs to acquire subscribers."

Ben's headquarters is in a small, two-storey building. The main floor is home to Reason, upstairs is *Good.* Twenty staff members buzz around in what might well be beach gear. Normally, Ben's dog is mooching and woofing around, too. "The only thing that matters at the office is that everyone believes, cares, and works their ass off to actualize our potential," Ben tells me.

"How old is your staff?" I ask Ben.

"All under twenty-nine. No, wait a minute." He yells out, "Matt, how old are you?" A voice yells back. "Okay, so, twenty-nine is the oldest. This whole thing is an experiment," he says. "What happens when a bunch of kids with money behind them bring their ideas to life? Every day we find out."

Ben's first film will hit the film-festival circuit next year and *Good*'s first issue is racking up raves. Starting a business is a hustle for anyone, Ben included: "There's a huge difference between how easy you think it's going to be, when you're just knocking everyone else, and when you're actually doing it yourself. But we have the confidence of the ignorant. I guess it just makes things that much more exciting."

THE PAID VOLUNTEER

"I'm five foot two and look like a seventeen-year-old," says Ceilidh McClurg, CEO of Extend Communications. She has a radiant smile, big blue eyes, long blonde hair, and a company that gets hired by businesses and agencies to assist with community development projects. "Even today, after five years in business, people still assume that I don't know what I'm talking about."

One director of marketing at a tech company was particularly obnoxious— doubting aloud whether Ceilidh could pull off the job she'd been assigned. He was angry that his boss had outsourced his project and to such a young woman at that. Ceilidh worked her butt off and put together a fantastic trade show booth that highlighted the tech company's impact on the local community. When it was all over, the guy took her out for lunch. He said, "I'm a jackass."

"What do you mean?" Ceilidh asked.

"I wouldn't give you the benefit of the doubt and I almost worked to prove myself right but you overcame that."

He ended up hiring Ceilidh for more work.

Ceilidh began Extend Communications at twenty-three years old. "I can't believe how lucky I am," she says. "I always loved organizing events for charities, but couldn't ever give it as much time as I wanted since I had to go back to my day job. Now I've just finished putting together an event for Raising the Roof, an organization that fights homelessness. We brought on board Direct Energy and the Royal Bank Financial Group as sponsors. My company got paid to coordinate and promote the whole thing. How crazy is that?"

Ceilidh's path to entrepreneurship was filled with seemingly odd zigzags. She ended up in places where she didn't expect to, but in retrospect every step was in sync with her abiding interests. After graduating from the Southern Alberta Institute of Technology, Ceilidh had hopes of becoming a journalist. "I wanted to teach people about what was happening in their communities, to expose problems that people didn't know existed," she says. She worked on a short-term contract at the *Calgary Herald* before a long, bitter strike put her out of work. Then she edited two small-town newspapers north of Calgary for a while, but quickly realized that journalism would either be freelance and financially unstable, or full-time/twenty-four hours a day.

Ceilidh figured that journalists know something about communications so she took a job in the communications department of a Calgary high-tech firm. Unfortunately, that was in the middle of the dot-bomb, the high-tech industry crash: "At 9 a.m. I had a job and was assured it was safe and by 11:00 a.m. I was unemployed," Ceilidh recalls.

With no jobs to be found in her field, Ceilidh knew it was time to take a chance on a business plan that she'd had in the back of her mind for a while. Her idea was to run trade show booths on a consultancy basis. She took advantage of a self-employment program to finish her business plan and then pulled in a loan for just under $15,000 from the Canadian Youth Business Foundation. She started Extend Communications to help firms prepare and coordinate their booths at trade shows. Although it was a good idea, and she had experience in the field, it turned out to be unfortunately timed.

Just as Ceilidh was getting her new business underway, the events and aftermath of September 11, 2001, sideswiped the entire trade-show industry. She needed to shift her focus fast if her company was going to make it. "If you're going to be an entrepreneur, you had better be adaptive," she says. And Ceilidh was determined to remain an entrepreneur, free from the "politics and bs" her friends were experiencing in large companies.

In the end, Ceilidh found her best idea through networking. One evening, she grudgingly attended a gala for the Canadian Youth Business Foundation. "My friend who was going had an extra ticket and dragged me along, kicking and screaming," Ceilidh marvels. Despite fine food and getting all dolled up, she wasn't in the best of moods. "I didn't know anyone else going and I wasn't feeling too confident since my business was going through tough times. I didn't know if I'd stay afloat or go under the next day," she remembers.

That was the night that Ceilidh met Dick Wilson, an adviser to the president of EnCana, one of North America's leading independent oil and gas companies. Because Ceilidh didn't know much about Dick, she was simply herself, chatting without being pushy. The two clicked and Dick soon came to visit Extend's tiny, shared office (in an industrial area) wanting to learn more about the business. After Ceilidh and her team had finished their explanation, Dick asked, "In your ideal world, what could I do to help?"

"Give us our first big job to use as a flagship. And help us to find mentors," Ceilidh said.

And that's what he did.

Impressed by the fact that Extend's employees were willing to roll up their sleeves and do community work, Dick handed the company a contract worth nearly $500,000 to develop what became "The Battle of the Border." EnCana was sponsoring Canadian female Olympic hockey players and wanted to leverage that into a profile-boosting community-oriented package. Extend arranged a series of six hockey matches, in small Western cities, between the Canadian players and top U.S. Olympians. The admission price was $10, which EnCana matched; the proceeds were turned over to local community groups working on women's issues or family concerns. Extend handled everything from publicity and logistics to ticket sales and sponsor relations. The event raised $101,299 in six communities across Saskatchewan, Alberta, and British Columbia.

Dick was so pleased with Ceilidh's work that he introduced her to other clients. She was able to fully transform Extend into a company that can help firms build up their profile in communities in Alberta and other Western provinces. Extend then bolsters that service by providing strategic counsel on the implementation of all the resulting events and programs. As Dick explains on Ceilidh's website, "Extend Marketing has found a niche in bringing the corporate and non-profit sectors together in a way that is mutually beneficial in support of the communities in which they operate."

Now Ceilidh always attends schmoozy events, no matter what mood she's in: "You never know who you're going to meet. Each person could be a new client. Network, network, network. I know it sounds like a cliché but it works," she says.

"The office is pure excitement right now," Ceilidh tells me. Extend is growing fast. In eighteen months, it doubled in size and revenues increased by more than 300 per cent. In one year, the Extend team moved offices three times to accommodate their growth, and finally moved into a custom-designed space for its seven staff and growing. In 2005, Extend won the Canadian Youth Business Foundation Business Award Winner in Alberta and Ceilidh represented Canada at the APEC Women in the Digital Economy Conference held in Seoul, Korea.

"On any given day I might be in the office of a VP of the one of the largest organizations in Canada," Ceilidh enthuses, "strategizing a community investment program. Or then again I might be putting together shelves or installing a dishwasher in our office. Ah, the life of an entrepreneur!"

Extend donates 1 per cent of its pre-tax profit back into the community by giving financially and also contributing time. "I love what I'm doing," Ceilidh says. "I always volunteered, but felt frustrated by how little cash there was. We needed to make cut after cut because there was never enough money. But now that I get companies to help with the budgets, we can actually realize great ideas and create projects that have a big and positive impact." Volunteering taught her how to bring people together and now she's using that skill in business: "It's good business for my clients, for the community, and for me."

Ceilidh knew to take on partners when she lacked experience and skill. "Don't be afraid to partner with people smarter than you," she insists. "Entrepreneurs like to be the person who knows everything. But you can't be territorial." Ceilidh knew she was strong when it came to event planning and dealing with people, but recognized that she was weak with finances and went looking for a money wiz. "I gladly leave those responsibilities to him," she says.

Ceilidh also finds mentors very helpful. She developed a team of advisers and calls on them for help not just at regular meetings, but whenever she's stuck. Late one night, her team was considering whether to move into a new office. They found themselves thinking in circles; should they get a space that they could grow into or a space that was okay for now but would probably be too small in a less than a year? Ceilidh picked up the phone—despite the fact it was 10:30 p.m.—and called one of her mentors, who immediately gave her a formula that solved the problem; get the space that is the right size for now but have a clause in the lease in which you have the option to expand within the same building within that year. "It was a decision made," she says.

Ceilidh credits her success with not being afraid to ask for what she needs. "Be intelligent enough to ask the stupid question," she insists. And in some cases you have to ask for what you want without an obvious invitation. "The worst thing that can happen is that someone will say no." Ceilidh has another great strength: she knows how to take no for an answer and move on. But she prefers yes.

THE FAST-FOOD REVOLUTIONARY

It's 12:30 p.m. and I'm starving. I have a meeting in thirty minutes at an ad agency. I want a quick lunch but the scene at McDonald's isn't inviting (major trans-fats.) A few storefronts along, I come to Lettuce Eatery. There's a long line but it seems to be moving quickly. The store colours are neutral white and soft green but the serving bar is a painter's palette of bright fruit and veg.

There are four kinds of lettuce: romaine, mesclun mix, iceberg, and spinach. Name a vegetable and it's in front fresh and diced: from asparagus to sun-dried tomatoes. There are chickpeas and mandarin oranges and red bliss potatoes. There are six types of cheese plus egg whites, grilled tofu, shrimp, steak, three types of chicken, and two kinds of tuna. There are toppings ranging from croutons to dried cranberries to toasted almonds to crispy noodles. And there are twenty different dressings: classic, light, and exotic.

I'm totally overwhelmed and it's already my turn to order. I opt for a chef special, the Protein Salad, and am whisked toward the cash. Before me is a guy with sandy blond hair and bright blue eyes. It's Matthew Corrin, the twenty-five-year-old owner and founder of Lettuce Eatery. He's stuffing clear take-out bags with clear salad containers, drinks, and napkins. He says a cheery hello, but his hands don't stop. I compliment him on the packaging. He responds, "Clear bowl, clear bag, clear conscience."

Matthew is changing what it means to get fast food. In less than two years, he's expanded his hip made-to-order salad, soup, and sandwich concept to four downtown locations, all on prime pieces of Toronto real estate. The first opened in January 2005 in the food court beneath the fifty-two-floor TD Bank Tower. Nine months later, the second opened in the middle of the advertising district. The third and fourth followed, the former in between fashionable shops and the latter back in the financial district. Matthew is serving salads for about $8 a pop to hungry salespeople, managers, and number crunchers who'd rather treat themselves to a few strips of chicken on spinach than a super-sized carton of fries.

But Matthew hasn't always been a fast-food revolutionary. In fact, three years ago he knew nothing at all about working in the food industry. He was born and raised in Winnipeg where he carried off his first entrepreneurial venture at the age of fifteen: compiling, printing, and selling a province-wide guide to Manitoba hockey rinks. The guide sold two thousand copies and won him an enterprise award from his high school. After high school, he moved to London, Ontario, to complete a bachelor of arts in media studies at the University of Western Ontario. During summer break, he worked in New York City as a runner for the *Late Show with David Letterman*. ("I got there during Dave's extra-reclusive phase, post-bypass and pre-fatherhood. My duty was to hold the door for him every day as he went from his dressing room to the stage. That was my number one priority for the summer. Open the door, watch Dave run out and then close it. Imagine trying to write an essay on that for course credit.")

The following summer, Matthew worked in the marketing department at the Oscar de la Renta fashion house and went back full-time after graduation. Manhattan inspired the Winnipegger. During his two-year stint at de la Renta, he'd lunch with his stylish colleagues on gorgeous custom-made salads, the fashion take-out indulgence of choice. "I was eating these incredible salads every day for lunch and loving them," Matthew says. "Growing up, I played hockey, like any other good Canadian boy, plus tennis and soccer. My mother owned a gym and my father ran marathons. We pretty well lived and breathed healthy." Matthew stuck to it as he grew up. But while he had no problem finding fast nutritious food in New York, he had a tougher time doing so back home: "In Winnipeg, we just don't have that alternative. You go to a food court and the majority of options are deep-fried. It's tough to find something healthy when you're in a rush. I wanted to provide that."

So Matthew decided to bring a healthy taste of Manhattan home to a Canadian city similar enough to New York to make it work. "Toronto isn't so different. Maybe it's a bit more price sensitive and there are fewer people, but rent and labour costs are lower," he says. "I knew that in New York the concept was successful in the financial, fashion, and advertising districts so I tried to mimic that."

Matthew would do one thing differently from his New York counterparts. His concept would be branded: "Fashion taught me how important branding is, the creating, fine-tuning, and protecting of the image. Branding is the only way to create a business making salads that has real growth potential and can drive off competitors."

"I researched every bustling Manhattan salad restaurant I could," Matthew recalls. "I watched how everything was done. What was their demographic? How fast were they getting people through the line? I learned about it all through the eyes of a customer. I considered what I liked and didn't like, what worked and failed and how comfortable I was with the price and speed of service."

Every Saturday afternoon for six months Matthew sat in a Starbucks with his laptop working on his business plan. He Googled sample plans and copied the template: "Once I saw a few and developed my own ideas, filling in the blanks was pretty easy."

Armed with his own business plan, his next step was to present it to potential investors and get funding to make it happen. "I didn't have money to invest myself but I had ideas and sweat to offer." Over the next two months, he made successful pitches to four private investors (whom he declines to name) and raised about $250,000 to start his business.

Matthew credits his first location as a critical factor in Lettuce Eatery's success. He got space in the food court of a posh tower in the heart of the financial district. It turned out to be a great business development opportunity. "I met so many contacts by being in a building where top businesses work. They became our consumers. In the first six months, I had four buyout offers, five partnership offers, and two offers to take the firm public," he laughs. "I was flattered but this was my business and I wasn't going to give it up."

Matthew learned a lot during his first few months. "I was negotiating the lease for the first location before I even knew what should be in a lease. I totally winged it. But after it was signed and done, the property management company told me that he had never had such a tough negotiation. I paid attention to every little detail." Matthew also had to learn at lot about money. "The very first day, after we closed I called my mother and said, 'Mom, we did $1,000 in sales today.' She said, 'Is that good?' I said, 'I have no idea!'"

Matthew learned quickly. After only six months of business, he was awarded the annual ARC award for achievement in new retail concepts by Cadillac Fairview, his building's property management company. Lettuce Eatery beat out its food court neighbour Hero Certified Burgers and clothing retailer H&M. When it came time to open the Bloor Street location nine months later, Matthew says, "We'd already recouped our initial investment and didn't have to go for a second round of investment."

Matthew is not only making money, he's also doing good—by helping people to make healthy meal choices. And it couldn't come at a better time. As the burger and fries backlash gains momentum, customers are looking for some wholesome crunch to counter skyrocketing obesity rates. One Lettuce Eatery regular lost nineteen pounds in three months. He wrote this to Matthew:

> I am not prone to writing letters to companies, particularly those in the fast-food service business. Usually an extra thank you with a smile on the way out would be how I would compliment this type of food experience. However, my experience with your product offering is uniquely different and deserves a letter. In short, you have helped me meet the most important personal goal that one can have . . . personal health. Since your operation opened, it has allowed me the opportunity to introduce a truly healthy daily diet. One that I have been religious in maintaining. So much so that I now have your menu taped to my fridge in order that my dinners have the same element of healthy eating. To date I have lost 19 of my 21-pound goal and have been motivated to increase my level of exercise as well.
>
> I know your reason to start the Lettuce Eatery was to create a business and make money. Well, I'm sure that will happen, but I wanted you to know that it did more than that to one individual's life.
>
> Thanks for providing such a great lunch experience.
> Sincerely,
> A Lettuce Fan

Making a positive impact in people's lives has helped build loyalty for the Lettuce Eatery brand. But Matthew also takes responsibility for his suppliers. Every morning, deliveries arrive from the nearby St. Lawrence Market, locally sourced whenever possible.

"I live and breathe this business," Matthew admits. Helping matters is the fact that his wife, Kate, is also part of Lettuce. "Before we were married," he explains, "I asked and asked and asked her to work with me and she kept saying no. Then I asked her to marry me and she said yes. And then when I asked her again to work with me she finally said yes to that too." Kate launched the Lettuce Eatery catering division. Office workers can now order wraps and fruit platters en masse.

I know from working with Mom that working with family can be challenging. Matthew says it's panned out well for him and Kate because they don't work directly together. "But we don't have any policies about when we can and when we can't talk about business," he admits. "Sometimes we wake up at 3 a.m. in bed and talk business, other times we're on treadmill and talk about it. But any time one of us wants to take a break, all we have to do is say so," he tells me. "Which maybe happens for five minutes every two weeks, or for the one hour we're watching *Desperate Housewives!*" Matthew does maintain a healthy balanced lifestyle to whatever degree he can: "I always make time to work out, no matter what. It keeps me in shape and it's a great way to get rid of stress," he says. "I never set up a workout schedule. I just make a point of going to the gym every day. I know that once in a while I'll have to miss one or two days and if I do, it's cool."

Matthew has his business challenges. "Staffing is the toughest part of my job," he says. "Especially since my industry is based on minimum wage, part-time labour so there's typically a high turnover rate." He's tried to overcome this challenge by motivating his staff—promoting from within, getting staff involved in decision making and establishing a bonus system. "Staffing is one of the most time-consuming tasks," Matthew warns. "But if your staff isn't happy and excited there's no way that your customer will be either, which means they won't be back." Matthew isn't involved in day-to-day operations anymore, he focuses more on expansion, but he still does all the hiring and staff management.

Matthew's goal is to remain the primary Lettuce Eatery corporate share-holder for as long as possible and to grow the business quickly. Any slowdowns could embolden competitors; as it is, he's already filed a few lawsuits against copycats. Matthew is also currently in talks with several interested parties who want to help with his expansion. He says he wants to pull "a Starbucks" with Lettuce Eatery and open numerous locations in every major Canadian and American city.

At this point, Matthew's reminisces almost fondly about his first week in business. On the third day he was open, he arrived at 6 a.m. to oversee the prep staff getting ready for lunch. But as soon as they got down to work chopping veggies, one cut himself and the other fainted at the sight of the blood, then fell and banged his head. Both were rushed to the hospital. Matthew was left alone at 6:30 a.m. with bushels of produce, six crates of lettuce, and thirty-six kilos of spinach. "I called Kate and said I was going to stay dark.' She was like, 'No way, I'm on my way,'" he recalls. "I realized then that this isn't rocket science. It's hard work. And if I could get through this crisis, I could get through anything. Nothing was going to stop me. I knew that if I failed, it wasn't going to be because I hadn't worked hard. I do work hard. Every day."

THE ENVIRONMENTAL ENGINEER

It's late afternoon in November 2005. Outside the window of Ben Voss's office, the farm fields have been sunburned orange and yellow. The wind tears through the fields, rustling and crackling. Ben leans back in his chair, feeling comfortable. He picks up a newly signed contract he wants to review. His phone rings.

It's a headhunter—wondering if the young entrepreneur would consider giving up his environmental company for a higher cause: helping other Saskatchewan entrepreneurs make their dreams come true?

It's one of the toughest decisions of Ben's life. For any entrepreneur, giving up the company is like giving up a loved one. He's spent seven years making mistakes and learning from them, so he knows he has a lot of first-hand experience to provide to people starting up new ventures. He runs his hand through his thick, black, curly hair and tucks his white dress shirt back into his blue jeans. He tells the headhunter he needs a day to think things over.

Ben is a true farm boy, born and raised on a cattle and grain farm in Spiritwood, Saskatchewan. His dad also ran a machine shop. Young Ben loved helping his dad fix and build things. But he never saw a career as an entrepreneur, let alone a social one. "Through most of my childhood, I was planning on becoming a farmer," he says laughing. "I had no idea what being an entrepreneur was even about. I don't even think I'd heard the word growing up." After high school he studied engineering at the nearby University of Saskatchewan, inspired by an engineer uncle. Ben went to school and he stuck to the farm, continuing to help out.

He became a front-line worker—or as he calls it a "soldier engineer." He was well paid but otherwise not very happy. "When you're in a large organization and have a lot of ideas, the bureaucracy stifles it and you can't take it forward. In most large companies the culture is: 'How can a young person who has been here only a few months have good ideas we didn't think of?'"

So Ben decided to put happiness ahead of money and went back to university. Not that he hadn't developed a passion for business; he couldn't get the adrenalin that comes with corporate life out of his system. He missed not only the action but the pace. He decided to include commerce courses in his curriculum: marketing, finance, and business planning to help lift his business off the ground. He was the first engineering student to take those classes, which meant getting special approval from the dean and carrying a load of nine courses. At the same time, he decided to set up his own engineering consulting firm.

Ben's focus on products, finance, and analysis didn't prepare him for the human-relations aspect of management. "Looking back, I didn't know enough about the business of business, about how to attract people and manage people. Business is 80 per cent dealing with people and only 20 per cent products." Ben's venture, called Ben-Don Innovations (BDI), was an engineering firm that carried out new product development for large firms in the farming industry. Companies that had an idea could contract BDI to turn a proposal into a workable product. Ben expanded the firm into a staff of ten and, for example, designed a complete line of grain-handling machinery that is being

distributed in Canada and the U.S. He also designed a harvesting and process-
ing machine for the medicinal-plant industry.

After a business trip to Europe, however, Ben switched his focus. He became
fascinated with new environmental technologies that clean up farm waste and
convert it into usable products. He decided to hand the consulting firm over to
his partner and start up a new business based on green technology.

Clear-Green Environmental Inc. develops products that convert organic
waste material from large livestock operations and meatpacking plants, such
as pig manure, into renewable energy that can replace natural gas. Ben
explains, "Where most people view organic waste as a problem, we see an
opportunity. Bio gas and fertilizer nutrients can be extracted from organic
waste. Large slaughterhouses, for example, find it increasingly expensive and
difficult to deal with waste." Ten Clear-Green projects have already been put
into operation across Western Canada. "I find these kinds of projects satisfy-
ing. They can make a profit, aren't dependent on government subsidies, and
can exist over the long term. I want to improve the environment but I want to
do it profitably."

Recycling agricultural waste isn't a new concept, but there was no market
for those kinds of products until recently. "In Canada, the missing link has
always been environmental pressure." Ben explains. "Until about five years
ago, there wasn't much value in something environmentally friendly because
the status quo was cheaper. But now that the status quo is getting expensive,
we provide a very competitive alternative." Ben says that too many companies
were selling environmentally friendly technology without training their sales
staff. "Consumers were frustrated because they weren't given any kind of guidance and support. That's another missing piece that we've tried to solve."

As Ben grew his firm, he brought mentors and advisers on board. But he
believes it's important to differentiate between the two. "You have to look
beyond your professional surroundings to find exceptionally talented and
savvy mentors whom you can level with honestly and who in turn will level
with you. There may be times when you can't open up to your accountant or
lawyer, or when their advice may be limited to their field of expertise." Ben
found individuals with a broad view of business and built an open, trusting
relationship with them. "A good mentor will give you frank advice and will

press you when you're hanging back." Ben's closest mentor was George Spark. "He had been through a bunch of businesses, experiencing all the ups and downs," Ben tells me. "I met him when I was seventeen years old. He hired me for my first job. George always said to me, 'Don't just follow the monkeys.' He wanted me to do things my own way, no matter how other people did things."

Ben also decided not to bring friends into the business. "Social relationships often don't translate well to business. The relationship falls apart when it's tested in a new environment," he says. "I went through an episode of having to lay off a bunch of friends and it was really hard to do. Our friendships were never the same after it." Now he hires people with skills that augment his own: "I've always been really good with the product development part of the business but not the accounting. So I brought in people who were great at that."

Ben believes his success has to do with his attention to relationships. "Businesses succeed through relationships, not just superior technology or better organization. And you need someone—if it's not you, because that's not your strength—to manage those relationships," he says. "Other companies will offer similar products to yours; it's trust that keeps them coming back. All business success is based on trust. Do what you say you will."

Ben also thinks a lot of his success has come by expanding his mind with travel. "You see how people do things differently. There are 450 million people in the European Union. We're thirty million in Canada. We can learn from them," he says.

Ben gets back into his office early enough the following morning to watch a red sun rise over the yellow fields. The evening had been busy: snowboard shopping, band practice, farm chores, dinner with Chris (to whom he is a Big Brother), and some much-needed sleep. Ben's made up his mind; he has an answer for the headhunter. He'll resign as CEO of Clear-Green to become CEO of the Entrepreneurial Foundation of Saskatchewan.

"A lot of companies stall, never making it out of the gates. I want to change that," he says. He's moving on from solving one social problem to solving another one. When he was twenty-three, building his first company, Ben ran into difficulty trying to raise funds from venture capitalists. "As a young person, your chances of success have an exponential figure with a negative attached," he says. Now that he's armed with a $50 million venture capital fund, he hopes to make it easier for those who follow in his footsteps. But he'll do more than just hand out money. He'll examine business plans and structures, assess management skills, and work with early-stage entrepreneurs to strengthen their chances of success.

"Eighty per cent of start-ups fail in the first five years. We want to prevent that from happening as frequently," Ben says. "Too many business plans are manipulated to satisfy the financiers' quirks or needs. I did that too. I wrote my business plan to fit what the investors wanted to hear." Ben suggests concentrating on the fundamentals of your business instead. Attract big capital afterward. "No matter how much money you raise, you're the one who'll make the business fly. You need to understand it best."

THE FOXY DESIGNERS

It's mid-afternoon in Bangkok and twenty-four-year-olds Jen Kluger and Suzie Orol are eating a late sushi lunch. Jen is wearing a bright blue tank top, a butterfly pendant hangs around her neck, and two gold diamonds dangle from her ears. Suzie's light brown hair is pushed back and she has on an army-green scoop-neck top and a pink heart necklace on a gold chain with matching heart-shaped earrings.

As they're about to dig into their dragon rolls and salmon sashimi, Jen's dark brown eyes and Suzie's bright blue ones become fixed on a commotion out on the street. People huddle at the sides of the road as an elephant lumbers past, pulled by a leash held by two men. Jen and Suzie stare at each other. Before either says a word, they grab pads and pencils from their bags and start to sketch an elephant necklace.

"It's very hard to predict what will inspire us," Suzie says, "but our eyes are always open and we're always prepared." Three months later, the Foxy Originals Monsoon Collection featuring elephant insignias is on display in jewellery cases across Canada and the U.S.

Jen and Suzie's passion for jewellery design started long before their visit to Thailand. In 1998, both women began their frosh year at the University of Western

Ontario, oblivious to each other but both with a love of jewellery. Jen had been selling her own pieces to a few Toronto stores since grade ten, after a friend wearing one of her designs went into a shop and the owner wanted to buy it. Suzie's grandfather had started a jewellery business, which her mother and step-father now run and she had worked at while growing up. Jen and Suzie had two other things in common: they were both from Toronto and both had a friend named Ryan.

The third week of school, Jen, Suzie, and Ryan all went home for the weekend. When Sunday night arrived, and it was time to make the commute back to London, Ontario, Ryan offered a lift to the others. Traffic was slow and the journey lasted longer than usual. But Jen and Suzie didn't notice. They were too busy bonding. "It was the quickest ride ever," Jen says. "We chatted non-stop. When we arrived, I felt like I'd just got in the car a minute before. Ryan couldn't get a word in edgewise." In two hours, they were instant friends and budding business partners.

Over their winter break, they designed some sample jewellery together. They started selling their stuff in dorms and in a few stores in London, Ontario. "The jewellery sold so well that stores were eager for more. It was viable to keep going," says Suzie. Still in their frosh year of university, they started up Foxy Originals. Suzie explains, "We didn't really think we were starting a full-on business at the time. We just both loved designing jewellery and other people wanted to buy it."

On campus, they became known as "The Jewellery Girls." Their dorm rooms became their showrooms. Students knocked at all hours to try on the latest necklaces and earrings. "One girl banged on my door at midnight. after a party and woke me up," Suzie says laughing. "I answered the door and she sat on my unmade bed and went through necklaces. After an hour she left with five."

They used their profits to buy supplies and employ themselves over the summer, selling their wares at summer concerts and craft festivals. They were rejected by the first craft show they tried to get into. The show traditionally didn't take jewellery vendors but Jen and Suzie wouldn't take no for an answer. They called the organizer, insisting that they were fresh and fun, and she asked them to phone back the next week. They did and scored an appointment to see her. That led to them being allowed into the show. That led to them being featured in a newspaper profile. "It's a good lesson on persistence," says Jen.

Suzie had been pre-accepted to the business program at Western, which begins in third year, and Jen had mildly considered enrolling. Even though they weren't set on continuing with the business after graduation, they both decided to enter the program, and take separate courses so they could cover the widest possible range of instruction, from taxes to sourcing.

One exception was a class on retail marketing that they both took, since it was fundamental to their operation. But they ran into a problem. They'd paid for a booth at the annual One of a Kind gift show in Toronto, the crown jewel of Canadian exhibits, and would need to miss two weeks of class to be there. But the prof was having none of that. "Business or no business, you've made a commitment to my class. You'll receive a failing grade if you miss any more than two days," he told them. Jen and Suzie thought fast. They quickly hired two friends to set up and manage the booth and shuttled between the show and school as often as possible.

Another business school prof was more understanding of the balance they were trying to strike between studying and business. He considered their efforts so exceptional that he wrote a case study on their company for other university students. One of the profs who taught the Foxy case study suggested they apply for the ACE and CIBC Student Entrepreneur of the Year Award, which they won in 2001. That was how I first met Jen and Suzie. They presented me with the same award the following year. The award garnered considerable publicity for Foxy Originals, as it did for me, and more retailers became interested in selling their jewellery.

Jen and Suzie decided to further their business knowledge by working at larger companies during the break between third and fourth year. Suzie worked in the marketing department at her family's firm, AT Designs. Jen joined the marketing department at Colgate-Palmolive, where she got to see how national brands are launched.

They returned to school in September, now as roommates, and had long discussions about the future. Their business philosophy so far had been to move methodically, step by step. But much like their time at school, this era had come to an end. They had to decide whether or not to keep the business running after graduation. Jen had the option of joining Colgate-Palmolive. Suzie was studying a semester in Prague and considering living and working abroad for a few years so she could travel, her long-time dream. But they had built this company, which was doing well, and thought maybe they should stick with it. "We had such momentum that we knew if we left and tried to come back we wouldn't get going again. We were young and energetic and needed to give it a try," says Jen.

So they decided to give Foxy Originals their combined 200 per cent. Suzie's parents let them use an empty room at the family company offices. "It was tiny," Suzie recalls to me. "There was room for just the two of us, staring across the table from each other." Jen and Suzie didn't spend a lot of time staring, however. Within a year they'd hired two sales reps and achieved full coverage in the Canadian gift store and hip boutique market. They then hired four more sales reps and expanded into the United States. They began to release a new line every six months for their target market of eighteen- to thirty-year-olds. They also started making custom jewellery for corporations and social causes. That's "taken off," according to Suzie. For example, they designed and produced the Rethink Breast Cancer Awareness necklace as well as one for all *Flare* magazine subscribers.

The Jewellery Girls are proud that they've never taken out a loan and have managed to build the company with a grand total of $900, invested by themselves. "We're very thrifty," says Suzie. "We're always thinking ahead of our business, but not spending ahead." As they grow, they think of their business as a large corporation that's only temporarily small and make policies, plans, and strategies with this big vision in mind. As Suzie says, "It's always easier to put a puzzle together when you've got the picture on the box."

"We couldn't have done our business without our families' support," Suzie tells me. "Both our parents were skeptical when we first started. My parents were probably a bit more supportive of the idea because they're both entrepreneurs. Jen's parents are both teachers, and so they were more concerned about her future when we decided to do this full-time. They wanted her to have a more stable job." But the ladies eventually had their parents convinced. "My parents let us use their fax machine, phone line," Suzie continues. "Jen's mom would sit in front of the TV and make necklaces for us." Today, their moms always get first dibs on whatever they want from the latest collection.

With so many clothing and accessory firms under attack for exploiting workers, Foxy stands out from the pack. All of its jewellery is made in Toronto by a small production team of skilled craftspeople who are paid fair wages and use materials purchased at fair prices. The Foxy products sell at a highly afford-able price point: $18 to $40. Many of the pieces are reversible so customers get extra bang for their buck. Of course, Foxy Originals are bettering the world aesthetically too, by designing some fabulous jewellery.

One defining aspect of Jen and Suzie's success has been that they did things their own way, no matter what others advised as the right way. For example, they were told by an industry professional not to invest very much in the design of their catalogue as the norm in the accessory industry is to distribute low-quality listings. They did the opposite, producing a high-quality catalogue that wowed buyers with its professional approach. "We listen to the advice of our mentors, but always remain confident to stray from it if need be," says Jen.

Jen and Suzie have also found staffing to be the most challenging aspect of running a business. Now they hire for traits, not skills. "A smart, eager person can learn most tasks but someone who is well-trained but has a negative atti-tude can't be taught to be kind and conscientious," says Jen. They've been lucky with finding some great people. "We had the two core girls who started with us up until six months ago," Suzie says. "One of them moved away and the other started her own PR company." (Foxy hired her new company to do its PR). "Two of our other employees brought in resumés from a friend. They had worked with them, trusted them, and wanted to work with them again. We ended up hiring both."

The office of Foxy Originals—still based in Suzie's parents' company but now expanded from one office space to four—is a hive of zestful activity. There are now eight staff members, in addition to Jen and Suzie, all less than twenty-seven years old. I walk over to a table displaying three necklaces. One is a blue and purple two-sided pendant, with a silhouette of tropical branches on one side and two birds chirping from a treetop on the other. Another is a black leather necklace accented with crystal stones. The last is a chandelier-inspired necklace in gold with a teardrop stone in the centre.

Jen and Suzie, Jen in jeans and a tank top and Suzie in a summer frock, both festooned in Foxy designs, sit at their desks (which still face each other) and discuss their travel plans. "We try and travel twice a year," Suzie says. "Travelling inspires our collection." Jen asks a staff member to contact the

Canadian consulate in Australia, their next destination. "We always contact the consulates before we visit anywhere. They hook us up with meetings with distributors. It saves so much time, especially since we have no idea who's who and who's good to work with in foreign countries," Jen explains.

Suzie grabs a thank-you card from the table beside her. "That reminds me," she says. "We need to get this off to the Canadian consulate in Japan. They were so helpful."

"Don't forget what mama told you," Jen says laughing. "We always send thank-you notes. It's amazing how many people don't and what a big difference it makes. When you're starting you own business, especially in the beginning, you'll have to ask many people for help and advice. If you have a question, and someone provides you with an answer, don't forget to say thank you."

Another Foxy staff member dashes into the room, "Guess what? I just found a picture of Tori Spelling wearing our stuff!"

"Cool," says Suzie. "We need to get that up on the website."

One of their main goals right now is getting their designs onto celebrities and thereby into the media. So far, they seem to be accomplishing that pretty well. Foxy fans already include Nelly Furtado, Sienna Miller, and Paris Hilton. Not to mention that *Flare*, *CosmoGIRL*, and *Fashion* feature their pieces as editor's faves. But the real acclaim is from everyday consumers. Foxy is currently sold in over 150 stores in North America and they've just hired sales reps for the U.K. and Australia.

"It's so busy right now," Suzie explains. "We have so many decisions to make and we need to make them so quickly."

"But we get a thrill from making decisions quickly," Jen jumps in. "You never know what will lead to what."

THE YOUTH EXPERT

I arrive at Tina Wells' New York office balancing a pumpkin spice latte in my left hand and a caramel macchiato in my right. Our love of Starbucks brought us together. Well, not exactly. Tina called and introduced herself after reading an article about me in *Teen People*. But our joint coffee-guzzling habit was a strong indicator that we were on the same page and set the tone for a great business friendship.

Buzz is buzzing with ringing land lines and cellphones and the chatter of people in their teens and twenties. The walls are exposed brick, and wooden beams run along the ceiling. Flat-screen monitors punctuate various work stations. One girl wears stretch skinny jeans, a jewelled tank, and purple stilettos. She's hammering away on a keyboard as she nods along to the tunes filling her headphones. A guy in baggy jeans, an oversized red hoodie, and copious bling chats intensely on the phone. "Ya, they dug the music, but not the album's wrapping," he's saying. A girl in a denim mini with black Jane Fonda workout leggings, and pink thigh-high sneaker boots huddles around a table with two other girls. They're sipping the new coffee-infused Coke and discussing an upcoming survey. "I think we need to switch up the language here," she says pointing to a list in front of her. "We need a more chilled word, one we actually use."

I spot Tina at the farthest workstation, furiously thumbing away at her BlackBerry. She has short black hair with bangs swept across her brow. She's in dark denim and a black turtleneck with killer black leather stiletto boots, legs elegantly crossed. "Ben, hey," she says, getting up to give me a big hug. I hand her a coffee, and she gives me another big hug. "I just need to finish this one email," she says. "Three questions," she says quietly to herself, as she taps out her message. Are we finished the proposal for *Essence*? When will the survey results be in for Interscope/Geffen? Am I confirmed for the marketing conference in Chicago? "Okay, done. Let go into the boardroom." We walk down the hall, swapping thoughts on a young Canadian singer whose album has just dropped in the States. Tina says the songstress is being considered as a spokesmodel for one of her clothing clients.

This morning, Tina and I are meeting to discuss a new project for a denim company that targets teens. The company wants to embark on a similar ad campaign to Dove's and use real teens as models. Tina and I work together regularly on fashion and beauty advertising concepts. She advises firms on the models and ads youth want to see; I find the models and then help develop the creative.

Tina is the twenty-six-year-old CEO of the decade-old Buzz Marketing Group (BuzzMG), a youth marketing agency that surveys teens and then advises Fortune 500 companies based on this research. She uses her in-depth knowledge of the youth market to make sure firms that reach out to youth do so effectively. That's the purest notion of marketing—a company not manipulating its customers; rather, trying to supply exactly what its customers want.

Tina is at a different stage than the other entrepreneurs I've described. After ten years of exhausting work building Buzz Marketing into a company with revenues of over $3 million, she's finally freed up time to learn French, become a Pilates instructor, head out on vacations, and take two courses per semester at the Wharton School of Business. Success took a lot of sacrifice; now it's time to correct the imbalance: "I'm in transition. I'm learning to embrace what I want, to do things for me. Too often, CEOs neglect themselves."

Growing up in New Jersey, Tina wanted to be a fashion editor. At sixteen she started writing product reviews for the *New Girl Times*, a national newspaper based in New York. She'd get free samples and rate them. It was all great fun until a marketing director confessed to Tina that her report was better than the one they'd just paid someone $25,000 to prepare. Tina realized there was a whole career out there that would earn her big bucks doing what she was already doing for free: "I didn't have a clue that people would actually pay me to tell them what I thought about their cool stuff. And I really loved having that opportunity. I felt young people should play a role in deciding how products and services are developed for them."

Tina started her company in 1996, as a high school sophomore, pitching clients and hiring friends to help with the research. She's the oldest of six so her brothers and sister were her first hires. (Some of them are still involved.) Their immediate specialty was that they knew the opinions of young people intimately because they *were* young. But Tina knew that her business had to be about more than just her friends and their ideas. She worked hard to develop a wide cross-section of teens and young adults from which to draw opinions and reactions—her BuzzSpotters.

Tina's BuzzSpotters serve as interpreters and ambassadors of youth culture. They keep Tina's clients up to date on trends in five key areas: fashion and beauty, religion and politics, music and entertainment, sports and travel, and pop culture. "I have about 150 teens on the Buzz Consultant Board and nine thousand on the Buzz Network," she says. "I feed a study to a teen who feeds it to two other teens, all peer-to-peer. It keeps the research honest. If it was me asking fifteen-year-olds about their experiences with drugs, obviously they wouldn't be as relaxed. When a peer is asking another peer, there's no reason not to be truthful."

Tina's studies don't hold back. "We hit hard issues like sex and drugs, and aren't afraid to go in front of people and say how teens feel. For instance, we went in front of the recording industry and said 99 per cent of the five hundred teens we'd talked to had downloaded music in the last thirty days and weren't going to stop. We had to tell them, 'You're going to continue to lose money.' It took guts but my job is to report the truth."

Tina does more. "Many times, clients come to us knowing that their brand is suffering, but don't know what to do about it or even what the problem is. Other times, our clients have specific problems and want specific suggestions. Our staff and teen consultants come together with the client to discuss the problem and brainstorm solutions."

Tina's ideas come alive in the Blue Room, the in-house think-tank: "Clients are often looking to create new brand extensions, give existing brands a makeover, or just looking to try something new. In the Blue Room, they communicate directly with our youth network."

The Blue Room all happens online. Clients gain access through a secure site and brainstorm with their team via email, instant messages, and message boards. It's a unique approach, different from any of Tina's competitors. She likes the way it drags clients out of their comfort zone: "I don't like a cookie-cutter approach. I like to think, and make my clients think. If you're feeling uncomfortable then I'm doing my job because the most incredible things happen that way."

Tina built up Buzz all through high school and her studies in communication at Hood College, an all-women university. Boxes of products to research piled up at her dorm room door while the hall phone rang off the hook with media wanting to talk to the teen marketing specialist. "By senior year, I was travelling to speaking engagements and client meetings every weekend. I rarely saw my friends. That was tough," Tina remembers. Countless times she had to be the first person to leave a table full of her buddies because she couldn't afford the time to linger. She needed three calendars to keep track of her schedule.

In her junior year, Tina took a detour. She moved to Chicago to form a partnership building a dot-com aimed at teenagers. It was all exciting stuff: getting in on the Internet boom, living in a Chicago high-rise, taking courses at Columbia College in the performing arts. But it was lonely. Especially because Tina started growing distrustful of her partner and her new business, which she worried was exploitive. "A lot of things weren't lining up," Tina says now. "I started looking closely at the situation and realized it wasn't good. My partner just didn't respect young people and their intelligence, and it showed. Obviously I couldn't stay." Tina made the toughest decision of her life—cutting her losses and going back to Buzz. "I went with my gut instinct," she says. "It was hard to realize I'd failed. But I've since realized that failure isn't always a bad thing. How do you know what success tastes like if you've never tasted failure?"

Today, Tina has a Manhattan office with a staff of ten. She spends three days a week working out of her New Jersey home office, twenty minutes from the family home. Her client list includes American Eagle, Aveda, Bongo, Candie's, M.A.C. Cosmetics, and Nike. Every month she publishes a Buzz report on hot upcoming trends.

Tina knows that her role could become precarious the older she gets, but board turnover and her peer-to-peer approach ensures Buzz remains sensitive to youth. She may have twenty-six-year-olds developing marketing plans, but they have to pass those plans past sixteen-year-olds—hitting the target cohort right where and when it counts.

Tina also uses Buzz to serve NGOs with marketing plans. Most recently, Buzz joined forces with Fight for Children (FFC), a Washington, D.C.–based non-profit that helps urban youth reach their full potential. Tina created a comprehensive PR and marketing campaign for FFC. She held multiple Blue Room think-tanks between investment fund partners—a seventeen-member advisory board of local-area youth—and FFC board members. Informed by those discussions, she revised the FFC website, launching "Create, Promote, Invest"—a new public service ad campaign—and a new FFC Youth Advisory Board, featuring Howie Dorough and A.J. McLean of the Backstreet Boys, plus a panel of high school students from public, private, and charter schools. The board will provide a forum for youth voices that's guaranteed to be valid.

One of Tina's greatest business lessons has been to hire great people, not to fill positions: "The tendency when hiring is to find somebody to fit a specific opening, but you can always rearrange work to accommodate someone great. You'll have a stronger overall team as a result."

Tina also believes in entrepreneurs continuing to educate themselves far and wide. "Wouldn't we all be boring if we were interested only in what we need for our job?" she asks. "Keep learning. Read the great books. Broaden yourself."

Tina can see how easy it is to be scared about being taken seriously in business because of your age. "Sure, there will be times when I walk into an appointment with older people and they're unsure whether I can help them. But as soon as I open my mouth and say something about their business that makes sense, then I'm in. They just want to solve a problem and get to the next step. If you help them, you'll be accepted," she says.

Although Tina knows a lot about her heritage, she doesn't focus on being African American: "Ever since I was very young, my parents made it their responsibility to teach us black history. I was fortunate enough to learn about great African Americans like Madame C.J. Walker and Dr. Drew. I was raised in an environment where anything was possible. My parents always told me I could achieve my dreams if I got an education. So I worked hard, and I was valedictorian of my class, and earned my degree in communications. I really don't focus on being a black woman. I just focus on being an expert youth marketer. I hope that if I do my best, people will respect my expertise. It's my philosophy that the only colour people see in business is green. Maybe it's a bit idealistic, but it's always worked for me."

Tina and I hash out notions for the print campaign across the boardroom table. We address typical jean ad conventions and how we can shake them up. I think Tina and I work so well together because we both really believe in consumers having a say in business decisions. In much the same way that I ensure that models are real representations of consumers' bodies, Tina makes certain that products and ad campaigns reflect authentic youth culture. "I expose young people to big business, empowering them to affect decisions made in boardrooms around the world. When their minds are valued, their self-confidence is developed. It's great to see."

Tina and I have to get back to work. We have a meeting with the client first thing in the morning and more concepts to flush out. But first we need more coffee.

THE COFFEE CONNOISSEUR

Whenever I'm in Ottawa, I stop for a coffee at Bridgehead. My favourite location is the one in Ottawa's historic Centretown. The front of the shop is all floor-to-ceiling windows, allowing light to radiate through the rectangular space with its natural gold and brown palate and moulded twelve-foot ceilings. Snuggled beside the windows are a dozen overstuffed chairs. Along the left side of the room is a long wooden bar where coffee brews and tea steeps. The right side is lined by a built-in bench with tables and stools pulled up to it. Electrical sockets dot the bottom of the walls, offering ample laptop power to go along with the free wireless. I order a green tea with a gluten-free peanut butter cookie and get cozy in one of the chairs overlooking the bustle of Bank Street.

Two clergy people originally founded Bridgehead as a "fair trade" operation. They paid above-market prices directly to coffee producers. In 1984, Oxfam-Canada (a non-profit organization that helps find lasting solutions to poverty) acquired the business and formally incorporated Bridgehead as a federal, not-for-profit company. The company reached $6 million a year in sales, importing coffee and crafts from developing countries and selling them through its own stores and mail-order catalogue. But for years the operation failed to make a profit. It passed through three collective not-for-profit ownership groups, meanwhile sinking deeper and deeper into debt.

That was until Tracey Clark came along. Tracey has a warm smile, vibrant brown eyes, short brown hair, and charisma to burn. When she speaks, her entire face runs a marathon of expressions. Listening to her makes you feel like you just had a double-shot-long espresso. At forty, she's older than the other entrepreneurs I've profiled in this chapter but I've decided to include Tracey because her story shows how the Balanced Contract can be applied to established organizations, and can grow and develop along with the entrepreneur.

As a youth, Tracey volunteered with the original Bridgehead. One summer, she travelled to Nicaragua with some other volunteers to work on the plantations where coffee beans were produced. She saw a lot of farmers working hard but being paid little.

After a few years of shift work and odd jobs, Tracey decided to return to school to get an MBA at the University of Ottawa. Upon graduation, she worked for a restaurant chain, making her way up the corporate ladder to become chief operating officer. Later, she was a store manager for a large camping and adventure chain. Still committed to social change, she joined Bridgehead's board. It was threatened with bankruptcy once again, and once again the board decided to put it up for sale.

This time, Tracey wasn't going to watch anybody else run the organization she loved into the ground. In 2000, she decided to take out a loan and ask family and friends to invest as well. For $30,000, she bought the Bridgehead name, trademarks, and customer lists. Since then, she's gone through several rounds of bank loans and financing to open up other Bridgehead locations. Tracey believed that the company was based on a winning idea but was poorly managed. "A good business doesn't have to go out of business," she told me.

But to stay in business, Bridgehead had to become a real business, not an activists' organization focused solely on a social agenda. Once she became the new owner, Tracey made two major decisions. She changed the organization from a not-for-profit to a for-profit venture, and she cut back the operation to coffee shops and mail-order coffee, closing the craft outlets. "People loved our crafts and craft catalogue but they didn't buy enough to keep that part of the business going. Other stores were doing it better," she says.

But Tracey didn't change Bridgehead's socially responsible roots. All the company's coffee and tea would still come from co-operatives—groups of farmers who elect a managing board to run the organization. Four per cent of the co-op's total revenue goes back into developing infrastructure for the business. Forty per cent of the profit goes back into the coffee-growing communities: health care, schools, and scholarships to high school or university. Moreover, all coffee, loose teas, milk, and sugar would be organic. "We're the first people in Canada to use fair-trade organic chocolate syrup," Tracey boasts.

As she grew the business, Tracey learned that while the socially responsible mission would attract consumers, she still needed to remain competitive in price, product selection, quality, and convenience. Tracey told me that mail-order customers, which now account for about 5 per cent of Bridgehead's revenue, are drawn predominantly from the socially committed. Eighty per cent of them report that their initial motivation for buying from Bridgehead was to support fair trade. But they also expect the quality and service to match competitive brands. In contrast, three-quarters of the coffee-shop customers originally drop in for a variety of other reasons: convenience, quality, brought by a friend. They return because Bridgehead meets their expectations for high-quality coffee with great service in pleasant modern surroundings. Over time, many become supporters of fair trade as well. About 25 per cent of Tracey's cafe customers care intensely about the fair-trade approach and prefer to come to her shop over others for that reason. A further 5 per cent are drawn to Bridgehead because they're committed to an organic lifestyle.

It was a tough go at first. Tracey went without a salary for two years. She moved back home with her parents while she worked sixteen-hour days to re-establish the business. Just as things were starting to come together, the price for coffee beans dropped from $1.40 a pound to fifty cents. For most companies, that would have significantly boosted the profit margin. But, committed to fair trade and to supporting the grower's communities, Tracey kept paying the higher price. Six years later, the company is now comfortably profitable. There are five bustling Ottawa stores and plans for more across Canada.

For Tracey, Bridgehead balances her two passions: the joy and challenge of getting a business right, and the satisfaction of making a contribution to others: "The business feels like a political vehicle to me," she says. Her mission also helps to attract top staff. "I find that if you speak to their interests and values, they'll want to get involved and will do a great job." Tracey's goal? "We want to get big enough that we can make even more of a contribution."

I'll do my part, by ordering another organic, fair trade green tea and plopping back in my chair to do some more writing.

Obviously, I'm not alone in fulfilling the Balanced Contract. Many others are choosing to run profit-driven yet socially oriented enterprises. At some point, each one of them has undoubtedly felt alone and on the losing end of a tough battle. But in the end, they prove their critics wrong and build profitable businesses that make positive social contributions.

Now, in the next two chapters, I'll add to the mix some thoughts of my own on running a Balanced Contract business.

CHAPTER FIFTEEN

BUILDING YOUR OWN RUNWAY

QUESTIONS ABOUT STARTING A BUSINESS

MOST ENTREPRENEURS SPEND a lot of sleepless nights and exhausting days asking themselves one question after another. Questions nag us, prod us, and yank our eyes open to matters that we need to be raising. The right question is halfway to an answer. Welcome or not, questions are valuable adventures.

I've asked myself, and I continue to ask myself, a copious amount of questions: How do I go on working in the fashion industry after learning all about my friend's terrible eating disorder? Should I go to university? Should I continue on to grad school at Cambridge? How can my agency change the face of fashion forever?

I'm also frequently posed questions. Young entrepreneurs, or business dreamers, or those supporting them, want to know what steps I suggest starting off with. I'm always reluctant to propose "Ben Barry's model of entrepreneurship." A lot of books offer systems for opening and running a business—I've read shelves full—but I've found that there's no real formula. Your path has got to be your own.

Okay, I've got no roadmap to offer but I will spring for a compass. Here's a series of questions that will help you sort your way through the intense business-creation phase. They're basically the same ones that I've asked myself. I'll tell you how I have answered them so far (and how I continue to do so day in and day out). You won't come up with the same answers as I did but you'll need to interrogate yourself in the same way. Failing to ask is asking to fail.

1. What issue matters to me? Does business matter to it?
2. Who am I? Who can I become?
3. What do I know? What must I find out?
4. For whom am I speaking? To whom am I speaking?
5. What little do I have? How can I make the most of it?
6. What do I have to offer? How is it better than what others offer?
7. How do I sell my product? Do I also sell myself?
8. How do I run my business? Am I the boss?
9. Is my life my business? Does my life include my business?
10. How do I make it to the top? How do I stay there?

Any entrepreneur can ask these questions, but they're especially useful for someone wanting to better society through business. Next up in this chapter, I'll tackle the first five sets of questions—the ones you ask when you've just started thinking about signing on to the Balanced Contract, the ones you ask before you've sunk in any real money or pinned on any real hopes. Your answers will confirm whether or not you're on the right track.

QUESTION 1: WHAT ISSUE MATTERS TO ME? DOES BUSINESS MATTER TO IT?

My values have always inspired my actions. I don't like to settle for the status quo; whenever I can opt for innovation I do. Once I start worrying about the way society is conducting itself, I don't let myself get away with squashing those worries: I take action. I transform the circumstances that upset me, or at least I try to. I firmly believe that the world can be improved as a result of one individual's actions, including mine and yours.

My values are deeply ingrained. They're not something I need to remind myself of or study in the abstract. They rumble in my stomach, they get my blood flowing, I feel them in my bones. They are who I am. These values propelled me toward entrepreneurship. They merged with issues that I wanted to learn about, wanted to talk about, wanted to be involved in—regardless of whether or not someone was paying me.

Your issue could be something you've noticed and cared about for a long time, or it could result from a eureka moment. Slowly, you'll find one smouldering idea taking up more and more space in your brain until it finally starts alarm bells ringing.

In my case, I'd been fascinated with the creative process pretty well all my conscious life. When I operated my little B&B at the age of eleven, I made sure the pillows were properly arranged on each bed, that the chocolate was placed in just the right spot, and that enough candles were present to create the desired atmosphere. Fashion and fashion photography played right into my passion for detail. At the end of the day, my interests were a perfect fit for the field I stumbled into. I guess the point I'm trying to make is that "stumble" is the wrong word.

While you may not yet be aware which industries spark your interests, you can start by asking yourself what activities you enjoy. What invigorates you? What would keep you up until 1 a.m. and then get you out of bed at 5 a.m. to start all over again? Being passionate is about a lot more than just intellectual engagement; it's also about being emotionally invested, about throwing your heart and soul into things. Passion happens when your values collide with an issue that personally affects you, or your family and friends. Your issue isn't something detached from you; your issue flows into and out of your own life experience.

Lauren was my personal connection to the modelling business. She needed help making her way through the industry. I started to help other people in similar situations. Then I lived through Mia's eating disorder. Gradually, I gleaned the negative impact my chosen industry was having on models, thanks to the spontaneous reactions of my friends, and women at large. Initially, I wasn't out to shake up the fashion world. As my business grew, however, the most important issues started penetrating both my head and my heart. It started to seem like there were some risks I was born to take.

By finding an issue that affects your life as well as provoking you intellectually, your business will be way more than just a job. It will become your mission. Plus, your cause acts as your guide, drawing out your instincts, telling you when and where to get involved. And it serves as your fuel, keeping you going throughout all the tough stuff. This is obviously not the same person who says, "I want to start a business so maybe I should get into a franchise; I hear they make lots of money with minimal risk." Nor is it the person who wants to be absorbed within a major corporation.

Once you've identified the issue that ignites your passions, ask yourself what role business can play in addressing and correcting it. Business influences issues in two main ways. First, business can contribute to problems: the manufacturing of clothing in overseas sweatshops supports unethical labour practices. Second, business can help solve social problems: providing a fresh and nutritious fast-food alternative to reduce obesity and increase health.

Ask yourself whether business negatively contributes to the social problem having an impact on your life and, if so, how? Then ask yourself how business could reverse that effect. Think about new products or services. Identify the relationship between those products and services and the problem itself: the cause and effect. Could what you're offering ameliorate people's lives? Business might not provide a solution to your problem and it's important to accept that. A not-for-profit non-government organization (NGO), or even government itself, might supply a better means to your end.

Remember that creativity is crucial when looking to solve a specific social problem. Not only will your products and services likely be new, so will your entire attitude toward them. Don't give up easily. Use your imagination.

Once you've come up with some ideas, you'll need to figure out whether your product or service would survive in the marketplace. Will it attract consumers and make money? This is the most critical question—you'll have to run a successful, sustainable operation, or you'll go under. Explore whether or not customers will buy your product or service. Why would anyone shop from you given the choice between you and your competitors?

How do you understand what people want? The best way is to talk with them, probing deep enough to understand not just what they say they want but also what they truly seek. With some products, it helps to watch consumers use them. You have to be careful not to universalize the experience of one or two people who happen to play into your own biases. If you keep an open mind and stick close to your customers you should be fine.

Remember when my friends discussed that *Seventeen* magazine in the lunchroom? I could have chosen to hear only their initial, positive comments and convinced myself I'd delivered the perfect fashion spread. But because I kept an open mind, I realized their reactions were turning out to be more negative than positive. In a sense, I was lucky: my gang started to spill their guts unprovoked. Nonetheless, it's a good lesson: if you take your idea to friends, don't be satisfied with the earliest reactions, which will likely be flattering. Push them. Ask what additions and improvements they would make. Ask what's wrong. Invite them to play devil's advocate. What are you missing? If Jason says something negative, don't let glares from the others shut Jason down. Welcome the comment and ask others to build on it. Dig and then dig deeper.

One helpful technique is the "five whys." Always ask why somebody feels the way they do. When you get an answer, ask why again. This will bring forth a deeper feeling. Then ask why again and again, until you get to root feelings, which often come only after the fifth why.

As well as talking to potential customers, it helps to put yourself in the consumer's place. Pretend you're making the purchase. What are your needs and wants? What matters to you? Think about current offerings and how they negatively impact on your issue. Ask yourself how your version would improve things.

It was critical for me to understand my industry from the point of view of both my models and my clients. After all, I was selling my services to both. I needed to understand their needs and decision-making processes. I put myself in their shoes; I listened carefully when they spoke. By shaping my business according to their perspectives, I was able to gain their confidence and patronage. My business operates as if it was designed and run by customers.

Keep in mind that you can't do it all. Often you will have identified a huge problem. Or, from a business perspective, *a very large market opportunity*. But you're likely to be a small operation—at least at first. Being a specialist in a small area is usually better than being a generalist in a large area. It gains you visibility. It provides focus. It reassures people you know what you're doing. Cut off a slice of the market that you can handle.

QUESTION 2: WHO AM I? WHO CAN I BECOME?

To be successful in business, to enjoy business, it's vital to know yourself. I've found business thrilling and enriching; I like how it draws on so many varying skills and talents. Business has thrust me into situations that push and pull at my value system, beliefs, and understanding. You've got to be flexible but you've got to be steadfast. Before you jump in, take stock of who you are.

Are you comfortable being *in* business, let alone at the top of one? Many individuals aren't. Maybe you don't want to face the daunting challenge of bringing in more revenues than your expenses? Perhaps you wouldn't enjoy being a boss? Some people view enterprise as inherently wrong. If you're hesitant, take some time to probe why. Ask yourself whether you could develop the skills and comprehension necessary to overcome your resistance.

I especially urge you to challenge your position if you identify with the idea that business is morally wrong. Under the guidance of the right entrepreneurs, business can do great things. If you have a vision of helping people, I'd argue that you, too, have the mindset to be part of the Balanced Contract generation of entrepreneurs. By opting for entrepreneurship, you could transform your own view of business and yourself. Remember: it will be your business, responsive to your values.

Obviously, I no longer consider whether business is the right path for me. But I did question that while visiting Mia in the hospital. I was unhappy with the modelling industry. But I loved the thrill of pitching and winning new clients. I loved planting ideas in the marketplace and cultivating them.

Entrepreneurs all have passion and determination, but beyond that they can be as different as Versace and Vera Wang. Some are loners; others work best with a team. Some are autocratic; others are consensual. Some like quick results and get bored easily; others prefer to dig in for the long haul.

Entrepreneurs also vary in their risk quotient. Some are bold gamblers and that's given rise to a stereotype that defines all entrepreneurs as oblivious to risk. Unfortunately, that's frightening off less-daring souls. The reality is that most entrepreneurs are pretty cautious. They don't want to expose their business—or livelihood, reputation, and staff—to undue risks. They do take risks, but conservatively.

Granted, failure is always possible. It's amazing how many budding entre-preneurs don't want to recognize that. They're convinced their idea will flourish—it seems so genius. Many entrepreneurs have failed at some point. They also succeed, sometimes in a huge way.

As I've said, building a business from a dream on up to a reality demands a wide range of skills and talents. Here are a few I needed as I built the Ben Barry Agency:

Vision: you should be able to see a glorious future, albeit in the distance.

Recognition of Reality: you should be able to understand your cur-rent reality and not gloss over unpleasant facts.

Organizational Ability: you should be able to organize yourself, and others, in order to pursue your goals methodically. If that's not your strength, you should be able to find somebody who organizes well, and be willing to delegate that task.

Empathy: to guarantee that you're aimed in the right direction, you must be able to understand your customers' feelings. And your staff's, to keep them energized.

Ego and Humility: it takes ego in the best sense of the term to be an entrepreneur: extreme confidence. But it also requires humility—to understand your limitations and win support. Balance is key.

Stubbornness and a Willingness to Admit Mistakes: another entre-preneurial yin-yang. You need to be obstinate, to hang in when everybody is telling you that you won't succeed. I displayed that stub-bornness when bigwigs told me my vision of diversity was wrong. But you also need the ability to know when you *are* wrong, and to reverse course. Remember how I had to evolve my business model?

Listening Ability: you need to be able to listen to others and grasp their advice. Even if you tend to advance your own points first in conversation—carried away by that entrepreneurial ego and determi-nation—you must be able to hear what other people say (even if you have to process it later).

Money Sense: you need to be able to handle money and to under-stand the financial side of your business. That means learning about accounting, the language of business, and the essentials of how your company can make enough money to thrive.

Marketing and Sales: you need to have a sense of marketing, either intuitively or from specialized courses. Who are your best customers and how can you best reach out to them? You'll be promoting both your company and yourself so you'll need a healthy comfort level and some expertise. Eventually, you might hire staff to handle sales, but as the owner you'll always be the company's main salesperson. And you'll always get called in when things get difficult or go off-kilter.

The majority of us don't possess all of these skills, at least not innately. That's the way it goes—you're good at some things and you need practise others. And in the end, some skills might elude you. Don't let that stop you. Successful entrepreneurs know their strengths, recognize their weaknesses, and find ways to compensate.

I constantly focus on what I do best. My strengths include vision, organization, and empathy. My weaknesses fall into the categories of money sense and recognition of reality. What I do is sit down, think hard about my weaknesses, and then ask others their opinions. I take my weaknesses extremely seriously; they could threaten what I'm building.

At the start of my business, I compensated for my inadequate money sense by learning about accounting and finance through courses, reading books, and setting up monthly meetings with my accountant. Obviously, back then I couldn't afford a full-time staff member to specialize in money issues. But as my business grew, I hired an accountant (in fact, that was my very first paid staff position) and eventually more staff with financial backgrounds.

As for my natural tendency to be idealistic, I've managed that by routinely questioning the validity of my goals. I also engage in constant meetings with my staff and advisory board to discuss and debate my ideas. My idealism frequently rubs up against reality that way; we develop plans for the agency that strike a balance between wishful thinking and the cold hard truth. I should add that this approach didn't cost me anything. I could discuss my ideas with my advisory board for free.

Take some time to understand yourself: your aspirations, your strengths and weaknesses. Take long walks or write in a journal. Ask those close to you for their thoughts. The better you know you, the better your business will be.

QUESTION 3: WHAT DO I KNOW? WHAT MUST I FIND OUT?

I leaped into business without any experience in either business or fashion but I quickly discovered that I already knew a lot that would help me run my company. I'd watched my friends read fashion magazines and buy clothes and makeup so I understood their needs as consumers. I'd worked on school projects so I understood how to operate in a team environment. I'd written essays so I knew how to develop a persuasive argument. And I'd been raised hearing stories of how my grandparents overcame enormous obstacles through hard work and determination so I knew how to be fierce and to never give up hope.

Even before we start our companies, life experience equips us with a lot of the knowledge that can make us adept entrepreneurs. Maybe we've seen through mistakes our former bosses have made. Maybe we know how to do in-depth research. You know what you know. Now know what you need to find out.

A lot of solutions come serendipitously as you run into challenges. At the start, however, it doesn't hurt to speak to people who have opened businesses, or to delve into a few books on entrepreneurship. Map out a list of what you need to find out to be successful. For example, you may need to learn where you can find the materials required to make your product, the best ways to manage consumer orders and the most effective marketing strategies for your industry (sometimes learning what's effective in other industries, too). I make a point of reassessing all these issues regularly in order to keep my knowledge fresh. Initially it was every month, then every three months, and now annually.

Research is an excellent way to discover the information we're after as well as information we didn't even realize we needed. I learned how to research in school but often left the information behind once my history paper was handed in and graded. In business, however, research is a routine activity for me. The information I gather informs constant decisions. Research helps me reach conclusions about major hurdles (the best way to develop an advertising program) as well as everyday matters (finding out about a client to whom I want to pitch).

I've gleaned knowledge from books, magazines, and the Internet, but I've found that the best information comes from talking with other people: network your way to informative contacts. I attend events all the time, from meetings of young entrepreneurs, to chamber of commerce breakfasts, to industry conferences, to gatherings of cycling and skiing buddies. Ultimately, good networking boils down to three points: be sincere, be yourself, and give in order to receive. Help others, and they will eventually help you. I've found that the best relationships are developed over time through regular communication. It's great to make contacts, but after doing so it's critical to keep them going. I frequently schedule time for one-on-one sessions with the people I've met, be it over coffee, lunch, or tennis.

Some of your contacts will become mentors: people who teach you about business in general and the ins and outs of your industry in particular. Potential mentors are all around you, at parties you don't want to attend, at seminars you don't want to make time for, at intimidating conferences. Mentors have been down your path before you. They can save you time, money, and headaches by sharing their experiences. You don't need to wait until you've started a business to find mentors—you can develop them from the moment you start considering your entrepreneurial mission and need to share your ideas.

Usually there is no one course or text that can teach you the in and outs of a particular field. Certainly there was nothing on how to set up a modelling agency, especially a non-traditional one. The key players in any given industry aren't listed in the phone book. The knowledge you need is usually locked inside people's heads. You have to find those people and extract that knowledge as you go. It's like reading a book about your industry that you're actually helping to write, chapter by chapter, over time.

One touchy aspect of mentorship is that eventually you'll move on. Your growth will take you beyond whatever guidance the mentor can provide. It's similar to what happens within our families as we grow up and move on to lead our own lives. I outgrew Elmer Olsen when I gradually learned enough about the business to be reasonably self-sufficient. More importantly, I developed my own notions about how my business would run and I had a vision that was substantively different from Elmer's. It's important to recognize when this is happening. Mentoring has two stages; the second is separation and redefinition. Remember what initially tied you to your mentor—treasure what he or she gave you, and let that be known so that you separate as close friends.

Mentors can also help with the personal, non-business aspects of your life. Where to go for graduate school stressed me out. My advisory board helped enormously, with many of them counselling me that I'd already developed a strong foundation for my business and should take advantage of the stimulating environment of studying in Cambridge to give me new ideas and different experiences. They said it would not only assist me personally but also help my business grow over the long term. They were right.

As you gain confidence and build your business, it's easy to think you can walk into a meeting with somebody new and handle it off the cuff or that you can stop learning from others' experiences. Be careful of this kind of overconfidence. Researching and preparing beforehand always impresses whomever you're meeting with. Keeping on top of current issues is a great foundation for doing good business.

QUESTION 4: FOR WHOM AM I SPEAKING? TO WHOM AM I SPEAKING?

When I switched to representing diverse models, one of the major issues I faced was how to promote them to the fashion and advertising industry. I started off by explaining to clients how models influence the public's self-esteem and body image. I shared Mia's story as an example. People's hearts went out to Mia, but most didn't see what her struggles had to do with their own positions.

My problem was that I was framing my argument in the language of social issues rather than the language of business. I had to translate my socially responsible ideas into business language. That meant showing clients how (by helping society) my product would help them meet their corporate goals and objectives.

I like to think of the language of business as similar to any other language; it has a grammatical structure and a vocabulary. The basic business message is as follows: you want to attract consumers to earn a profit (or better yet, attract more consumers than your competitors to earn more profit than they do). To complete the equation, you need to explain how your approach will attract potential consumers more efficiently than what's out there and thereby add to profits. Once you've got that far, expand into the deeper reaches of the business vocabulary. How does your offering provide a "competitive advantage," leading to increased "market share," favourable "brand attitude," "consumer loyalty," and, eventually, increased and "sustainable profits"?

Speaking in business terms, I'd explain that individuals who felt negatively about their body image after viewing models weren't just random people in society but rebuffed consumers. I'd explain that negative feelings about body image often translated into negative attitudes toward a brand. Consumers would relate better to models who reflected real customers, and subsequently the brand, which would convert into increased loyalty and purchases.

You may need to consider a staggered strategy. While your new product or service may offer great benefits to consumers, its differences may also scare them off. You may need to gradually introduce consumers to the new features of your product or service, offering them a chance to try it, or parts of it, without completely switching to something new. This approach will allow them to develop confidence in and loyalty to your offering. Hopefully, they'll soon make a complete swap to your new way of thinking and doing.

If I had started with only diverse models and abandoned the traditional ones, I'm sure my business would have gone under. My way of thinking would have been considered too untested—clients would have been scared right off. Instead, I initially offered clients the opportunity to book traditional models. That allowed them to slowly develop trust and confidence in my firm, my models, and me. Over time, that trust transformed into confidence in my business that I could leverage to convince clients to include a few diverse models in their bookings. Once clients experienced the benefits of diverse models and developed a solid relationship with me, they could completely switch over. My staggered strategy allowed me to develop a customer base, create a market for diverse models, and make sure my business maintained financial viability.

Just make sure you also stay fluent in social-issues talk. It's easy to lose that facility as you become more immersed in the business world. Staying on top of social-issues language will ensure you always consider and understand the social perspective—the impact of your business on people and the world.

QUESTION 5: WHAT LITTLE DO I HAVE? HOW CAN I MAKE THE MOST OF IT?

One advantage for young entrepreneurs is that we're forced to be creative when it comes to acquiring resources. Banks won't loan to a teenager. Obviously, that limits your options. You're not going to start a construction company, for example. (Although you could begin a handyperson service.) Not having easy access to money is actually an advantage. You have to ask yourself, "If I can't get any money, how am I going to make this business work, anyway?" You have to think things all the way through.

The first step in the search for capital is to approach your personal contacts: family, friends, and people you know. Remember that capital doesn't always mean money; it can also be goods in kind, or skills. I was helped enormously by the lawyer who loaned me his office in the evening. I was bailed out of difficulty by friends who were willing to serve as reception staff. A friend's mother let me use her photocopier at her office. Others offered to help me pick up clothing for photo shoots and fashion shows, using their parents' cars. My friends with graphic-design skills volunteered their time and ability to design my business card and marketing materials. Figure out what you need and then think creatively about how people you know could help.

I found that being young was a massive advantage when I was looking for help. You'll probably find the same thing. My guess is that your peers are proficient and up to date with technology, have some cutting-edge design and artistic talents, and possess high energy levels and a willingness to help. They're excited about using their talents to gain experience in the working world, experience for which they're normally told they're too young. Your shout for help will open up a lot of opportunities for them.

Adults will want to help you, too, because of the very fact that you're young. You'll be seen as the "future." Many adults will feel emotionally and intellectually invested in seeing you excel. It's important to be completely upfront about your needs. Requiring help won't devalue your business. Sometimes, the most unexpected people will volunteer assistance if they know what you require. Make sure to thank them, repeatedly. I left a note of thanks every single time I used that lawyer's office.

Government grants can also be a substantial source of support. Many are directed specifically at young people, small businesses, and socially responsible ventures. I didn't receive my first loan until I'd been in business five years but I secured my first grant much sooner. The government had an equal-opportunities program to support companies helping disadvantaged groups enter the workforce.

Finding out and applying for government grants can seem daunting. Governments have many different departments, and applications are often detailed and complicated. Sometimes, it's hard to know where to begin. I've found that developing a relationship with your elected representatives and their staff can simplify the process. Elected representatives are there to help. And their staff generally knows the bureaucracy inside out. They can pass along the special phone number that actually gets you to the person in charge instead of the one that gets you the automated attendant.

I've received help from municipal, provincial, and federal politicians. You may not immediately connect with the representatives in your area, but start with the person who answers the phone, explaining who you are and what you're doing. In a quiet moment, they will likely share your story with the boss because it's unusual, inspirational, and important to the community.

The member of Parliament in my constituency was approachable. We developed a strong relationship. He didn't have time to help me personally but he made sure his staff did. I got to know Marilyn, his assistant. I'd call her with questions. I might say, "Marilyn, I need to hire a new staff member. Are there any government programs?" She'd call back in an hour to inform me of a program specifically aimed at young entrepreneurs. She'd help me complete applications. "You have to hire someone under twenty-five but the government will pay 75 per cent of their salary," she'd say. "Stop by the office; I'll give you the forms and help you fill them out. Once you're finished, I'll send them off on your behalf." The forms were always accompanied by a supportive letter from the MP. It was all much more effective than any web search.

Developing knowledge is about having access, and while money can buy access, so can our age. Because we are young, we're generally not perceived as direct competition. We're just kids wanting to learn. Most people will share willingly if you're not perceived as a threat. They'll be quite relaxed about it. A lot of businesspeople remember those who gave them a hand on their way up, and they want to give back. They'll be happy to share their experiences and their contacts and some of them will become your mentors, imparting even more details and advice.

I got invited to the L'Oréal shoot in New York by a woman willing to share her experience and knowledge. She didn't need to invite me anywhere to get access to my models. She offered the invitation simply to help. Elmer also taught me valuable information about scouting and booking models—information gained only from working on the inside—and he personally introduced me to key decision-makers within the fashion world. Ironically, because of labour laws, at age fourteen I couldn't even have worked in Elite's mailroom. Yet I was able to learn from the country's top talent manager simply because I asked and because he was graciously willing to help. Interestingly, I was invited to judge the Elite model search in my first year in business, but two years later I was not invited. By then, I was a viable competitor.

Once you are established in business, remember to pass along your own knowledge through mentoring. As much as I can, I help young people who want to get into the fashion industry or start their own business. I speak at schools and conferences, and I respond to every email asking for my advice. My company also offers internships to young people who want hands-on business and fashion experience.

If you've come this far and still think that a Balanced Contract business is for you—go out and make it happen! Once you make headway, you'll need to focus on the questions addressed in the next chapter.

CHAPTER SIXTEEN

EXPANDING YOUR RUNWAY

QUESTIONS ABOUT RUNNING A BUSINESS

YOU'VE ISOLATED YOUR ISSUE and decided to tackle it through business. You're ready to begin your own Balanced Contract venture. Your website is live and you have your first client. Now what? Keep questioning yourself if you want to survive and thrive.

In this chapter, I'll finish answering the questions that I ask myself on a daily or weekly basis—the ones that have helped me successfully grow my company over the last ten years. Innovative ideas are no guarantee of success. Success in business is based on an ability to effectively promote and execute these new ideas.

QUESTION 6: WHAT DO I HAVE TO OFFER? HOW IS IT BETTER THAN WHAT OTHERS OFFER?

I quickly discovered that being young is a competitive advantage in the business world. In the previous chapter, I explained how being young was beneficial when developing in-kind support and mentors. But the power of youth goes further than that: it helps us to fashion what Thomas Kuhn would call a "paradigm shift."

In 1962, Thomas Kuhn authored *The Structure of Scientific Revolution*, which argued that science changes when a new paradigm replaces the old. Young scientists aren't pre-committed to established laboratory methodologies. They haven't yet built careers and reputations on a particular set of ideas. They don't have an emotional investment in the status quo. All this makes them much more open to change.

What goes for science goes for business. Business thrives on constant innovation and change. That's how the free market works—each firm competing to outperform the other by surpassing the current form of thinking and doing, producing a better product at a better price. As a newcomer to the market, without any routines (or routine assumptions) you'll be well positioned—intellectually and emotionally—to innovate solutions.

As a high school student, I had insights into the marketplace that few people in Manhattan office towers shared. I realized I had a problem when I brought a *Seventeen* magazine to my friends in the lunch hall and caught their spontaneously mixed reactions. I came up with solutions that shed some bright new light on my industry. You make previously unseen connections when you see things in new ways. You won't be boxed in by tradition either.

I had other age advantages as well.

I could walk around high schools and scout models with no one questioning me. My friends around the city were constantly alerting me to events I should scout—a basketball game or a play. No other agent had equivalent access.

I was the same age as a lot of the models I was representing; as a result, they weren't nervous or closed with me. They didn't worry about what to say (or not to say).

Younger businesspeople have an insider's knowledge of youth culture trends that companies pay consultants big money to snoop out. We understand the information fully and can act on it fast.

In order for companies to be successful nowadays, they have to embrace new technology and new global markets. Okay, that's become a cliché. But embracing the BlackBerry (etcetera) and Beijing (etcetera) remain a constant

challenge for most executives. Young people are raised with the latest technologies; using it in daily life is second nature. We've also been raised with
global awareness: media, communication technology, and schools have taught
us that we live in a borderless world, yet one that has deep differences and
divisions. Our parents struggle much more to incorporate the global mindset
into their lives and businesses.

One word of caution: while taking full advantage of your youth, you still
have to adapt to business convention. If you don't dress and act professionally
in certain situations, for example, you won't get in the customer's front door.
And if you don't talk like a professional then the individuals with whom you
seek to do business won't understand you. I've always dressed in attire that is
appropriate for my particular field, and developed marketing materials and
budgets using business language whenever I've presented my services to
potential clients. If I had come off completely as a kid, clients would have been
overwhelmed by my age and not seen what I had to offer. They would have
worried that I couldn't match the quality of my adult competitors. By operating according to certain conventions, I was able to keep clients from being
overly distracted by my age and land them.

QUESTION 7: HOW DO I SELL MY PRODUCT? DO I ALSO SELL MYSELF?

People need to know about your services. That can be hard if you don't have
funds for advertising. How will you get your message out? For me, the media—
from local news to *Oprah*—was a critical tool when it came to spreading the
word about my company across the city, the country, and eventually the world.
The media lend credibility to any new business, especially a youth-run operation. Once I'd been profiled in the local newspaper, prospects who'd never
returned my calls started requesting my models.

To gain media coverage, you have to understand what the media want. The
average producer needs to come up with loads of stories with little time for
research. Make it easy for them. Give them your idea, provide background
material (without deluging them), and be accessible when they're ready to talk

to you. You can reach out to them through a phone call or email. The initial contact will generally involve a "pitch," a short explanation as to why their readers or viewers will be interested in what you're up to. That's a key point. Keep the readers or viewers front and centre. It's all about them.

Sometimes, you want the media outlet to get wind of your story from someone they know or respect. See if you can make a connection that leads to somebody else promoting your story. For example, one of your advisory board members can make an initial phone call to the media, talking up your venture.

The media are generally interested in young entrepreneurs; youth is newsworthy. Play up your age when developing your pitch. But when you're finally interviewed, make sure to talk about more than just your age. Your age will be a great hook but it can also hamstring you. I was able to do find a balance by focusing on my age for my first couple of years of media coverage. Then, as my business advanced, I began to pitch different angles for stories, focusing on how my firm was changing the fashion industry, or how it was growing internationally, or how my models were gaining prestigious contracts. It was easy to pitch follow-up stories because I'd already developed a relationship with reporters and news outlets. They wanted to update audiences who were already familiar with me.

My key advice for dealing with media is to be proactive. You can't wait for journalists to come to you; you have to go to them, at least initially. It might take a while for them to get back to you, and sometimes you'll have to try again and again. Without being a bit of a pest, you won't get a story—they know that so don't let it hold you back.

You also need to be a bit of a pest when you promote your services to a customer. So often, entrepreneurs make the sales pitch, but don't close the deal. The customer says she'll consider it, and the entrepreneur is left waiting. Time passes, other things come up, and the deal is lost—along with important revenue.

Don't be embarrassed to ask for money for your product or service. It's your right as a for-profit entrepreneur. That's why you put all of your time and effort into establishing your company. Customers know this. There's nothing rude about asking for their business or trying to make a sale.

After I make a pitch, I'll always call the customer to ask, "What can I do to get your business and close the deal?" For example, one time, a client said he was waiting for another estimate for my competition before he would make a decision. I said I would cut my estimate by 10 per cent if he committed to my agency on the spot. He said yes, and I closed the deal.

Another important way to promote your company is through connections with other businesspeople. That includes other young business owners. Suss out groups that support young entrepreneurs and join them. I benefited enormously from ACE, the Advancing Canadian Entrepreneurship organization. I won its CIBC Canadian Student Entrepreneur of the Year Award, which got me networking with business kingpins. ACE puts on frequent events and conferences. One year, I was the master of ceremonies at the ACE gala dinner in Toronto. When I took my seat at the dinner table, Isadore Sharp, the founder and CEO of Four Seasons Hotels and Resorts, was sitting next to me. We chatted up a storm. He offered me and my models a discount anytime we stayed at one of his hotels. (So now, of course, we stay only at the Four Seasons when we travel. Sweet!)

The contacts I've made from ACE are frankly invaluable—new customers, professional partnerships, advice and support, friends with similar interests and passions. Enter contests if you can; even if you don't win, the people who run the awards will still be impressed that you applied and may well become valuable contacts. And you never know who might be sitting in the chair beside you.

I've found that when promoting your company, whether in the media or at conferences, it's important to promote yourself as its leader and visionary. A unique product or service gathers attention, but a unique personality stays in everyone's mind. Give a human face to your business. Customers develop relationships with people not things. Let your character, style, and habits speak loudly. At the same time, don't plan everything out—just be your genuine self. People connect with sincerity and will in turn connect with your company. Similarly, people sense when someone isn't comfortable in their skin, so don't fake anything. But have fun. A quirky, eccentric, or eclectic personality can work! It makes you—and therefore your business—stand out from the competition. Things you might find weird about yourself (extreme marathon running, a vegan diet, an Italian furniture habit) might be what other people are totally into. The best firms are known for having the best staff. In the public's mind, your business doesn't get better than you.

QUESTION 8: HOW DO I RUN MY BUSINESS? AM I THE BOSS?

Your ideas can only carry you so far. You need the help of other people, in particular your staff and an advisory board. You want them talented, passionate, and loaded with vision. I could have never built my agency alone (whether or not I was splitting my time between work and school). The Ben Barry Agency hinges on a terrific team, collectively implementing a mission that we all work together to develop.

When I need to hire staff, the first question that presents itself is where to find the right person. I've never sought people by advertising in newspaper classified sections. Instead, I tend to make targeted efforts on one hand and take advantage of happenstance on the other. For example, I meet individuals in the industry or at entrepreneurship conferences. If I sense they could make a valuable member of my team, I approach them when a position opens up (or needs to be created). I also post job openings on bulletin boards in fashion, business, and women's studies departments. I opt for email listings. Some of my staff originally approached me for a job, excited by my goals and willing to offer support. One of our scouts, who eventually became the director of scouting, got in touch because she'd been inspired by a newspaper profile describing my mission (she had previously suffered from body image issues when working as a model).

Always keep your eyes and ears open for potential staff members, even when you're not looking to hire. Ask your current staff and your contacts to do the same. (As you grow, your own eyes and ears won't be sufficient.) I make a point of meeting with each applicant—not for a formal interview but a more informal chat. Then I add their resumé and contact info, and my personal observations to a database. Each time I look for new staff, I review the database. My system saves me time and risk. I don't need to go over tons of applications, or spend energy (and money) on a time-consuming search process. When I need to hire someone, I already have candidates whom I like. Take the time to meet with people who you think would make ideal staff members. Create your own database of potential hires. It really helps you find the right people at the right time.

The next issue I face when hiring a new staff member is figuring out if the applicant is right for the job. A person may come off as qualified—a strong resumé, great references, and personality—but how can I be as sure as possible that she'll be the best fit of all? Truthfully, it's always a risk. You can never be sure about someone's performance until they've been on the job for three months.

Okay, here are a few techniques that I use to reduce risk. When I interview a person I've never met, I conduct the first interview by phone. That way, I'm not swayed by appearances. I also put the candidates through several structured interviews; they're asked the same questions by several different people. I find it important to get additional opinions and perspectives. Others often see things that I miss. All of us then collectively evaluate each candidate. When you are your only employee, or you have only one other, ask a mentor to conduct the interview as well.

There are two other useful tactics to increase your odds of hiring the right person. Most jobs make things hard for people in one way or another. In one job, for example, you might be expected to follow a routine while in another, flexibility and initiative are key. Somebody who is a terrific employee in a very structured company might not work out at your firm. Consider what things might hold people back in particular jobs at your company. Possibly, a promising candidate has failed in the past because the structure of the job didn't fit with his or her working style.

Evaluate how the candidate will mesh with your company mood. Will he or she integrate well with the other staff and take to the atmosphere you've created? Performing well in a job isn't just about skills; it's also about attitude and personality. Learning new skills is easy, actually, but changing attitude is next to impossible. Make sure you spend some time thinking through each candidate's attitude and how it works with your company culture, the nature of the job, and the dispositions of your other staff members.

I learned that technique the hard way. One of the first employees I picked for our Toronto office met all the qualifications for the position and came with glowing recommendations. When I met her, I worried that she was overly sure of herself, but her background and experience spoke volumes. Within the first week, I knew I'd goofed. Although she certainly had skills, she thought she knew more than all the other staff and came off as condescending and conceited in meetings with colleagues, models, and clients. My fellow interviewers and I could have picked up on that weakness if we'd evaluated her attitude and considered that relevant.

However, even using all these techniques, you can never be certain a person will be right for the position and your company. After you've exhausted the objective measures, trust your gut. You came up with your business idea, understood what about it would work, and ran with it at least in part on instinct. There were no certain answers. In the end, you need to follow your gut feeling when hiring as well. Do you like the person? Would you like to spend time with her or him? You'll need to be working with this person every day; make sure you get along.

Venture capitalist Guy Kawasaki recommends the "shopping mall test." These days, it's the final question I ask myself before any hiring. It helps me to confirm my gut reaction. Before making an offer, I assume I'm in a shopping centre and that I see the candidate fifty feet away. Would I (a) rush over to say hello; (b) figure if I bump into him I'll say hello and if not, that's fine; or (c) get in my car and go elsewhere. I don't hire unless my response is (a). Kawasaki would approve.

Another staffing issue that often arises for young entrepreneurs is the age difference between you and your staff. At the Ben Barry Agency I'm the boss, yet I've been much younger than some of my team. I believe age makes no difference when it comes to job performance, but the situation does contradict social convention (older equals knowledge, experience equals authority).

Sometimes it's a shock when a candidate first meets me. When they start work it can lead to tension, especially if the new hire is substantially older. I always acknowledge the issue in the interview, and again on their first day on the job, rather than simply pretending it doesn't exist. I ask whether the person senses any discomfort working for a company owned and managed by someone young. I explain, sometimes in a joking way, that while I don't believe age makes a difference in job performance, I recognize that the age difference goes against expectation so it might feel strange off the top. And I stress: "It's cool if it feels strange at first, but we should talk about it so it doesn't come between us." Then I explain that I believe we each make different contributions thanks to our varied experiences. I emphasize that I hope we can each learn from each other, that I value what they bring and I hope they value what I provide. As long as age is recognized instead of ignored, it shouldn't be a big deal.

Sometimes during an interview you can just sense that the age difference is an issue for a potential staff member. They may be uncomfortable talking about it, or just feel uncomfortable with having you as a boss. Try to catch this in the interview. If you don't, and it emerges on the job, you may find yourself in a position where you have to let someone go. And it's better to drop someone rather than try to make the best of a bad situation. The latter option only creates negativity and slows down everyone. At the end of the day, it's your company and you're the boss: your staff needs to respect your ability.

Surrounding yourself with great people also means having seasoned minds to advise you on the many decisions you will face in your business. I put together an advisory board in order to have experienced people offer me professional counsel. We meet together regularly and sometimes my board members offer advice individually. My advisory board has no legal power, unlike a board of directors; it's simply there to help me.

Try to recruit advisers from different fields, not just from your industry. You want to find other entrepreneurs, strong managers, experts in finance and law, maybe people from not-for-profit organizations. If you have an accountant—and you will need one—he or she can join the board. If you know an astute business professor, there's another addition.

These days, "consensual management" is a widespread practice. It's important to share power, delegate responsibility, and be diplomatic with your team: influence rather than instruct. But you also need to remember that you're the boss. It's your company. You're ultimately responsible for your success or failure. Sometimes—maybe often—you'll have to act against the crowd, driven by the courage of your convictions. You might even have to act against the advice of your advisory board, as esteemed as they are and as attached to them as you might be. It's important to seek advice, to ask and listen; it's also important that you make final decisions based on what you feel is right.

One last suggestion: retain legal control. Don't give that up at any cost. As you grow, investors will often offer you funding in exchange for control. Understand what you're giving up to grow, whether it's worth it, and where it will lead you and your company down the road. An injection of quick capital might permit your short-term expansion, but it could limit your long-term potential. Look for other ways to obtain capital; ways that don't require you to give up ownership and control. These avenues invariably exist, although they may be harder to access or take more time.

Remember—it's not just giving up your ownership and all the benefits it entails; it's also giving up your decision-making power. Others will be in control of your vision. How does that sound?

QUESTION 9: IS MY LIFE MY BUSINESS? DOES MY LIFE INCLUDE MY BUSINESS?

It's very easy for your business to take over your life and become a twenty-four-hour-a-day operation. Trust me, it can consume your every waking hour and haunt your dreams. It's important to have balance in your life. Balance doesn't have to prevail every day, or even every week, or month. (Starting a business will probably require a period of serious imbalance.) Over the long haul, however, you need equilibrium to be successful. Figure out how best to get it. What other pursuits are vital to maintaining your energy and sanity? Swimming? Snowboarding? Coffee at the diner? Plan time for those. Put them in your schedule and don't cancel easily, as if your pet pastimes are somehow secondary and to be pursued only if you're not busy. You'll always be busy; they aren't secondary.

As a student entrepreneur, I was lucky. Being a student forced balance in my life. I couldn't always be in the office, surrounded by business associates. I had to get to class, or hit the library. No matter how much I might have wanted to entrench myself at the office, I had papers to hand in and exams to write.

Studying also ensured that my mind had balance. I read, wrote, thought, and talked about ideas and issues, important ideas and issues that had nothing to do with fashion. I took a class in contemporary art history, for example; something I knew nothing about and that had virtually nothing to do with my business. I loved it.

I have a tendency to view my business as the most important thing in the world. School kept my life in perspective. It's easy to get caught up with being the boss, being the one who makes all the decisions and who holds the final answers. In class, my knowledge was no more valuable than the person's beside me. I had the same rules and deadlines as everyone else, with no control over them, with no exceptions made because I'm the chief. When your business becomes successful, many people will tell you how great and wonderful you are. But in school, sometimes you get a good mark, sometimes you struggle with the material and need help from a friend who gets it. Everyone is on an equal footing, the kind of footing that really keeps you grounded.

Making friends in class and through clubs has helped me remember my age. Sometimes, I forget I'm only in my twenties. It's easy to grow up too fast. School allowed me to meet people my age who had nothing to do with business. They invited me to parties, clubs, concerts; stuff where I could just hang out and talk about moving away from home, dating, or what band was the coolest.

Higher education may not be the best option for all young entrepreneurs. Tina Wells postponed Wharton. Each business, and person, is different. But if you want to attend school, you don't have to postpone running your business or give it up altogether. You can do both, and do both well.

And if you don't choose school, find other ways to get balance.

Maintain friendships and connections beyond business. That won't happen without commitment on your part. It's easy to lose friends when you get busy, and develop new, seemingly more important business relationships. But there's an old proverb: "Make new friends, keep the old. These are silver, those are gold." Do your part to keep old friendships alive. They'll keep you connected to yourself, your values, and your interests. Remember, these golden friends knew you before your business took off and don't define you by it.

I've already urged you to join entrepreneur groups and associations. You should also think about activities that provide relief from work, be it sports, a book club, or a regular movie night. Do things that get you circulating with people you wouldn't meet through your work, and particularly with people your age.

Volunteering is another great way to maintain balance and to give back to the community. I've volunteered with an organization called the Metropolitan

Action Committee on Violence against Women and Children and with the Toronto Youth Cabinet. I met lots of people whom I would have never met in business or school, had the opportunity to learn from them and their experiences, and learned about my community. On the Toronto Youth Cabinet, for example, I worked with young people from across Toronto and with city councillors. I learned about municipal politics in practice, and about the issues facing other young people in my city. I loved working on a team where I wasn't the boss; where no one was the boss.

Why not apply your management skills elsewhere by volunteering to serve on the board of a non-profit? I acted as a board member for a national not-for-profit called Meal Exchange. I was able to share my experience in marketing and strategy and help the organization develop five-year plans in both these areas. It also gave me the chance to meet and work with individuals from different businesses, government departments, and not-for-profits. Serving on boards can give you useful perspective on your own company.

Ideas need to be inspired, souls need to be nurtured. Otherwise, we aren't curious, we aren't happy, and we're definitely not fulfilled. I often attend lectures, book launches, concerts and plays, and visit galleries and museums. I'd classify these as events and outings that are completely unrelated to my business yet completely related to my soul. I'm exposed to new knowledge and connected to new feelings. And I always invite someone to go with me—a mentor, a staff member, a client (to cultivate our relationship outside business), a friend, a date. Even Mom!

Balance also means taking care of your body. Sitting in an office all day enduring meetings can make you feel tired and grumpy, and your body feel weak and stiff. Try to do something physical: evening walks, tennis, biking, your call. Four times a week I head off on a long run myself, or hit the gym. It's stress relief, it's an energy boost, and I get some time and space to think without interruption (or groove to the latest downloads on my iPod). When I take business trips, my running shoes and shorts are at the top of my bag.

Make sure that you eat well. It's easy to eat anything that is quick...I know! There are times I forget to eat because I'm on the go. Then I'm starving so I grab the quickest closest item, usually not very high on the nutrition scale. Mostly, I try to eat three square meals a day—lots of fruits, vegetables, and protein with healthy fats. I also try to go for small, healthy snacks: yogurt or my favourite trail mix. And I drink lots of water, and juice it. Find out what works for you, but remember: you are your business. If you aren't in great shape, your company won't be either.

The people who do the best at their businesses are not the ones who devote all their attention to it. Instead, they seek balance through family, friends, life-long education, sports and recreation, and volunteering. Work can be draining. Consider how to recharge your batteries and balance your life.

QUESTION 10: HOW DO I MAKE IT TO THE TOP? HOW DO I STAY THERE?

So you've started your own company. Now what? How do you make your business succeed and grow?

I've developed a few techniques—some that I follow on a daily basis—to make sure that the Ben Barry Agency not only gets to the top of the fashion industry but also remains there. As my agency grew and I hired more staff and opened more offices, like many CEOs, I began to focus more and more on long-term strategy, finances, and major decisions. My interactions primarily involved our key executives. I didn't work on anything filed under day to day. That was so *not* how I had ever wanted to operate! I had developed my business based on connecting with what was happening with everyday people. I knew that if I was going to keep succeeding and growing, I needed to keep that connection alive and make it part of my job all over again.

In so many companies, the head honchos are isolated in their high office towers, removed from the action on the street. That was what I sensed with many of the fashion executives I met in New York. There was not only a task divide between the executives and the frontline workers, there was a perspective divide as well. The executive was removed from the customer in a practical sense while the frontline workers dealt with their real issues. This division harms growth and limits success.

Yes, long-term planning needs to be based on an understanding of the firm and the market as a whole; strategic decisions require a broad perspective. But that's not enough for maximum success. Understanding what the customer wants (and where their wants are headed) can be developed only by seeing and interacting with the customer. A business needs to be grounded in everyday actions and interactions, through and through.

Management guru Jim Collins sums up this idea with a good analogy. A great CEO, he says, is one who has the dance floor covered (where the action is, knowing how things work in detail) while also getting the view from the balcony (knowing where the action is going). I think good entrepreneurs actually have to be down on the dance floor and up in the balcony simultaneously. They can't just think. They have to do.

Stay intimate with your customers. Talk to them and to your frontline staff about them. Listen and learn. I make sure that I spend at least half of my work time personally involved in our frontline business operations—searching for models with my scouts, booking models for jobs, and developing new pitches—and the other half dealing with the bigger strategic decisions and planning. On many afternoons, I'll go into a bookstore and chat with consumers about the magazine images they're perusing, just like I first did with my friend Mia.

Whether I'm at the magazine stand, in a staff meeting, or at the bank, I ask myself what is happening and why. It's important to make questioning and learning a continual process—a pattern in your life. It's the only way to stay competitive and be on top of changes in your industry and the environment at large. I question all the stakeholders I meet—the people affected by my venture. Those include my friends, my customers, and the woman beside me on the bus. I also regularly read the media, books, and expert studies, questioning their findings and arguments. I come at them from every angle I can. I want to discern their significance and figure out their impact, and discover how I might be limiting myself.

Once I start questioning, I find things keep changing. That's good. It means I'm learning. And I'll keep pressing for more information, going back to talk to people over and over again. No matter how much information you assimilate, it's vital never to think you know it all—that can be the beginning of the end. As soon as you stop listening to others, you become inflexible. Knowledge is an ongoing process. New ideas need to be put into practice. Staying competitive means constant evolution.

As you implement your new ideas, you need to continue to take risks. In business, risk never goes away. In fact, it's an important criterion for long-term success and growth. You begin your business by taking a risk, and you improve it by taking further risks. Otherwise your business will stagnate and eventually die. Thomas Edison said of his efforts to make the light bulb, "I never really failed. I just found ten thousand ways that didn't work." Mistakes are a way of figuring out what to do next.

I once made a big mistake while scouting new models during an Elite model search. I told the potential models that their local agency was ripping them off by charging them lots of money for photos and modelling classes. I told them if they signed with Elmer, he'd make them lose weight and change their look. I promised that my firm treated models better. Many of them signed contracts with me on the spot, right while the search was going on. Their agents and Elmer were watching exactly what was happening! It wasn't professional or appropriate business practice. Elmer drew this to my attention. I apologized to Elmer and the other agents, immediately adjusted my scouting techniques, and tried not to lose confidence because of my naive botch-up.

Now, when I scout a model who is currently represented, I tell her or him that it's great that they're currently represented because they should be in the business and they have the look and personality to be successful. I also tell them that should they ever have any questions about modelling, or find themselves considering a switch in agencies, they should feel free to give me a call because I'd be happy to help them out.

Sometimes people will warn young entrepreneurs against taking some course of action with a fledgling business. They'll say you're taking a huge risk and might "lose everything." But what are you really going to lose? In most cases, all you have to lose is time and maybe some money. Even if you do miss out and the idea flops, the return in terms of learning and experience outweighs the cost. Successful entrepreneurs don't make fewer bad decisions than their less successful counterparts. The difference is that they learn from the bad decisions and correct them faster.

Business success is about more than implementing new ideas. It's also about constant re-evaluation. In the same way I watch the gauges on a dashboard when I drive, I have a set of measurements that I keep regarding my own performance. "Outputs" are my contracts signed, or my sales in the last month. My other measurements include the number of prospective clients with whom we've met recently. You have to measure the right things or you'll waste resources.

Periodically step aside and ask yourself some hard questions about your business. I sometimes do this alone on a long Sunday morning run. Occasionally, I involve others at a strategic retreat. At the same time, don't make recharting your course a daily event. I make mine an annual one. That might work for you, too.

No matter how strong your connection to consumer reality or how much you question and re-evaluate, the key to making your business a success is hard work. Business is gruelling and it never stops. It challenges you on many fronts simultaneously. So be prepared for work, work, and more work. And don't be deceived by glamorous stories about the life of a CEO. Being a boss is about a lot more than fancy lunches and stockpiling Air Miles. But the hard work is all worth it when you see how your vision changes your world. Your efforts are making the world a better place. What could beat that?

CONCLUSION

WHERE WILL YOUR RUNWAY LEAD?

There are some intense moments just before a fashion show, a panic backstage: designers make their final adjustments to their outfits, hairdressers give the hair spray one last whiz, makeup artists re-apply bronzer for the last time, and the choreographer shushes the chattering. Then the lights dim. The crowd hushes, eager to be wowed and transported. Well, life is like that. When you're young, there's a flurry of preparation, you get ready to make your big entrance, you arrive on the scene, and hopefully you start convincing people to see things your way.

Change is driven by young people more often than not; people who don't need to accept the world as it is. Change takes a lot of energy, and it's never over. With enough insight, sincerity, and conviction, you can lead change— change that's focused within your own organization, change that nudges a whole industry, or change that transforms society. With enough attention, enough action, enough co-operation, anything can change and usually does.

REFASHIONING BEAUTY

The fashion and beauty industry needs to change. The images it spreads are harmful, counterproductive, and damaging. That goes for Mia, for the thousands she represents, and for all of us who struggle with distorted pictures. We need to create a more diverse, healthier set of images in fashion and beauty advertising.

I hope a lot of you agree. I realize fashion might not be your main focus. Still, there are things everyone can do to help. Please start by being alert to the power of beauty images. They affect us all, whether we're persuaded of an overly narrow view of what's attractive, or buy products that don't provide the satisfaction seductive ads promise, or worry too much about our looks and see our friends or children struggling the same way.

You can help promote a more realistic and positive image of beauty by articulating where you want the beauty and fashion industry to go. Visit online chat rooms, write letters to newspapers and magazines, contact head offices. Vote with your wallet and buy from companies that use realistic models, that promote a true and full understanding of beauty, that respect you and listen to you. Be a customer for what is right... or at least for what is better.

If you're in the fashion and beauty industry you can take direct action. Many companies that have dispensed with the current model are doing great: from international leaders like Dove and The Body Shop to national chains like Harry Rosen to regional firms like Panda Plus. This won't be the first time society rejects a fashion myth: anybody remember bustle skirts? Whalebone corsets? Bound feet? The woman who posed for what is regarded as the most beautiful and alluring female sculpture in Western history, the Venus de Milo, wouldn't make it as a model today: "Not tall enough, too big in the hips."

We're off track; it's time to get back and get real.

BUSINESS IS A VEHICLE FOR SOCIAL CHANGE

Society needs more socially relevant enterprises. It needs more people making more changes. Address the problem that ignites your passion then start a business that seeks to right the wrong. Make a profit to sustain both you and your cause. Learn from other young entrepreneurs around the world—they operate on principles that will work for you, too.

Why strike out on your own when there are traditional ways to achieve social change? True, you could join a non-profit that's a standard-bearer for your ideals, or donate to the cause. You could work politically, striving for policy changes, getting ideas built into party platforms and helping to get your party elected. You could join the public service. Or you could opt for activism.

Each of these has its advantages and disadvantages. Governments create the programs and policies that affect society overall, but the law and policy-making processes are slow and tedious. And when policy is changed, it doesn't always translate into change in daily practice. Social agencies and non-governmental organizations can be powerful forces of change through their influence on governments and industries. But their efforts can also run up against tough, frustrating roadblocks. A lot of the work of NGOs hinges on the political climate. Funding is often short term; worthwhile projects are abandoned when funds are diverted to the newest loud lobbyists by the latest new government. As for the public service, it can be slow, reactive, and burdened by the need to forge compromises between various interests. And public service generally doesn't give voice to young people. You have to work in the system for years before you have much influence.

The Balanced Contract calls for a profit-driven socially oriented entrepreneurial model—and recognition that while making a profit is the rightful end of business, creating a better world is the most rightful of all ends. The Balanced Contract is the path to both ends.

Three factors unite to make the Balanced Contract achievable now:

1. Social issues influence consumers' purchase intentions. Many consumers now demand that companies embed social responsibility into every aspect of their operations. A growing number of consumers will support—go out of their way to support—good-conscience firms. But they won't compromise on quality just because you're serving a good cause. Social issues are a route to the bottom line, not an obstacle to it.
2. Business can be a vehicle for social change. Governments and social agencies play important roles, but they have limited funds and competing objectives. They can't be doing everything. In contrast, business has the efficient and innovative economic and creative resources to solve complicated problems.

3. Young people are in the best position to initiate the Balanced Contract. We're up-to-the-moment educated, media-savvy, and technologically adept. And we see the world in a different way: we're acutely aware of the impact of industry and globalization; we don't recognize geographical borders. And we believe in the power of one: the idea that a single individual can initiate change.

ACT NOW

You don't have to live in a state of suspended animation, waiting until later in your life to construct something yourself. That's a social myth. Getting an education, doing an apprenticeship, and paying dues before making changes might work for some professions; no one wants to go to a fourteen-year-old doctor. But that doesn't work for entrepreneurs. Jump in. Act now.

Think Wayne Gretzky and Sydney Crosby—identified as hockey stars by age fifteen. Nobody asked Tiger Woods to put away the golf clubs until he had a degree. Similarly, Keisha Castle-Hughes was nominated for an Oscar for *Whale Rider* at thirteen, and Vanessa-Mae was recording Tchaikovsky violin concertos at twelve. They were all given the best training, the best opportunities, and an environment in which to succeed.

Young entrepreneurs are made of similar stuff. They get the drive early. They're profit-driven and socially oriented simultaneously, and they can also combine running a business with going to school and maintaining a balanced life. The establishment must start encouraging people to pursue business ventures, no matter their age.

SIGN HERE

When you see a problem—something you feel isn't working and needs to be confronted—don't waste time talking about it. Do your part to solve it. Take action. As the great philosophers Thomas Hobbes and John Locke once wrote, all of us are living in a social contract with each other. No matter who you are or what you do—and no matter what your age—you're part of that contract. Society can function only if everybody holds up their end of the bargain. Creating a business that follows the Balanced Contract is the best way I know of doing so.

I'm trying to do my part by working to change an industry that promotes a destructively narrow view of beauty. Other young entrepreneurs are creating their own vital businesses. You can do the same, addressing any number of issues that matter to you by making that your work. Together, we'll create a world in which we all really want to live.

We can fashion reality.

SOURCES

Many fearless individuals within the fashion and advertising industries work in the face of convention to confront the oppressive images we see. I am appreciative of the business and media leaders who share their strategies in this book: Manjit Basi, Catherine Lawson, Mike Hemingway, Amy Jasmer, Erin Iles, Wendy Naugle, Nancy Monsarrat, Kevin Roberts, and Alex Spunt. I am also grateful to those who advance positive body image within community health and education, and especially to Ann Kerr and Susie Orbach, whose vision and commitment push me to continue my battle within the industry.

I am especially thankful to the young business owners who share their stories in this book: Tracey Clark, Matthew Corrin, Ben Goldhirsh and WorldChanging (www.worldchanging.com/archives/003504.html), Amy Jasmer, Jen Kluger, Ceilidh McClurg, Suzie Orol, Ben Voss, and Tina Wells. Your lessons have greatly enriched this project.

I am grateful to the many academics whose research and theories shed new light on media, body image, and entrepreneurship and collectively call us to action. Your work enriches my own understanding as well as helps me persuade the fashion industry to diversify its images. Excerpts from the following sources appear with permission.

Bornstein, David. *How to Change the World: Social Entrepreneurs and the Power of New Ideas*. New York: Oxford University Press USA, 2004.

Collins, Jim. *Good to Great: Why Some Companies Make the Leap and Others Don't,* New York: HarperBusiness, 2001.

Cortese, Anthony. *Provocateur: Women and Minorities in Advertising,* New York: Rowman & Littlefield Inc., 2004.

D'Agostino, Heidi, Nancy Etcoff, Susie Orbach, and Jennifer Scott. "The Real Truth about Beauty: A Global Report: Findings of the Global Study on Women, Beauty, and Well-Being," commissioned by Dove (Unilever), September 2004. Available online at http://www.campaignforrealbeauty.ca/uploadedFiles/dove_white_paper_final.pdf

Gill, Rosalind. "From Sexual Objectification to Sexual Subjectification: The Resexualisation of Women's Bodies in the Media," *Feminist Media Studies,* Spring 2003.

Klein, Naomi. *No Logo: Taking Aim at the Brand Bullies,* Toronto: Random House, 2000.

Orbach, Susie. *Fat is a Feminist Issue,* London: Arrow Books, 1978.

Roberts, Kevin. *Lovemarks: The Future Beyond Brands,* New York: Powerhouse Books, 2004.

Pope, Harrison G., Jr., Katharine A. Phillips, and Roberto Olivardia. *The Adonis Complex: The Secret Crisis of Male Body Obsession,* New York: Free Press, 2000.

Wolf, Naomi. *The Beauty Myth,* New York: Anchor Books, 1992.

INDEX

ABOUT THE AUTHOR

Ben Barry began the Ben Barry Agency, Inc. at age fourteen. Today, the agency scouts and sources models of all ages, colours, sizes, and abilities for fashion and beauty brands. Ben Barry models have appeared in ads for Max Factor, Nike, Dove, L'Oréal, and Sears, and on the pages of *Vogue*, *Elle*, and *Seventeen*.

Ben has been featured on CNN, FOX News, CTV National News, Fashion Television, CBC Morning, Vicki Gabereau, and *The Oprah Winfrey Show* as well as in the *Toronto Star*, *People* magazine, *National Post*, *Globe and Mail*, and *Profit* magazine. He has won numerous awards, including the CIBC Student Entrepreneur of the Year Award and the Queen's Golden Jubilee Award for making an outstanding contribution to Canada. Ben has been recognized as "One of 20 Teens Who Will Change the World" by *Teen People* magazine and "One of the 25 Leaders of Tomorrow" by *Maclean's*. He frequently lectures on entrepreneurship and diversity for associations, businesses, and schools, and has developed and facilitated workshops on men and body image, and media and body image.

Ben holds an honours bachelor of arts in women's studies from Trinity College at the University of Toronto where he studied on a four-year Millennium Scholarship. He is currently a graduate student in innovation and strategy at Judge Business School at Cambridge University where he studies on an Ogilvy Foundation Research Grant. He divides his time between Toronto, Ontario and Cambridge, UK.